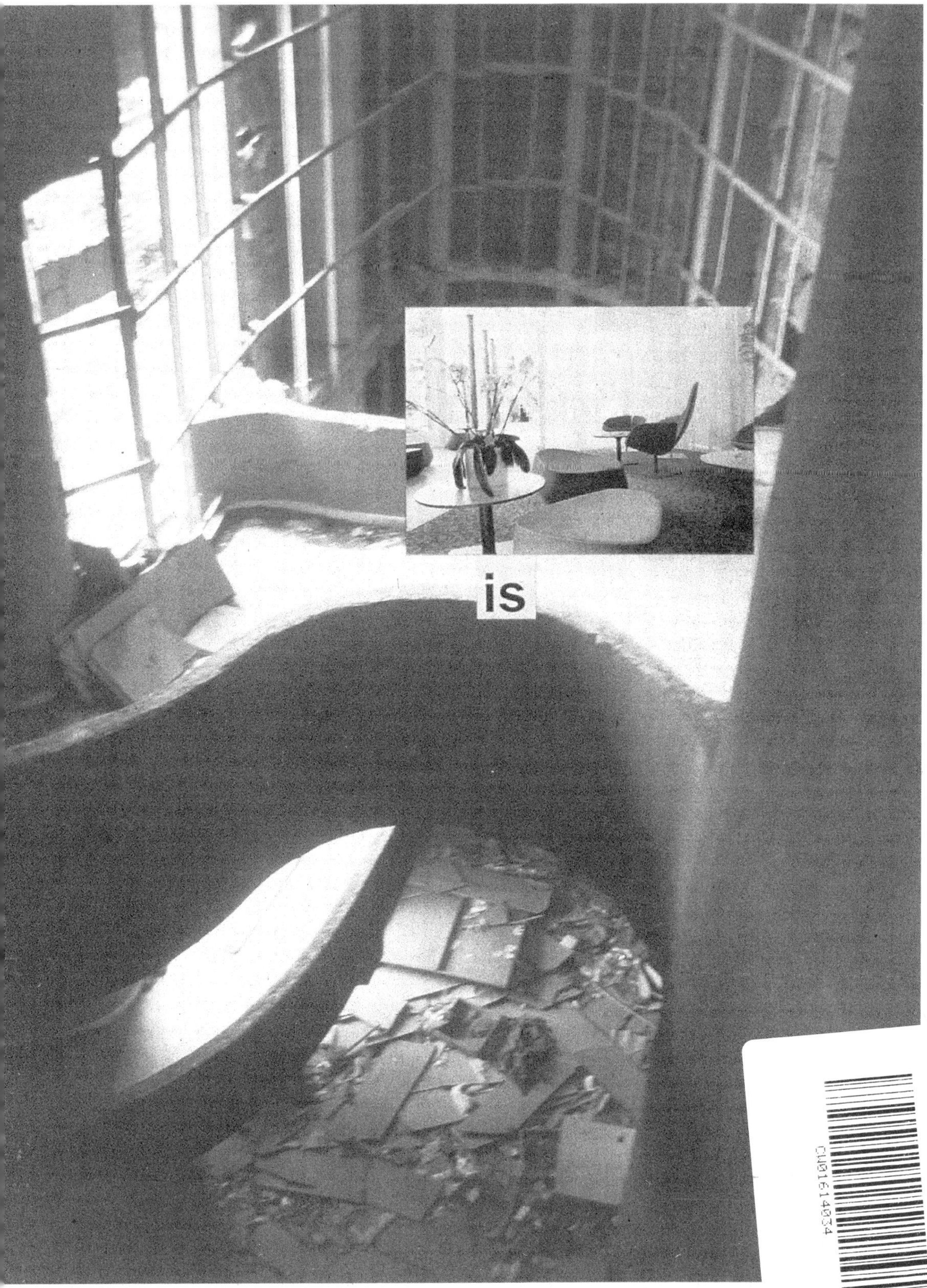
is

# David Maljković

## Almost Here

ALMOST HERE

Kunstverein in Hamburg

DUMONT

This publication was supported as Catalog No. 111 by the Alfried Krupp von Bohlen und Halbach-Stiftung under its program *Catalogs for Young Artists.*

Diese Publikation wurde als 111. Katalog von der Alfried Krupp von Bohlen und Halbach-Stiftung im Programm *Kataloge für junge Künstler* gefördert.

# ALMOST THERE

## Contents / Inhalt

# BACK TO THE FUTURE

## YILMAZ DZIEWIOR

> Collage technique is the systematic exploitation of the accidental or artificially provoked coincidence of two or more essentially alien realities on an apparently inappropriate plane – and the spark of poetry which leaps over as these realities approach each other. (Max Ernst) [1]

When Filippo Tommaso Marinetti published his Futurist Manifesto in the French newspaper, *Le Figaro*, almost one hundred years ago, he could not have known of the subsequent two world wars or the establishment of a socialist Eastern Europe under the leadership of Russia, and its collapse at the beginning of the 1990s. On this day that has entered into the history of art as the beginning of futurism, 20 February 1909, he proclaimed militantly the beauty of speed and praised the aesthetic superiority of a racing car over Nike of Samothrace. Dissociating himself from cultural history that reaches far back into the past and is felt by him to be a burden, he made a plea for not looking back, but for breaking open the 'mysterious gates of the impossible' because 'time and space died yesterday'. Since everything past was anathema to him, he demanded as a consequence the destruction of places where history is remembered, namely, museums, libraries and academies. What counted for Marinetti was 'eternal, omnipresent speed,' a desire which even today, in the twenty-first century, in post-Fordist and neo-liberal society, is omnipresent in efforts for a continually advancing technology of communication and the development of ever more efficient means of transportation.[2]

The sparkling visionary prospects of a supposed future and the constructively prismatic formal language of installations and collages of David Maljković could tempt us to make the assumption that the futurists' program still possessed great attraction for him, especially because motor-bikes and racing cars are among the standard repertoire for his works. And the artist really does mention in his associative text on the work, *Again for Tomorrow*, that on his journey in time through history he also encountered the futurists, but that he had tried to avoid any kind of nostalgia in doing so. In this sense, the dashing motor-bike in *Again for Tomorrow* can only be interpreted as a transfigured symbol of progress in a limited sense because its front wheel is held fast by a simple telescopic funnel construction made of wood- and plasterboard, and therefore a real ride on it is impossible. Rather, the installation creates the impression of a time machine, as if a force would pull the motor-bike with its rider through the funnel-shaped opening into another dimension. Perhaps directly into the video shots from alienated film material of simple domestic appliances and domestic activities which can be seen on a flat screen immediately opposite the motor-bike, accompanied by digitally generated music reminiscent of tribal rhythms. The whole thing is embedded in a space whose walls are completely covered with collages, drawings, photographs as well as dynamic networks of rhombi made of adhesive tape, and whose front wall is overgrown completely with crudely carpentered plasterboard. One year after its first presentation in the artist's studio at the Amsterdam Rijksakademie, the installation, *Again for Tomorrow*, travelled to Montenegro for the Cetinje Biennial, where it was presented more puristically, without the works on paper and the mural drawings made of adhesive tape, in the room where, it is said, the last Presidium of Yugoslavia convened. And again one year later, in 2005, Maljković showed two variations of this work, one in Amsterdam and another one at the Prague Biennial. This is significant insofar as the constant further development of installations in his case does not necessarily lead to ever more elaborate versions, but rather emphasizes various facets of an engagement with similar subjects. Thus, for instance, in Prague, the motor-bike, now wrapped in aluminium foil and without a construction surrounding the installation, was combined with posters from travel agencies. Of these posters, which were found on a walk through Zagreb in a deserted shop that had become the victim of economic processes of transformation, some advertise, significantly, holiday trips to Prague and Amsterdam. In this context, collages came about into which some of the posters, along with cut-outs from previous installation shots of *Again for Tomorrow* were integrated.

If the term 'Gesamtkunstwerk' had not been so discredited by totalitarian regimes, it would be a suitable description, not only for this installation, but also for other voluminous arrangements by David Maljković consisting of drawings, collages, objects, sculptures, videos and sounds. But precisely because of the specific historical frame of reference for his works in which Eastern Europe and especially his home, Croatia, assume a key position, the concept of intermediality seems more apposite for describing the linking of various kinds of expression. These include in their broad expanse also his own texts which open up his works to a partly fictitious hermeneutic context which, however, is populated also with many real persons and events. In their sum, the various media in Maljković's work join together to form a whole which is more than the sum of its parts. As such, his work is entirely in the tradition of art of the 1960s which wanted to work against social and aesthetic alienation by employing individual media in parallel, thus overcoming the single medium. But this interpretation becomes more complicated precisely because Maljković puts these art movements arising originally with a Utopian, revolutionary impetus into relation to the history of his home country which, in the twentieth century, is characterized above all by the failure of precisely these political pretensions. On the other hand, this is understandable insofar as his works are never completely absorbed by their subject and references to real events and places, but bring an abstract plane into play through temporal and spatial displacements. Even if, for instance, in *Scene for New Heritage* or *These Days*, aspects of the chequered history of Croatia are recognizable as a subtext, and the effects of the transformation from a communist form of society to a capitalist one, and the associated economic and cultural repercussions, can be read off indirectly, these real connections are overshadowed by elements of the unreal that make any too straightforward interpretation difficult. Thus, for instance, *Scene for New Heritage* begins with a definite specification of place, Croatia, but the temporal location of 2045, and especially the exact date of 25 May, which is not merely fortuitously the birthday of Yugoslavia's long-ruling president, Tito, makes the situation uncertain. Tito, who is a highly controversial historical figure, is honoured for his anti-Fascist commitment and what he achieved for a bloc-free Yugoslavia, and also criticized for his repression and authoritarian style of leadership. The concrete specification of a time thus becomes historically charged, but obtains at the same time, through its projection into a future whose reality from today's point of view is not really imaginable, a fictitious element.

Maljković proceeds in a similar way with his selection of film locations. They are frequently deserted buildings and monuments from the 1960s and 1970s which impressively mirror the promise of a better future and, because of their ruinous state today, simultaneously make the failure of this promise apparent in a melancholy mood. In their equally futuristic and historical architectural language, they are ideal settings for the occasionally strange and not clearly explicable actions which are acted in the videos by amateur actors. In the juxtaposition of spectacular architecture with persons in contemporary clothing who seem completely everyday, sustained confusion arises, especially by mixing staged and accidental actions. For instance, the young men and women in *These Days* speak their sluggish monologues by relating them to each other and complementing them, but in doing so, they do not come into any real interaction. Despite communicative gestures and actions that relate to each other, most of them run more or less parallel to each other.

Similar to the combination of different, chronologically incompatible moments, this adjacency bolsters the impression that in Maljković's works the relationship between time and causality has been suspended. If one proceeds in principle from the dependency of the concept of time on the concept of causality, roughly in the sense that the cause occurs before its effects, and the past cannot be changed and influenced from the present, with his idiosyncratic intermeshing of future, past and present, Maljković seems to question these reciprocal interactions.

This holds also for his own production, which never runs in a linear fashion, but rather in the form of a spiral. Thus, his series, such as *Scene for New Heritage*, do not arise immediately one after the other, but are interrupted by other works which in part are also conceived serially. Maljković also mixes different times in the presentation, for instance, when he integrates into his exhibition architectural models for the Petrova Gora Park memorial from the 1970s which are conspicuous in the videos and collages from *Scene for New Heritage*. A basic trait exemplary for his way of proceeding is reflected in combining historical models with his own, present-day works, thus incorporating research as well as interweaving various realities.

His approach makes it apparent that not only the future is influenced by the present, but also the past is dependent upon the present and the present's interpretation of the past. In relation to the historical, political and cultural contexts in which Maljković's work comes about, it mirrors the categorial transformation of an understanding of East and West, of communism and capitalism.

In his book, *Icons of the Left*, the art historian, Otto Karl Werckmeister has portrayed in a graphic way how the identification of communist political repression and a socialist planned economy, on the one hand, and democratic freedom and capitalist market economy, on the other, is today in a state of flux. The ascriptions are not at all so unambiguous, as Werckmeister shows convincingly using the examples of China and Russia and their adaptation of capitalist practices, as well as the example of the crisis in traditional capitalist industrial countries and their massive problems with keeping their social orders intact.[3]
In this sense, a work such as *These Days* can also be interpreted as the expression of the antagonism which is reflected, partly humorously and partly oppressively, in the clash between the promise of the future of a capitalist West with English as lingua franca, and the unwillingness or inability to fulfil the requirements of efficiency. In this contradiction and the necessity of an updated re-evaluation of historical formations, social forms and political systems there is also an opportunity which the work of David Maljković follows up.

Notes

1 Max Ernst *Biographische Notizen. Wahrheitsgewebe und Lügengewebe*, in: Werner Spies (ed.), *Max Ernst. Retrospektive zum 100. Geburtstag*, Düsseldorf 1991, p. 291.

2 Filippo Tomaso Marinetti's *Futurist Manifesto* has been reprinted in several places including Evelyn Benesch, Ingried Brugger (eds.), *Futurismus. Radikale Avantgarde*, exhibition catalogue, BA-CA Kunstforum Wien, 7.3–29.6.2003, Vienna, p. 264.

3 Otto Karl Werckmeister, *Linke Ikonen. Benjamin, Eisenstein, Picasso – nach dem Fall des Kommunismus*, Carl Hanser Verlag, Munich, Vienna 1997, p. 229. Translated into English, *Icons of the Left (Benjamin and Eisenstein, Picasso and Kafka – After the Fall of Communism)*, Chicago, University of Chicago Press, 1999.

# ZURÜCK IN DIE ZUKUNFT

## YILMAZ DZIEWIOR

> Collage-Technik ist die systematische Ausbeutung des zufälligen oder künstlich provozierten Zusammentreffens von zwei oder mehr wesensfremden Realitäten auf einer augenscheinlich dazu ungeeigneten Ebene – und der Funke Poesie, welcher bei der Annäherung dieser Realitäten überspringt. (Max Ernst)[1]

Als Filippo Tommaso Marinetti vor fast einhundert Jahren sein futuristisches Manifest in der französischen Zeitung *Le Figaro* publizierte, konnte er weder um die folgenden beiden Weltkriege, noch um die Etablierung eines sozialistischen Osteuropas unter der Führung Russlands und dessen Zusammenbruch Anfang der 1990er Jahre wissen. An diesem, heute in die Kunstgeschichte als den Beginn des Futurismus eingegangenen Tag, dem 20. Februar 1909, verkündete er kämpferisch die Schönheit der Geschwindigkeit und pries die ästhetische Überlegenheit eines Rennwagens über die Nike von Samothrake. In Abgrenzung zur weit in die Vergangenheit reichenden und von ihm als lähmend empfundenen Last der eigenen kulturellen Geschichte, plädierte er dafür, nicht zurückzublicken, sondern die ›geheimnisvolle(n) Tore des Unmöglichen‹ aufzubrechen, denn ›Zeit und Raum‹ seien ›gestern gestorben‹. Da ihm alles Vergangene verhasst war, forderte er folgerichtig die Zerstörung der Orte, an denen Geschichte erinnert wird, namentlich Museen, Bibliotheken und Akademien. Was für Marinetti zählte, war die ›ewige(n), allgegenwärtige(n) Geschwindigkeit‹, ein Verlangen, das auch heute, im 21. Jahrhundert, in der postfordistischen und neoliberalen Gesellschaft in dem Bemühen um eine stets avanciertere Kommunikationstechnik und der Entwicklung von immer effizienteren Fortbewegungsmitteln allgegenwärtig ist.[2]

Die aufblitzenden visionären Ausblicke in eine vermeintliche Zukunft und die konstruktiv prismatische Formensprache der Installationen und Collagen von David Maljković könnten zur Annahme verführen, dass für ihn die Anliegen der Futuristen nach wie vor große Attraktivität besitzen. Zumal Motorräder und Rennautos zum festen Repertoire seiner Arbeiten zählen. Und wirklich erwähnt der Künstler in seinem assoziativen Text zur Arbeit *Again for Tomorrow*, dass er auf seiner Zeitreise durch die Geschichte auch den Futuristen begegnet sei, er habe jedoch versucht, dabei jede Nostalgie zu umgehen. In diesem Sinne kann denn auch das schneidige Motorrad in *Again for Tomorrow* nur bedingt als verklärtes Symbol von Fortschritt gedeutet werden, da sein Vorderrad durch eine einfache, aus Holz- und Gipskarton bestehende teleskopartige Trichterkonstruktion fixiert, und somit jede reale Fahrt unmöglich ist. Eher erweckt die Installation den Eindruck einer Zeitmaschine, so als würde ein Sog das Motorrad inklusive Fahrer durch die trichterförmige Öffnung in eine andere Dimension befördern. Vielleicht direkt in die Videoaufnahmen aus verfremdetem Filmmaterial einfacher Haushaltsgeräte und -aktivitäten, die auf einem Flachbildschirm unmittelbar gegenüber dem Motorrad zu sehen sind und von digital generierter, an Stammesrhythmen erinnernde Musik begleitet werden. Das Ganze ist eingebettet in einen Raum, dessen Wände mit Collagen, Zeichnungen, Fotografien sowie dynamischen Rautennetzen aus Klebebändern übersät ist, und dessen Stirnwand von kruden zusammen gezimmerten ausufernden Gipskartonplatten überwuchert wird. Ein Jahr nach ihrer ersten Präsentation im Atelier des Künstlers an der Amsterdamer Rijksakademie reist die Installation *Again for Tomorrow* nach Montenegro zur Biennale von Cetinje, wo sie puristischer, ohne die Papierarbeiten und Wandzeichnungen aus Klebeband in dem Raum präsentiert wird, von dem gesagt wird, dass hier das letzte Präsidium Jugoslawiens getagt haben soll. Und wieder ein Jahr später, 2005, zeigte Maljković zwei Varianten dieser Arbeit, eine in Amsterdam und eine weitere auf der Biennale in Prag. Dies ist insofern aufschlussreich, als die permanente Weiterentwicklung von Installationen bei ihm nicht unbedingt in eine immer elaboriertere Fassung mündet, sondern verschiedene Facetten einer Auseinandersetzung mit ähnlichen Themen hervorhebt. So wurde zum Beispiel in Prag das nun mit Aluminiumfolie verkleidete Motorrad ohne installative Umbauung, jedoch gemeinsam mit Plakaten von Reisebüros kombiniert. Von diesen Plakaten, die auf einem Spaziergang in Zagreb in einem verlassenen, den wirtschaftlichen Transformierungsprozessen zum Opfer gefallenen Geschäft gefunden wurden, werben einige bezeichnenderweise für Urlaubsreisen nach Prag und Amsterdam. In diesem Zusammenhang entstanden Collagen, in die teilweise die Plakate wie auch ausgeschnittene Fotos vorhergehender Installationsansichten von *Again for Tomorrow* integriert sind.

Wäre die Bezeichnung Gesamtkunstwerk nicht durch totalitäre Regime zu sehr korrumpiert, so könnte sie eine geeignete Umschreibung nicht nur in Bezug auf diese Installation, sondern auch für die anderen, raumgreifenden, aus Zeichnungen, Collagen, Objekten, Skulpturen, Videos und Sound zusammengesetzten Arrangements von David Maljković sein. Aber gerade aufgrund des spezifischen historischen Bezugsrahmens seiner Arbeiten, in dem Osteuropa und vor allem seine Heimat Kroatien eine Schlüsselposition einnehmen, scheint eher der Begriff der Intermedialität angebracht, um die Verknüpfung der verschiedenen Ausdrucksarten zu umschreiben. Zu ihrem weiten Geflecht zählen auch eigene Texte, die seinen Arbeiten einen teilweise zwar fiktiven, jedoch mit vielen realen Referenzpersonen und Ereignissen versehenen interpretatorischen Kontext eröffnen. In ihrer Addition fügen sich die unterschiedlichen Medien im Werk von Maljković zu einem Ganzen, das mehr ist als die Summe seiner Teile. Damit steht es zwar ganz in der Tradition der Kunst der 1960er Jahre, die mit der parallelen Anwendung und somit Überwindung des Einzelmediums einer gesellschaftlichen und ästhetischen Entfremdung entgegenarbeiten wollte. Verkompliziert wird diese Deutung jedoch, indem Maljković gerade diese eigentlich mit einem utopischen, revolutionären Impetus auftretenden Kunstströmungen zur Geschichte seiner Heimat in Beziehung setzt, die im 20. Jahrhundert vor allem durch das Scheitern eben dieser politischen Ansätze geprägt ist. Andererseits ist dies insofern nachvollziehbar, als seine Arbeiten nie vollkommen in ihrem Sujet und dem Verweis auf reale Ereignisse und Orte aufgehen, sondern durch zeitliche und räumliche Verschiebungen eine abstrakte Ebene ins Spiel bringen. Denn auch wenn beispielsweise in *Scene for New Heritage* oder *These Days* Aspekte der wechselvollen Geschichte Kroatiens als Subtext erkennbar, und die Auswirkungen der Transformation von einer kommunistischen zu einer kapitalistischen Gesellschaftsform und die damit verbundenen ökonomischen und kulturellen Auswirkungen indirekt ablesbar sind, werden diese realen Zusammenhänge von Momenten des Irrealen überschattet und erschweren jede zu geradlinige Interpretation. Zwar beginnt beispielsweise *Scene for New Heritage* mit der eindeutigen Ortsangabe ›Croatia‹, jedoch verunsichert die zeitliche Lokalisierung in das Jahr 2045 und erst recht die genaue Datumsangabe des 25. Mai, bei der es sich nicht zufällig um den Geburtstag des langjährigen Staatspräsidenten Jugoslawiens Tito handelt. Die in der Rezeption äußerst umstrittene Figur Tito wird für sein antifaschistisches Engagement und seine Verdienste für ein blockfreies Jugoslawien ebenso verehrt, wie für seine Repressionen und seinen autoritären Führungsstil kritisiert. Die konkrete Zeitangabe wird so zum einen historisch aufgeladen, erhält aber gleichzeitig mit ihrer Projektion in eine Zukunft, deren Realität aus heutiger Sicht noch nicht wirklich vorstellbar ist, ein fiktionales Element. Ähnlich verfährt Maljković bei der Auswahl seiner Drehorte. Es sind häufig verlassene Bauwerke der 1960er und 1970er Jahre, die eindrucksvoll das Versprechen auf eine bessere Zukunft spiegeln und gleichzeitig aufgrund ihres heutigen ruinösen Zustandes dessen melancholisch stimmendes Scheitern verdeutlichen. In ihrer gleichermaßen futuristischen wie historisch erscheinenden Architektursprache sind sie ideale Schauplätze für die zuweilen befremdlich anmutenden und nicht eindeutig zu erklärenden Aktionen, die von Laiendarstellern in den Videos ausgeführt werden. In dem Aufeinandertreffen der spektakulären Architektur mit den in ihrer zeitgenössischen Kleidung vollkommen alltäglich wirkenden Personen entstehen insbesondere durch die Mischung aus inszenierten und zufälligen Handlungen nachhaltige Irritationen. Beispielsweise sprechen zwar die jungen Männer und Frauen in *These Days* ihre schleppenden Monologe, indem sich diese ergänzen oder aufeinander beziehen, trotzdem treten sie dabei in keine wirkliche Interaktion. Ungeachtet vermittelnder, aufeinander Bezug nehmender Gesten und Aktionen laufen die meisten Handlungen eher parallel zueinander.

Dieses Nebeneinander unterstützt, ähnlich wie die Kombination verschiedener chronologisch unvereinbarer Momente, den Eindruck, dass in den Arbeiten von Maljković das Verhältnis von Zeit und Kausalität relativiert wird. Geht man grundsätzlich von einer Abhängigkeit des Zeitbegriffs von demjenigen der Kausalität aus, also etwa dergestalt, dass die Ursache vor ihrer Wirkung auftritt bzw. die Vergangenheit unveränderbar und von der Gegenwart nicht zu beeinflussen ist, so scheint Maljković mit seiner eigenwilligen Verschränkung von Zukunft, Vergangenheit und Gegenwart die gegenseitigen Wechselwirkungen zu hinterfragen.

Dies gilt auch für seine eigene Produktion, die nie linear, sondern eher spiralförmig verläuft. So entstehen seine Serien, wie zum Beispiel *Scene for New Heritage* nicht unmittelbar nacheinander, sondern werden durch andere, teilweise ebenfalls seriell konzipierte Arbeiten unterbrochen. Verschiedene Zeiten mischt Maljković auch in der Präsentation, wenn er beispielsweise Architekturmodelle der Gedenkstätte des Petrova Gora Parks aus den 1970er Jahren, die in den Videos und Collagen von *Scene for New Heritage* prominent zu sehen sind, in seine Ausstellung integriert. In der Kombination der historischen Modelle mit seinen eigenen, aktuellen Arbeiten spiegelt sich ein seiner grundsätzlichen Vorgehensweise exemplarischer Grundzug, zu dem das Einbeziehen von Recherche ebenso zählt, wie die Verflechtung unterschiedlicher Realitäten.

Sein Ansatz macht deutlich, dass nicht nur die Zukunft von der Gegenwart beeinflusst wird, sondern ebenso die Vergangenheit auch von der Gegenwart und ihrer Interpretation derselben abhängt. In Bezug auf den historischen, politischen und kulturellen Kontext, in dem das Werk von Maljković entsteht, spiegelt es den kategorialen Wandel eines Verständnisses von Ost und West, von Kommunismus und Kapitalismus.

Der Kunsthistoriker Otto Karl Werckmeister hat in seinem Buch *Linke Ikonen* anschaulich dargelegt, wie die Identifizierung von kommunistischer, politischer Unterdrückung und sozialistischer Staatswirtschaft einerseits und demokratischer Freiheit und kapitalistischer Marktwirtschaft andererseits heute zur Disposition steht. Längst sind hier die Zuschreibungen nicht mehr so eindeutig, wie Werckmeister am Beispiel China oder Russland und deren Adaption kapitalistischer Praktiken ebenso schlüssig darlegt, wie an der Krise traditioneller kapitalistischer Industriestaaten und deren massiven Problemen, ihre Gesellschaftsordnungen intakt zu halten.[3] In diesem Sinne kann eine Arbeit wie *These Days* auch als Ausdruck des Antagonismus gedeutet werden, der sich im Aufeinanderstoßen des Zukunftsversprechens eines kapitalistischen Westens mit Englisch als Lingua franca und dem Unwillen oder Unvermögen, den Effizienzforderungen nachzukommen, in teils humorvoller und teils bedrückender Stimmung spiegelt. In diesem Widerspruch und der Notwendigkeit einer aktualisierten Neubewertung tradierter Größen, Gesellschaftsformen und politischer Systeme liegt auch eine Chance, der das Werk von David Maljković nachspürt.

Anmerkungen

1 Max Ernst, *Biographische Notizen. Wahrheitsgewebe und Lügengewebe*, in: Werner Spies (Hrsg.), *Max Ernst. Retrospektive zum 100. Geburtstag*, Düsseldorf 1991, S. 291.

2 Das Futuristische Manifest von Filippo Tomaso Marinetti ist unter anderem abgedruckt in: Evelyn Benesch, Ingried Brugger (Hrsg.), *Futurismus. Radikale Avantgarde*, Ausstellungskatalog, BA-CA Kunstforum Wien, 7.3–29.6.2003, S. 264.

3 Otto Karl Werckmeister, *Linke Ikonen. Benjamin, Eisenstein, Picasso – nach dem Fall des Kommunismus*, Carl Hanser Verlag, München, Wien 1997, S. 229.

# AGAIN FOR

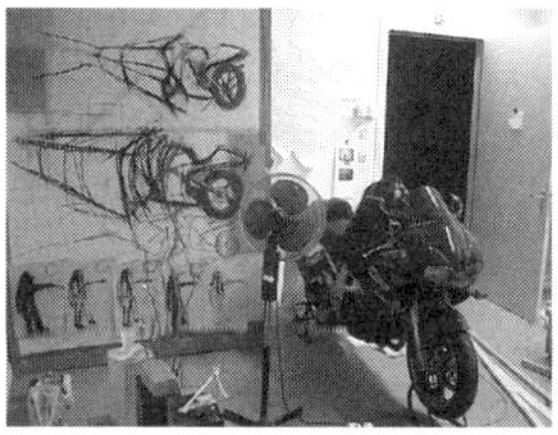

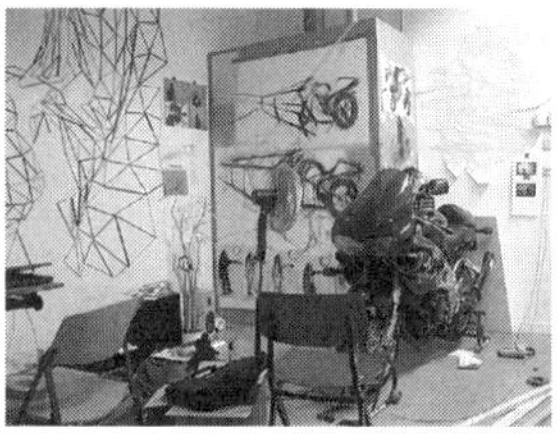

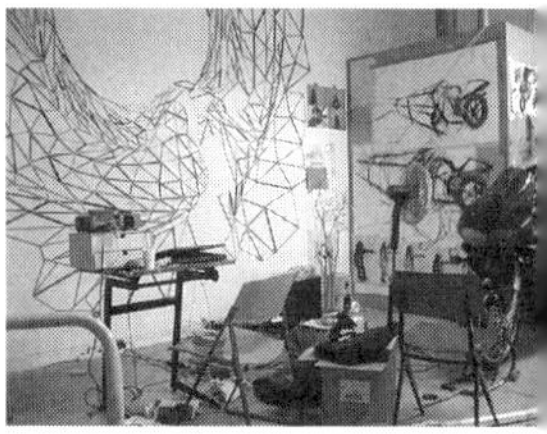

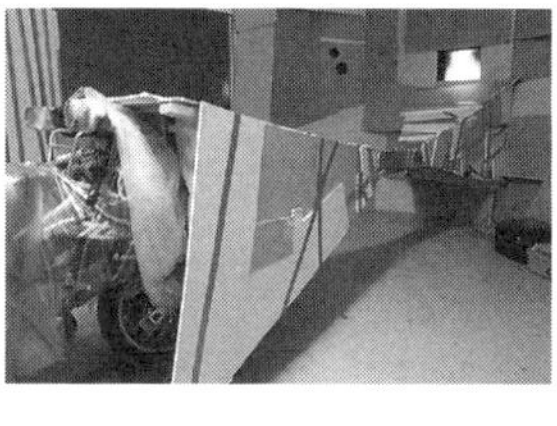

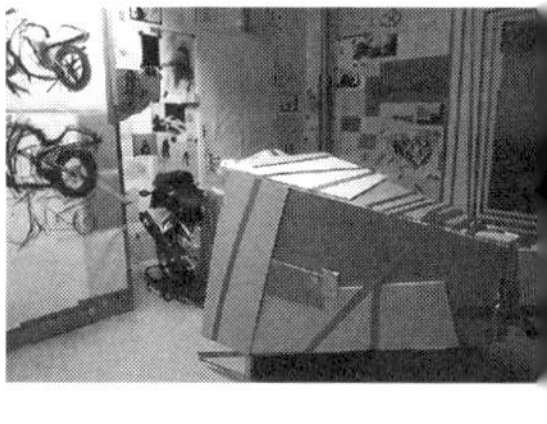

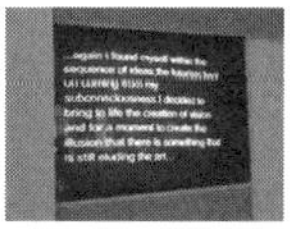

*Again for Tomorrow 1*, studio at Rijksakademie van beeldende kunsten, Amsterdam, 2003

# TOMORROW 1

This time I was really well prepared long before I started. Sketches, models, re-examinations alternated for several months. Finally, after six months, the static journey began. I had protected myself against romanticism and set forth, although there was no wind in my hair. The quest for vision had begun, of course; the images of history appeared at once, the futurists were the first to appear, to remind me how, after all, this was their journey ... I know, I know ... I have skilfully slipped away from nostalgia.

The journey got longer and longer as well as the questions and with them the fear. My *Again for Tomorrow* machine raised the question of the existence of a vision. Although the question seemed general, individuality had to appear, but so did the panic. I stepped on the gas and the static speed increased in an attempt to reanimate the visionary moment. Everything seemed hopeless. After some time I became reconciled with that. Personal exploration accumulated as well as visions of the future in a naive desire to create an illusion of something still elusive ...

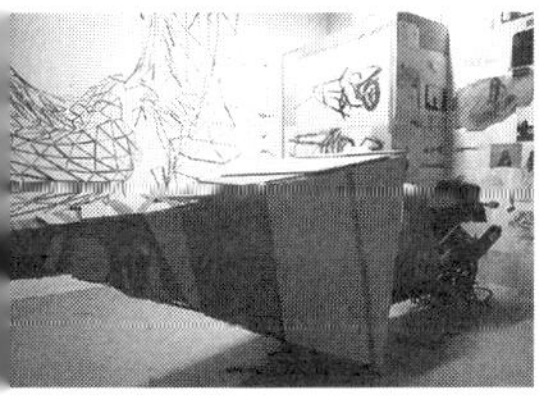

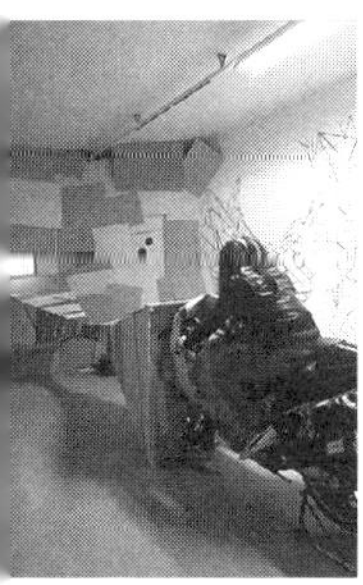

# SCENE FOR

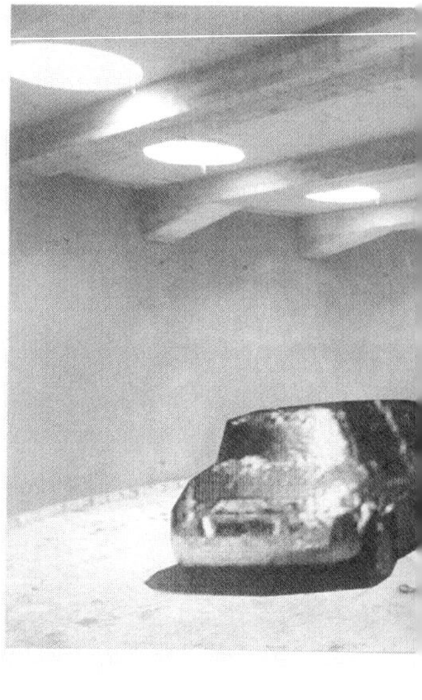

# NEW HERITAGE

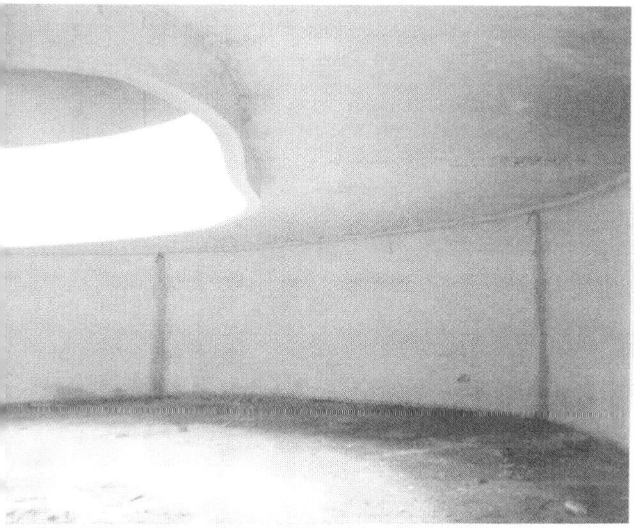

*Scene for New Heritage*, 2004, collage

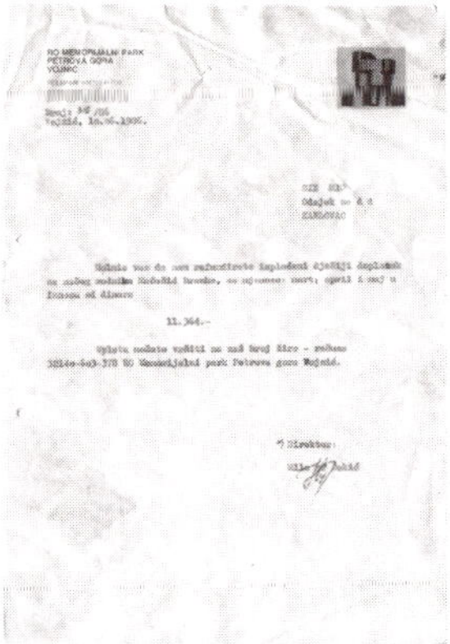
RO MEMORIJALNI PARK
PETROVA GORA
VOJNIĆ

11.364.-

Direktor:

Petrova Gora Memorial Park letterhead

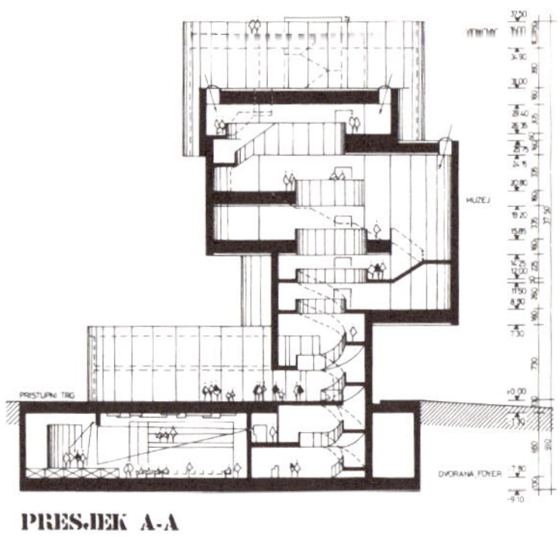


Monument section

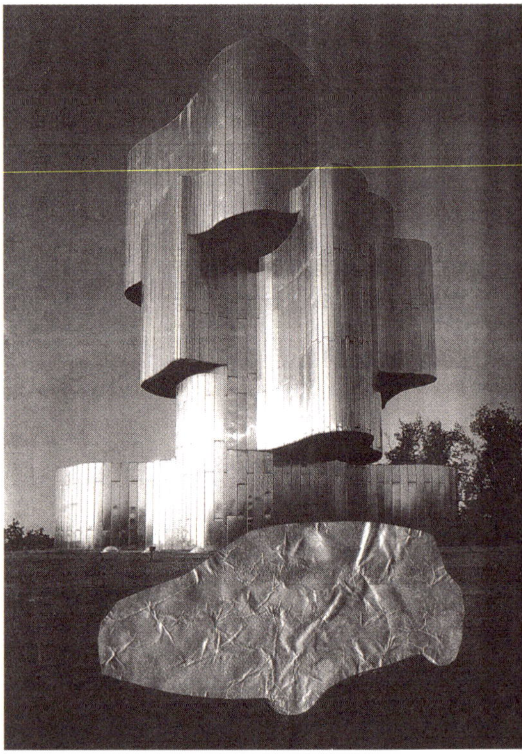

*Scene for New Heritage*, 2004, collage

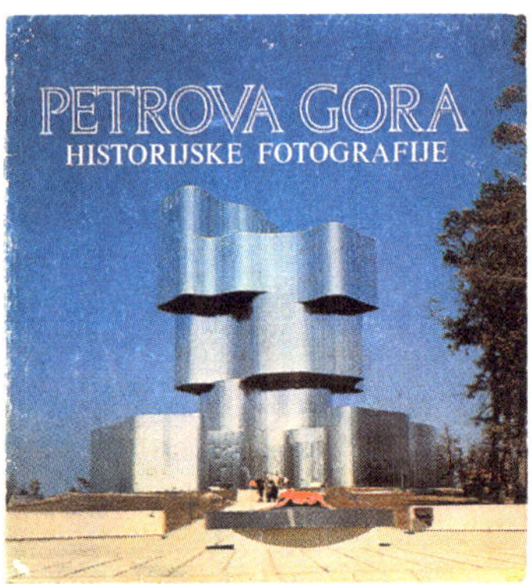


Petrova Gora Memorial Park catalogue, 1982

It all began a year ago when I made the video-installation *Again for Tomorrow* in my studio. This is where the static futurist journeys started and where questions were asked concerning the vision's bare existence as well as the creation of an illusion of it. After some time, the travel started again but this time it headed backwards, into the past.

I reached the forgotten place that used to be a memorial park to the victims of the Second World War under the Communist regime, or to be more precise, the Central Partisans' Hospital. The monument's designer, Vojin Bakić, worked on it for ten years, from 1970 to 1981, in collaboration with his son Zoran and the architect Berislav Šerbetić. I remember that this was one of the places that had to be mandatorily visited in elementary school. It is interesting that a long time ago, the last of the Croatian kings, Petar Svačić, was killed on this very spot in May 1097, and it was even named after him.

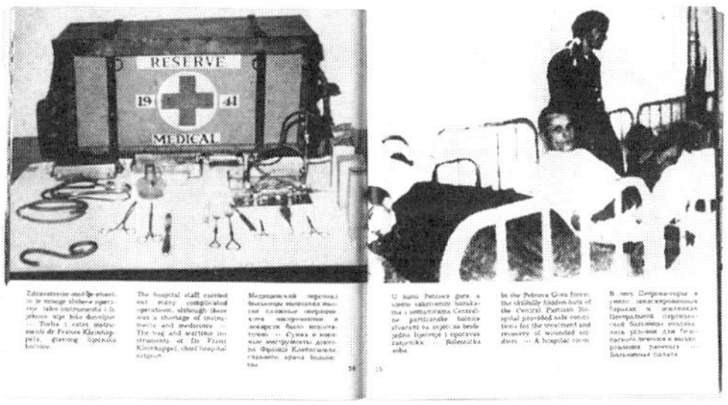

Petrova Gora Memorial Park catalogue, 1982

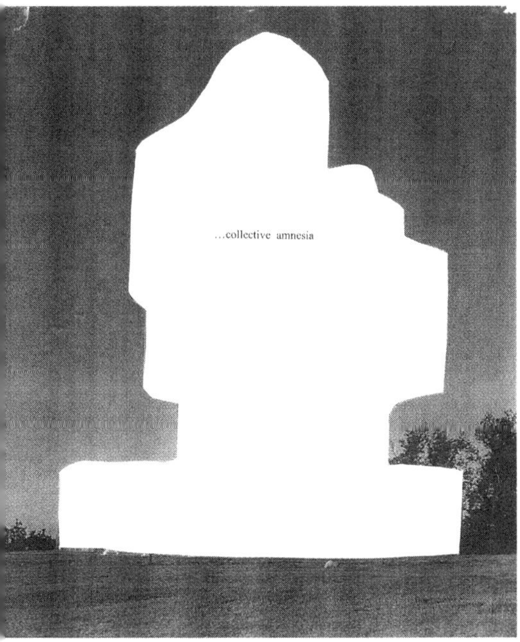

*cene for New Heritage*, 2004, collage

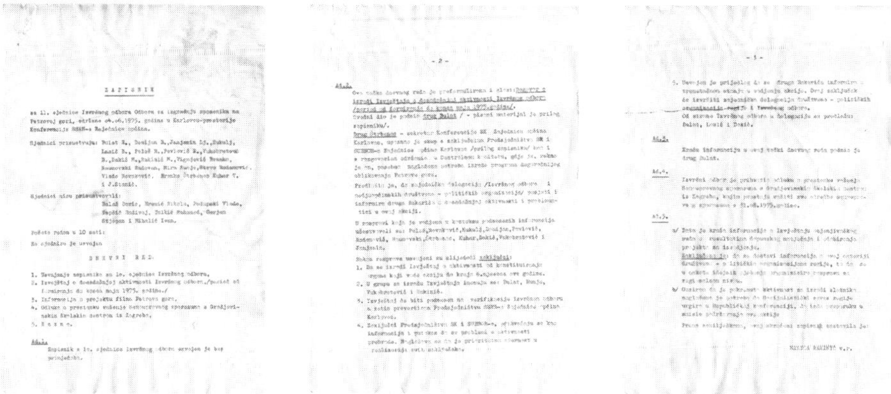

Meeting notes concerning the development of the Petrova Gora Monument, 4 July 1975

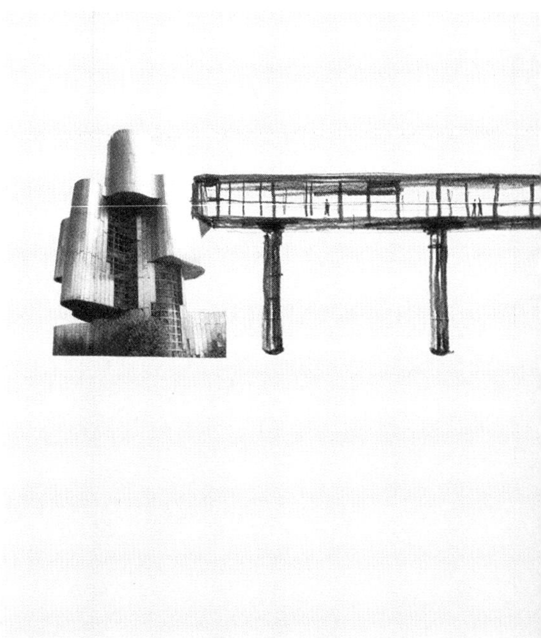

*Scene for New Heritage*, 2004, collage

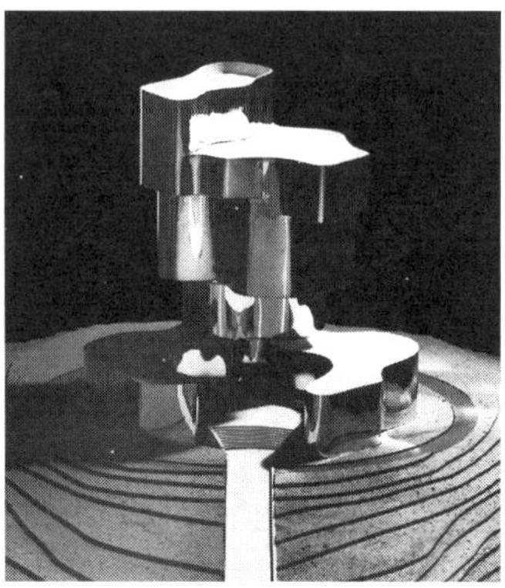

Vojin Bakić's model

Let us go back to the period between September 1991 and August 1995 when the memorial park was within the occupied part of the Republic of Croatia and completely devastated at the time. Today it exists as an artefact, a structure without function, if we disregard the repeater for Croatian television and a T-Mobile transmitter. I don't know how I found myself in that place. Probably the unconscious again directed the course of my journey. I only know that I stood looking at the sight of the monument for a long time. Suddenly I succeeded in finding a narrow slit to escape from all these historical facts and the journey started. I returned to the future and was in 2045, on the 25th of May. I followed a group of people who set out in quest of their heritage and everything seemed without pressure; history became an issue of fiction, and time created a collective amnesia.

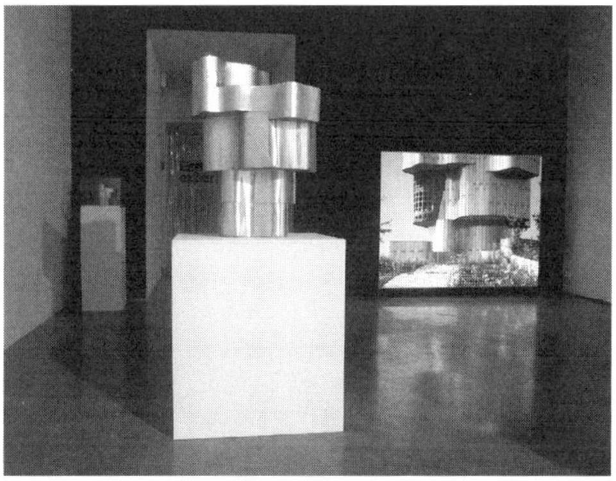

*Scene for New Heritage*, installation with Vojin Bakić's models, Le Plateau, Paris, 2005

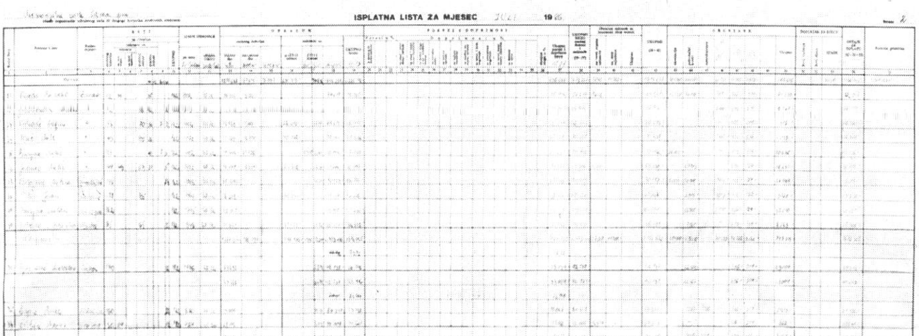

ISPLATNA LISTA ZA MJESEC 1986

Petrova Gora Memorial Park workers pay-list for July 1986

They reached Petrova Gora, an old place unknown to them laden with historical facts not visible to them and they were perplexed by its monumentality. They tried to identify it. It was interesting that they spoke the tongue of Ganga, 'a folk song performed in the manner of a primitive polyphony', most often a rhyming decasyllabic verse revealing a moment of good or bad mood caused by a person or a manifestation. It took a long time to identify the forgotten place and their ignorance made them nervous. It looked as though the issue of heritage would remain unresolved and that this moment was their heritage.

**... your mome**
**your heritage**

**r moment is**
**tage**

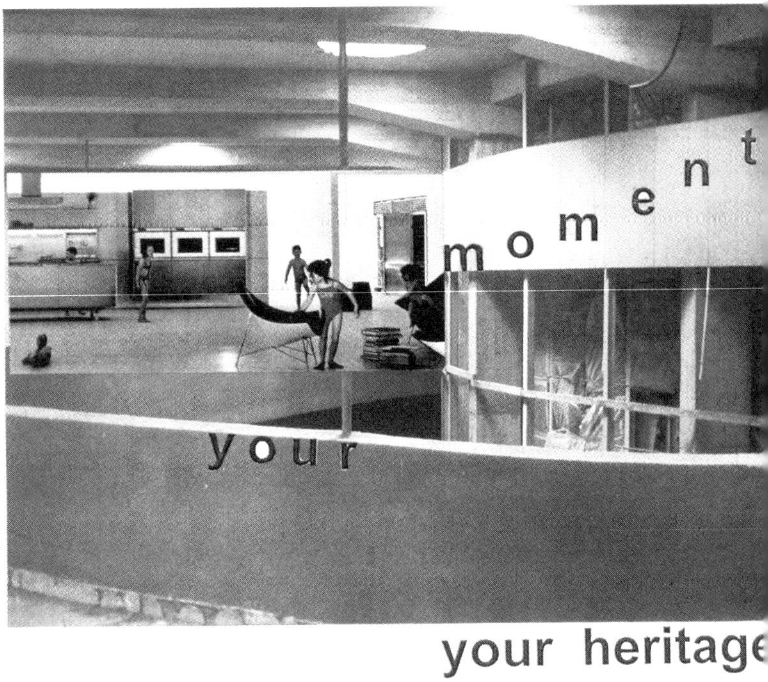


*Scene for New Heritage*, 2004, collage

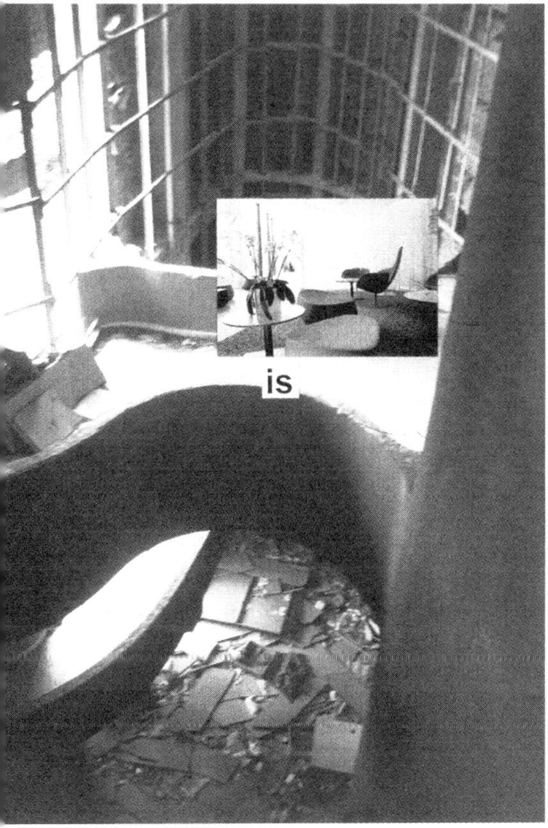
is

Do you think we should
have stopped?

But we set out in quest
of heritage.

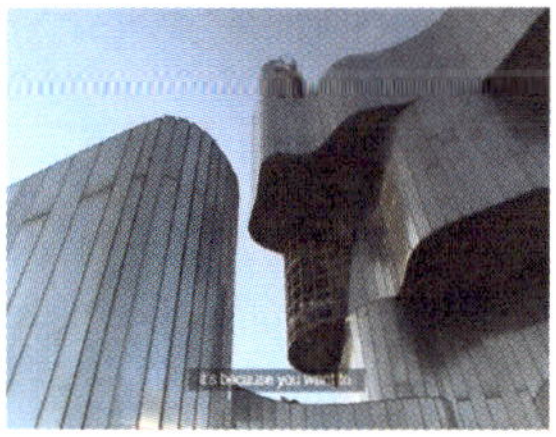

It's because you want to.

It doesn't matter to us.

That was just an excuse
to go on a trip.

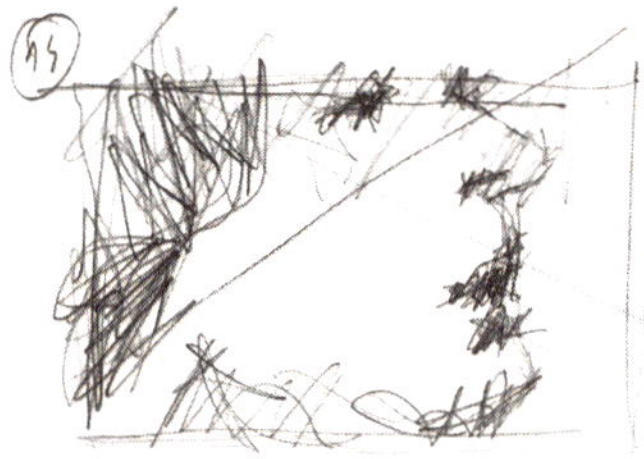

Maybe we should give
ourselves some time.

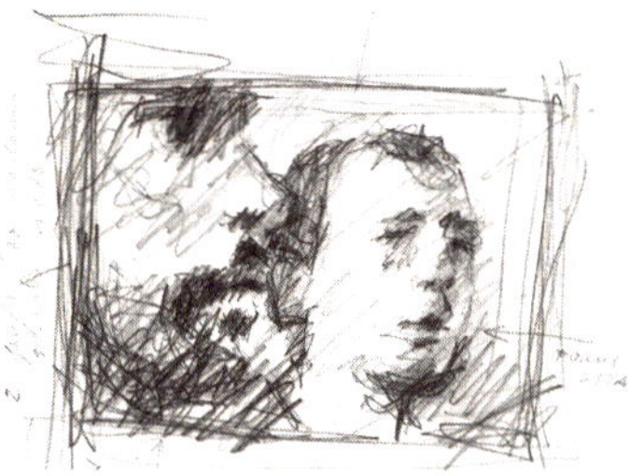

What do you mean?

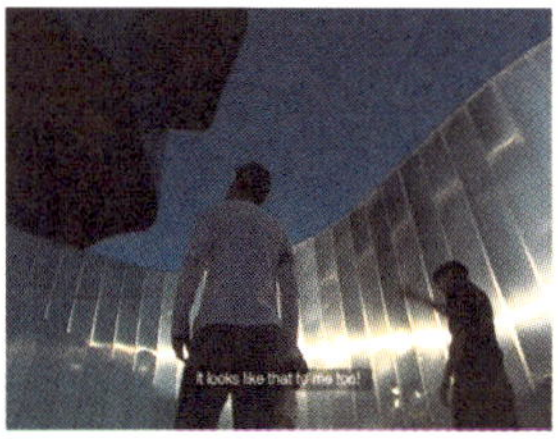

It looks like that to
me too.

We haven't got time,
but OK.

What is this except that
it's big and built in a
strange place?

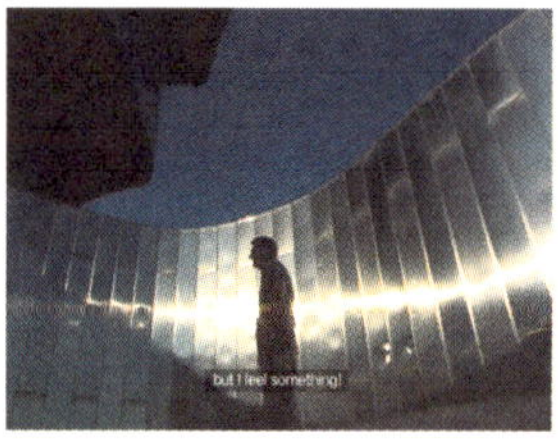

But I feel something.

It looks absurd.

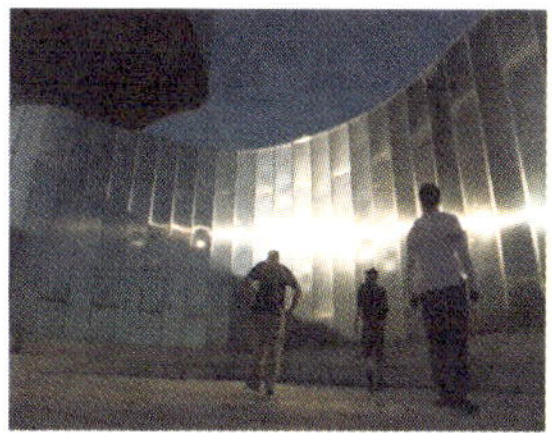

I think it carries a strong message.

And I can't recognize a thing.

Come on, we're tired, we'll come again.

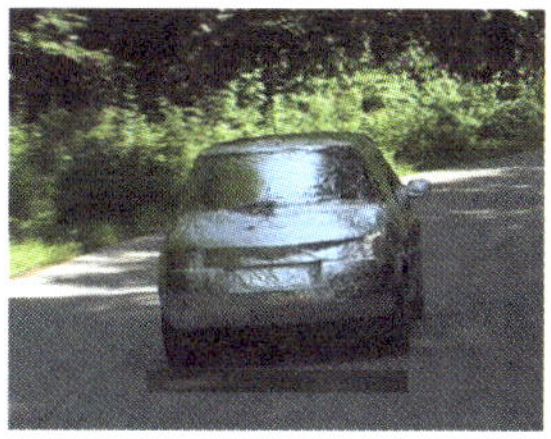

If it were strong, we would see it.

I suggest we change the function of this building.

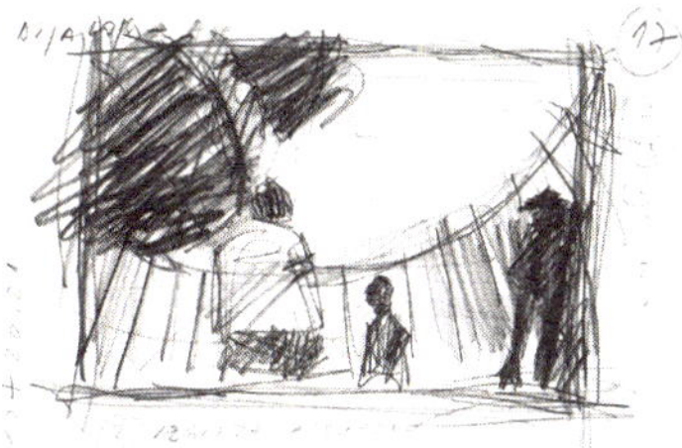

Times were different back then, that's all.

We can't, this place is sacred.

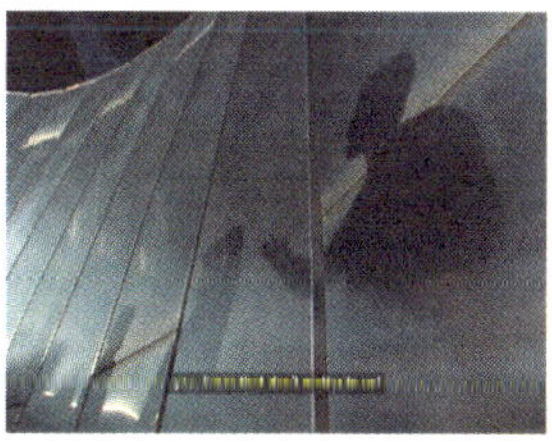

Yes, times that don't matter to us.

It looks to me like there's no god in here.

*Scene for New Heritage*, 2004, stills, sketches and dialogues

## New Possibilities

After I had followed a group of people I returned to my studio but the experience I shared with them changed much. After 25.05.2045 things simply haven't been the same. I thought that the journey had finished and the trip to Petrova Gora would be easy. It seems that a parallel life of the Memorial Park has just started and that the monument does not care about the historical facts any more. The monument has suddenly come to life and has started to seek new possibilities. The time for shutting myself in the studio confronted me again, making sketches/collages to satisfy the monument's need for a new life.

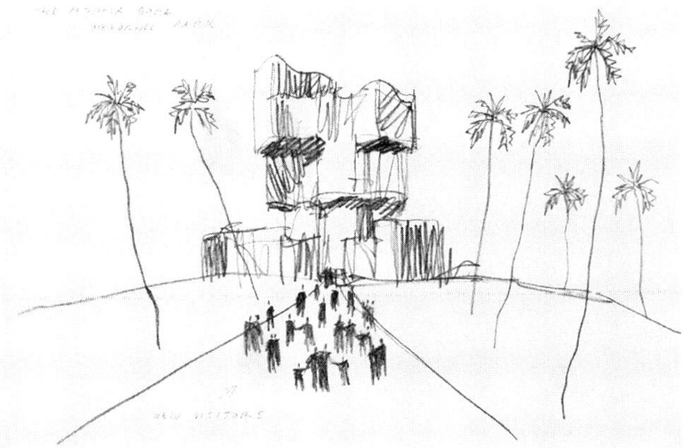

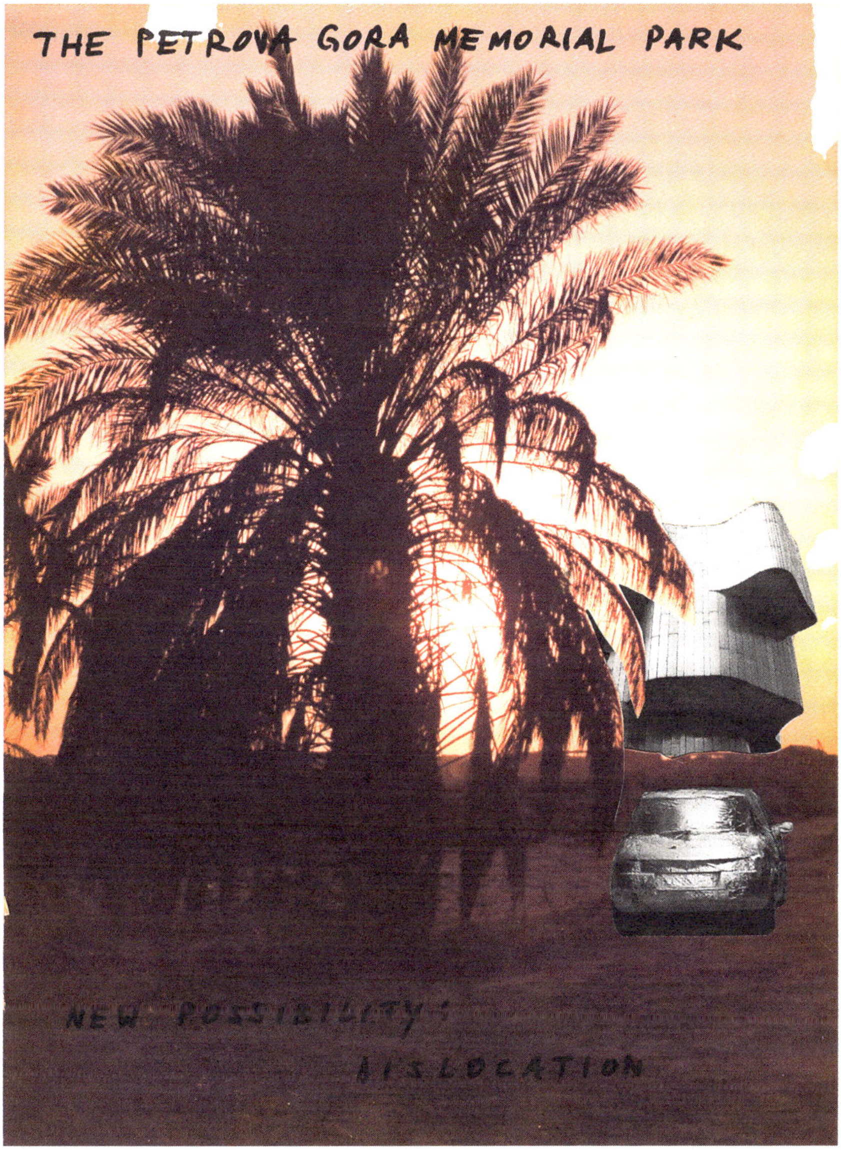


*Scene for New Heritage – New Possibilities for the Petrova Gora Memorial Park*, 2004, drawing and collage

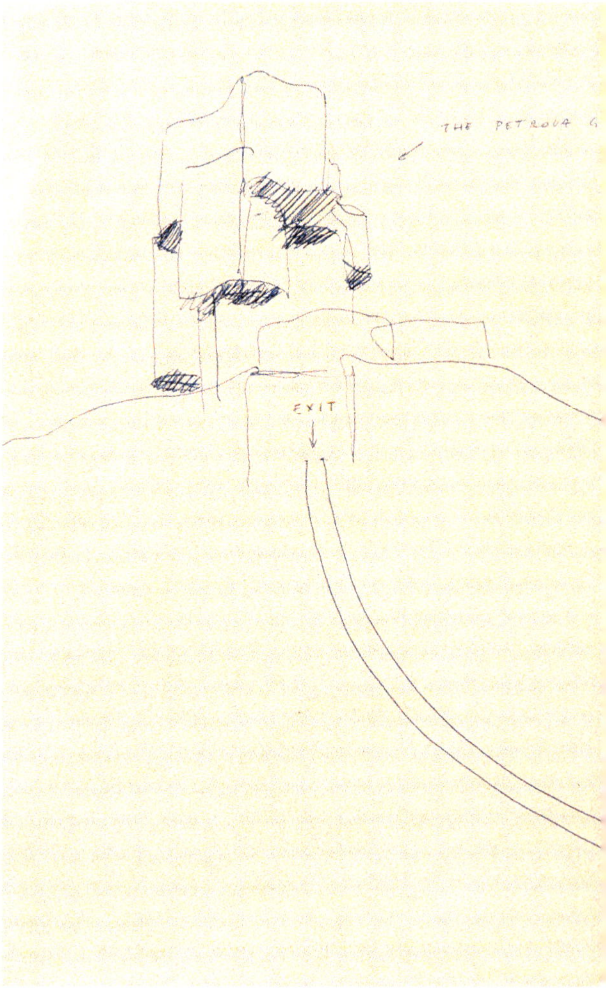


*Scene for New Heritage – New Possibilities for the Petrova Gora Memorial Park*: *Secret Tunnel for a Better Life*, 2004, collage

RIAL PARK

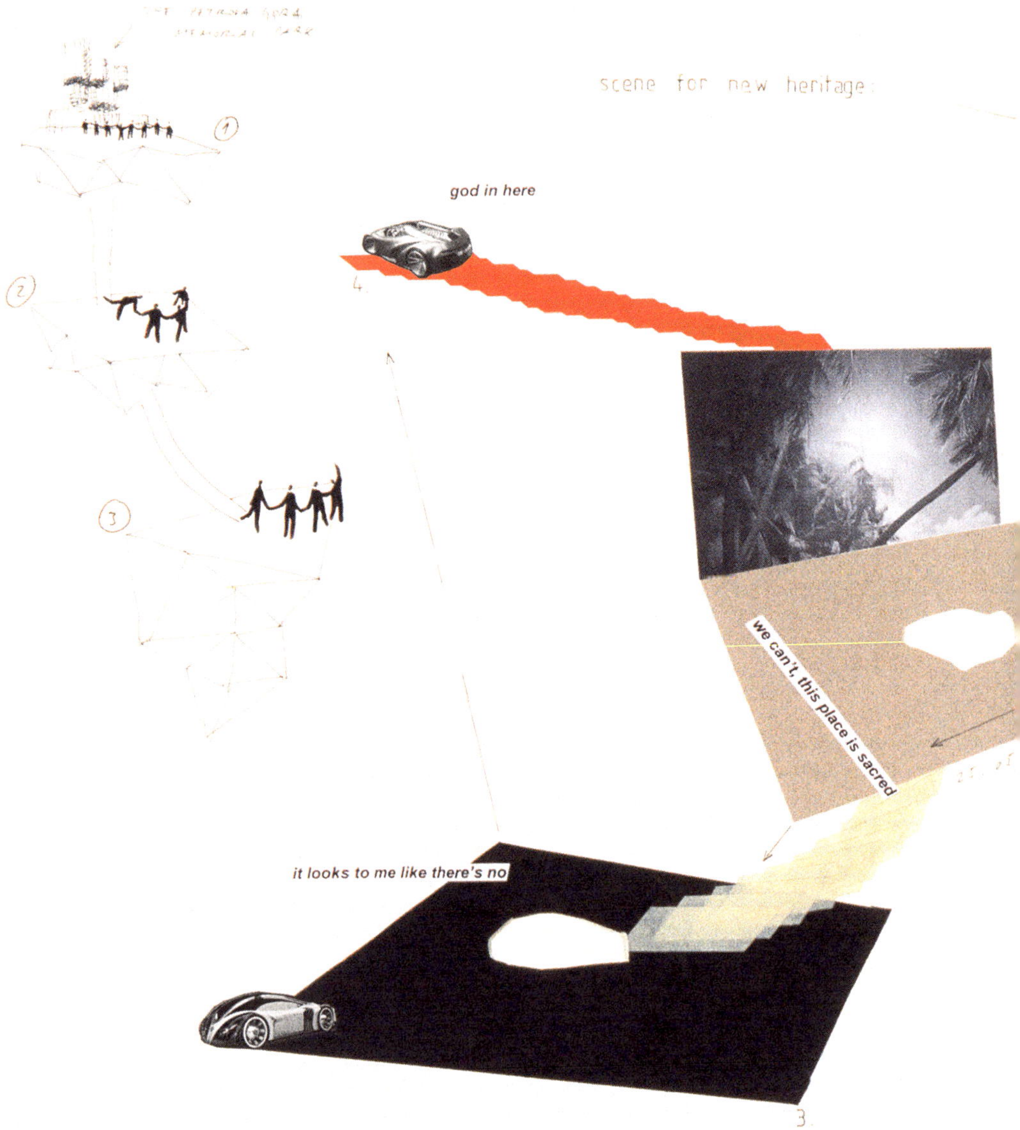


*Scene for New Heritage – New Possibilities for the Petrova Gora Memorial Park: Attempt to Create Platforms for New Visitors*, 2004, collage and drawings

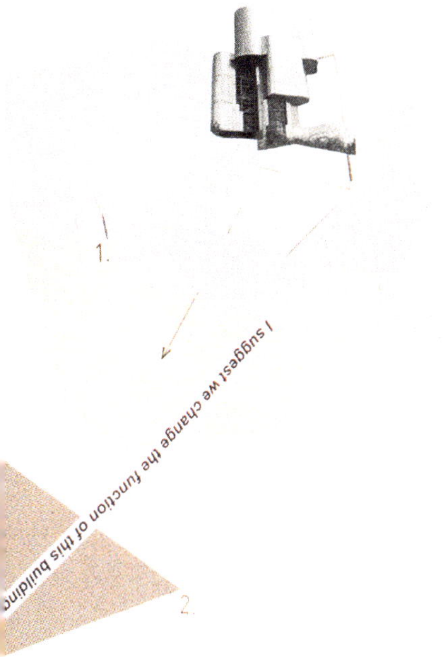
1.
I suggest we change the function of this building
2.

1
2
3
4

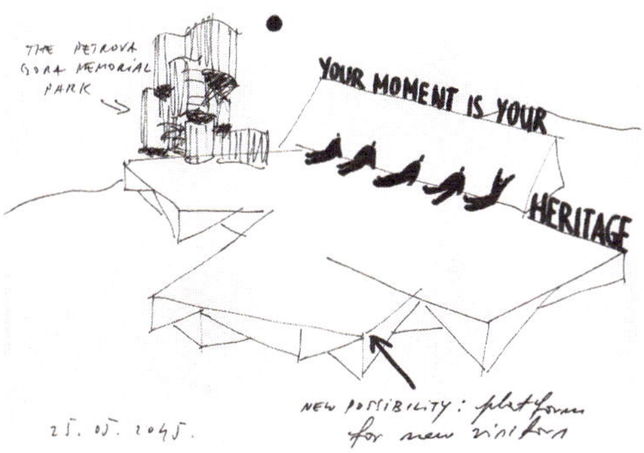
THE PETROVA GORA MEMORIAL PARK
YOUR MOMENT IS YOUR
HERITAGE
25. 05. 2045.
NEW POSSIBILITY: platforms for new visitors

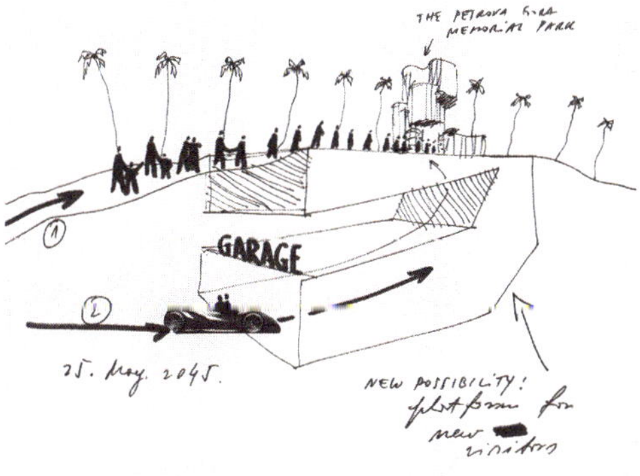
THE PETROVA GORA MEMORIAL PARK
1
GARAGE
2
25. May. 2045.
NEW POSSIBILITY!

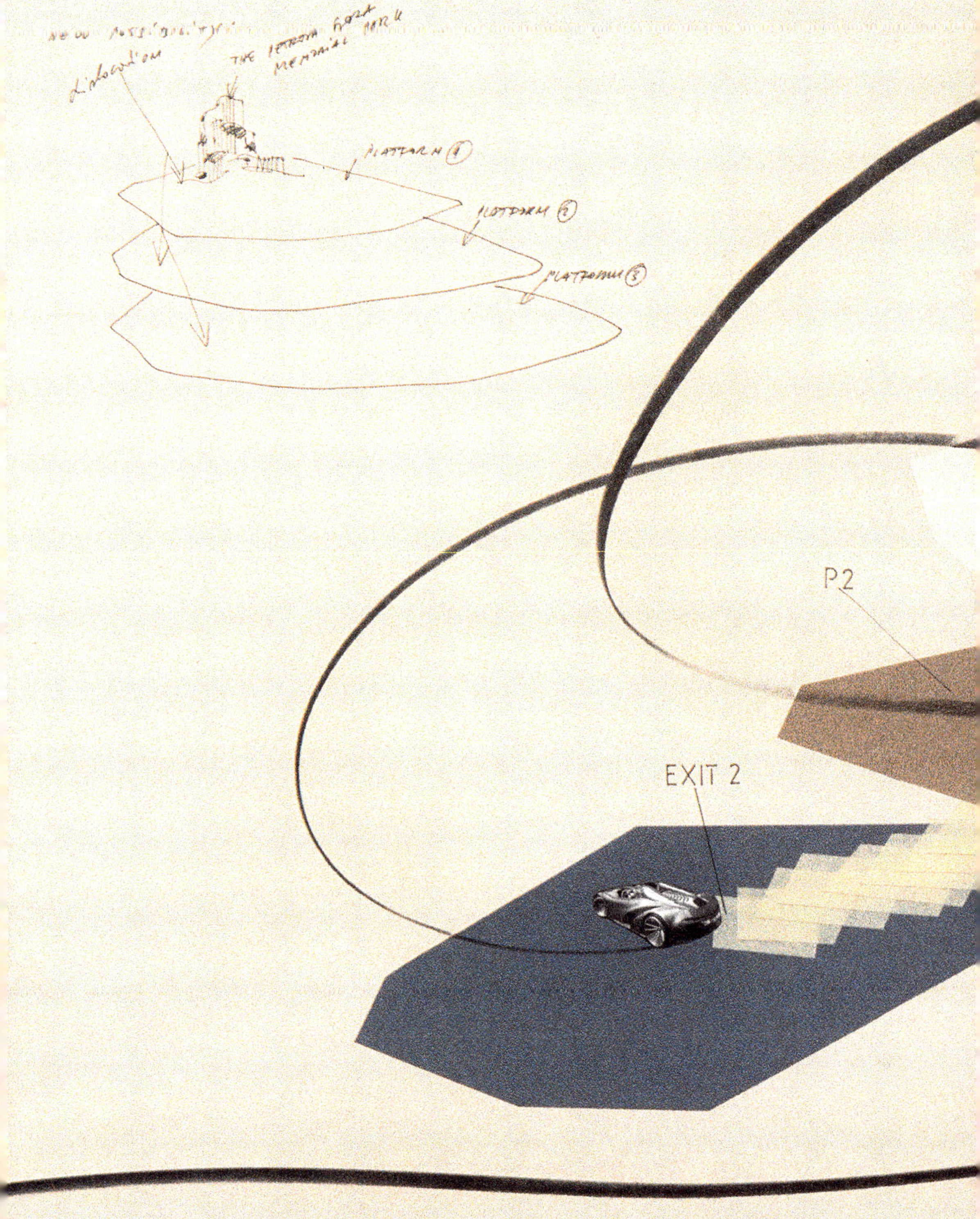
P2
EXIT 2

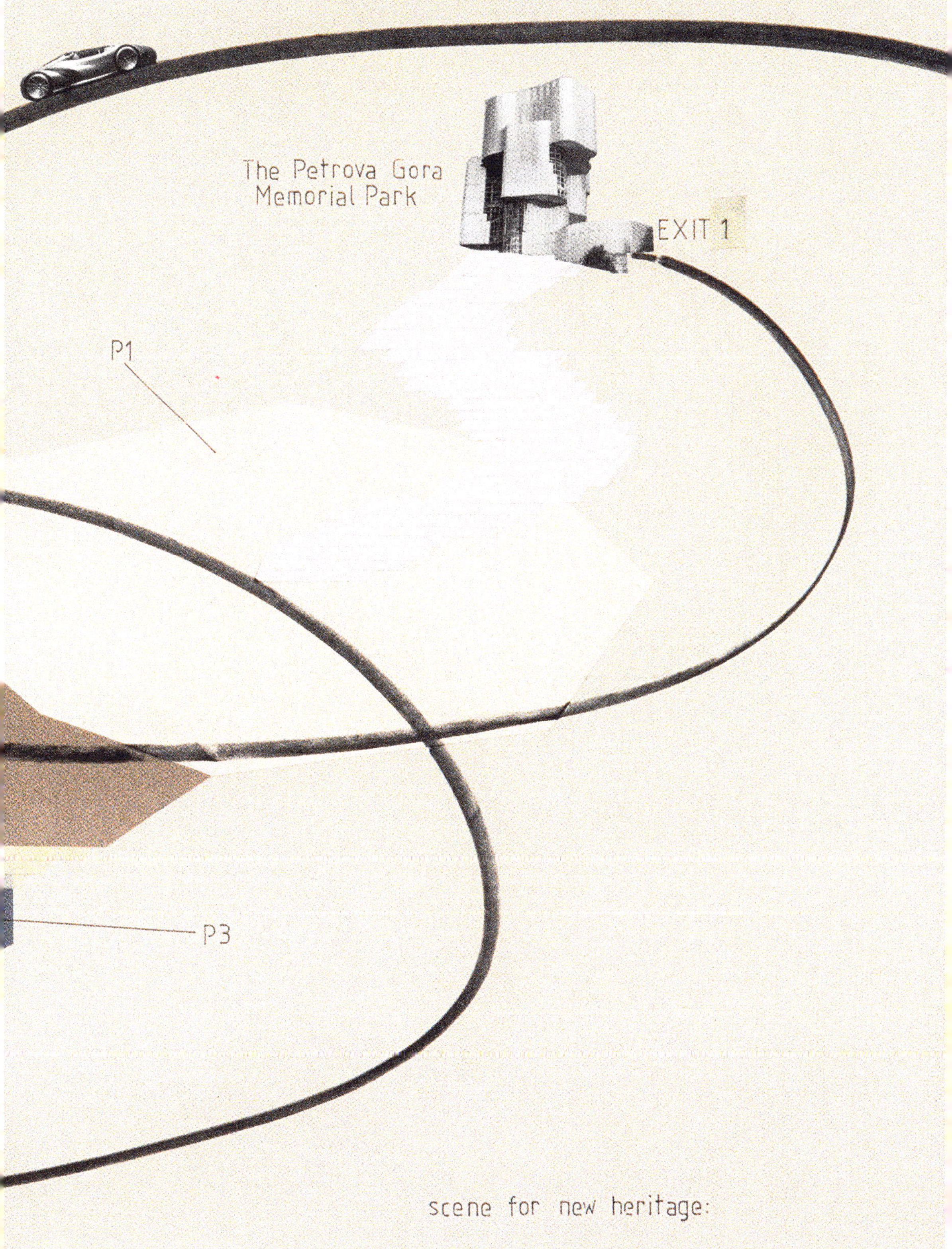


*Scene for New Heritage – New Possibilities for the Petrova Gora Memorial Park: Attempt to Create Platforms for New Visitors*, 2004, collage

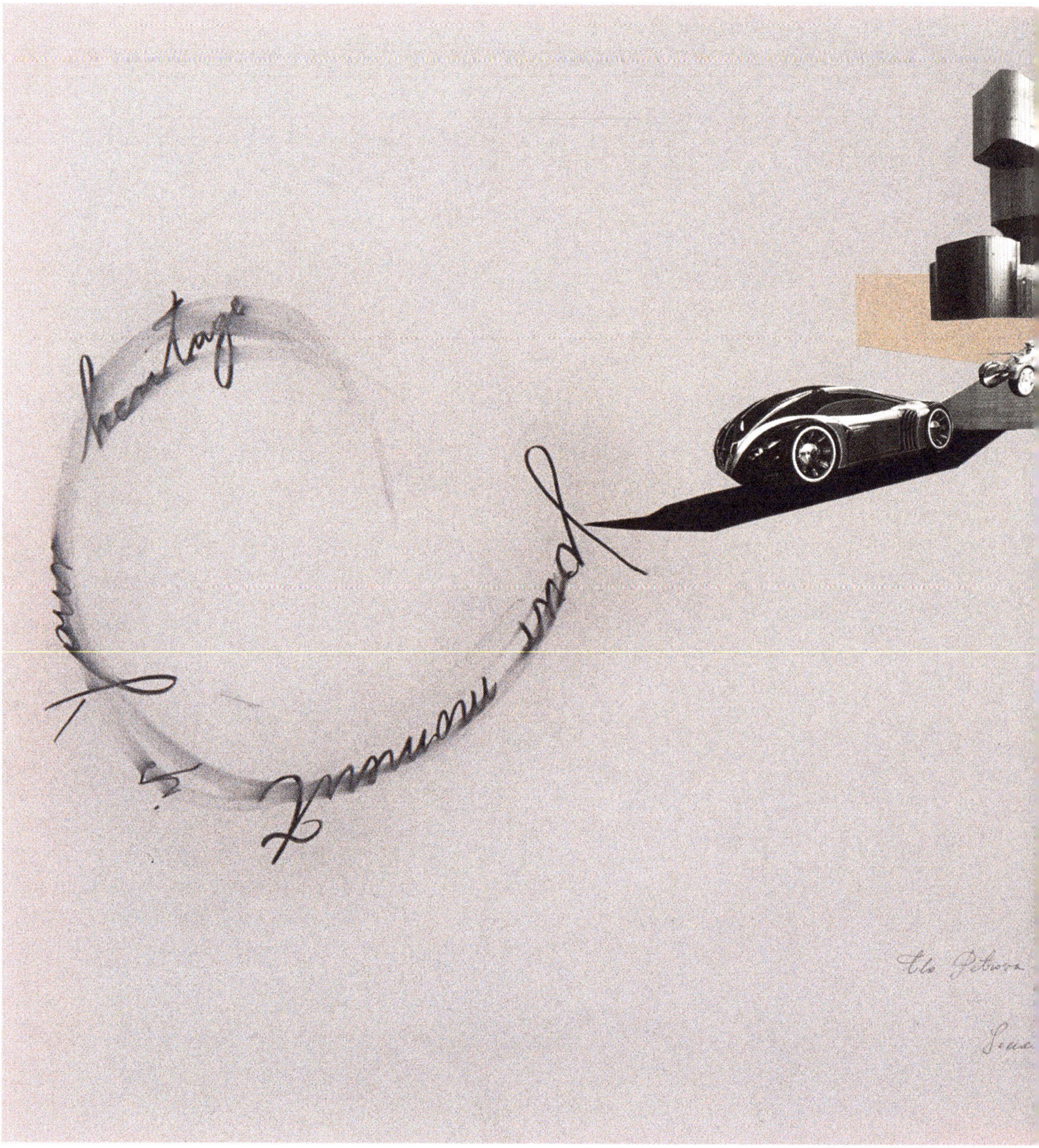

Above: *Scene for New Heritage – New Possibilities for the Petrova Gora Memorial Park: Platform with Peugeot Concept Cars*, 2004, collage

Opposite
– above: *Scene for New Heritage – New Possibilities for the Petrova Gora Memorial Park: Hotel Option*, 2004, drawing
– below: Peugeot 4002 Concept Car, 2002, by Stefan Schulze

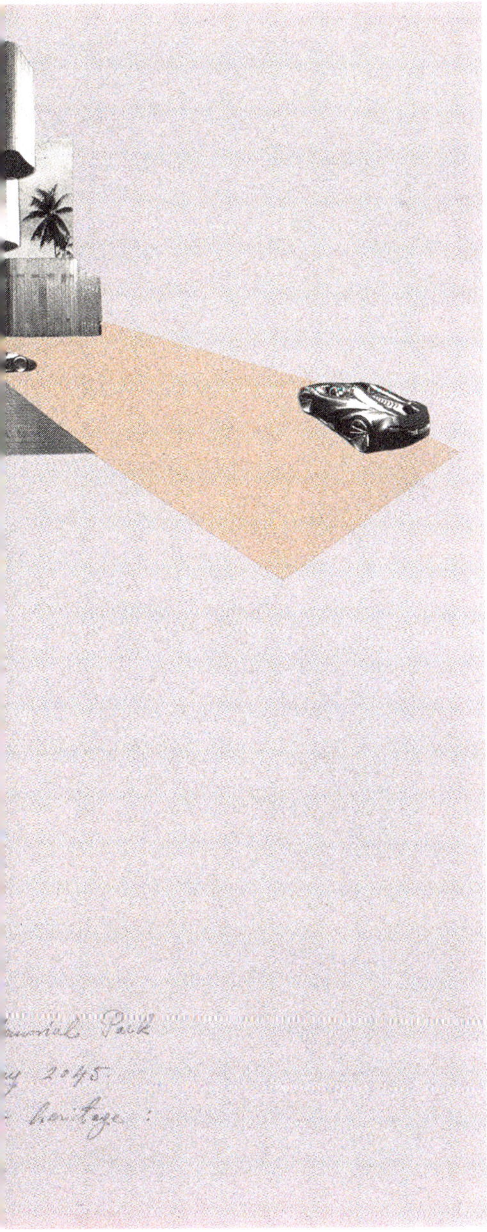

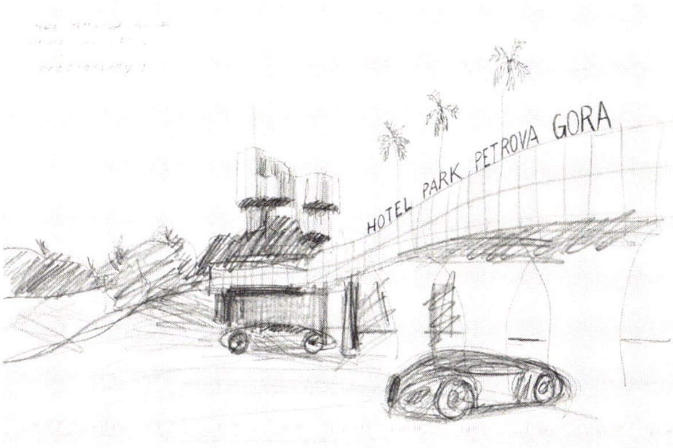
HOTEL PARK PETROVA GORA

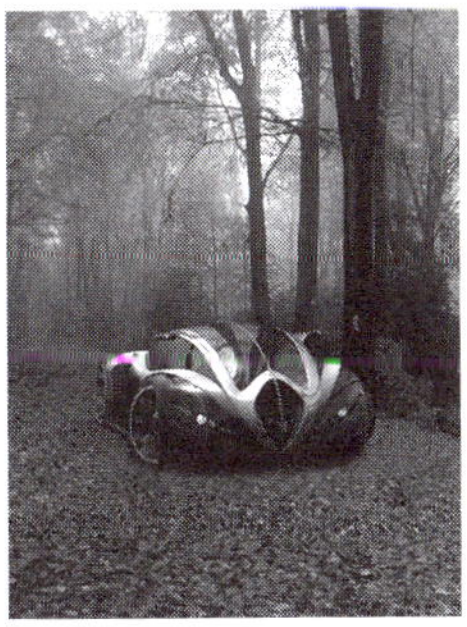

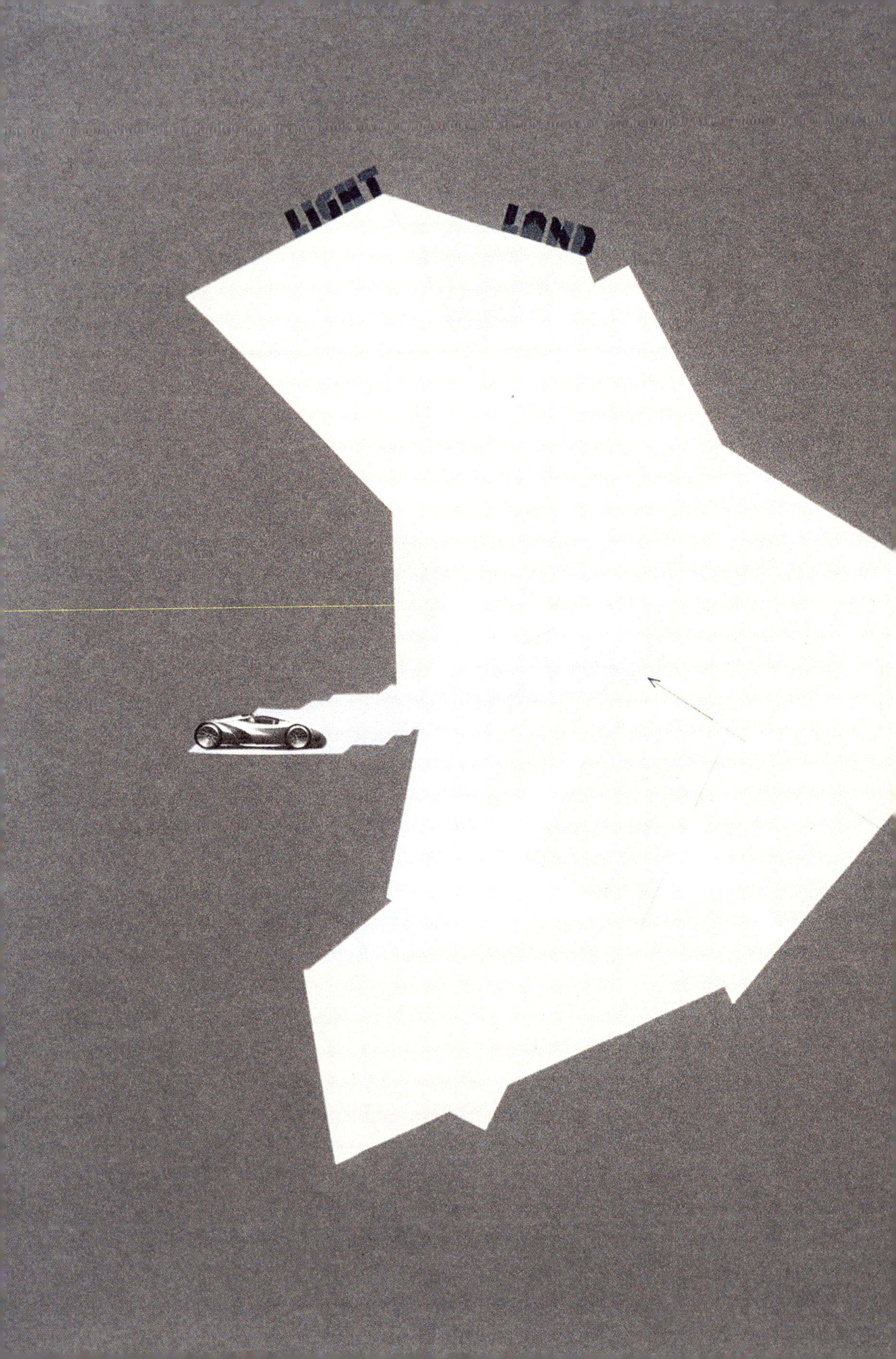
LIGHT
LAND

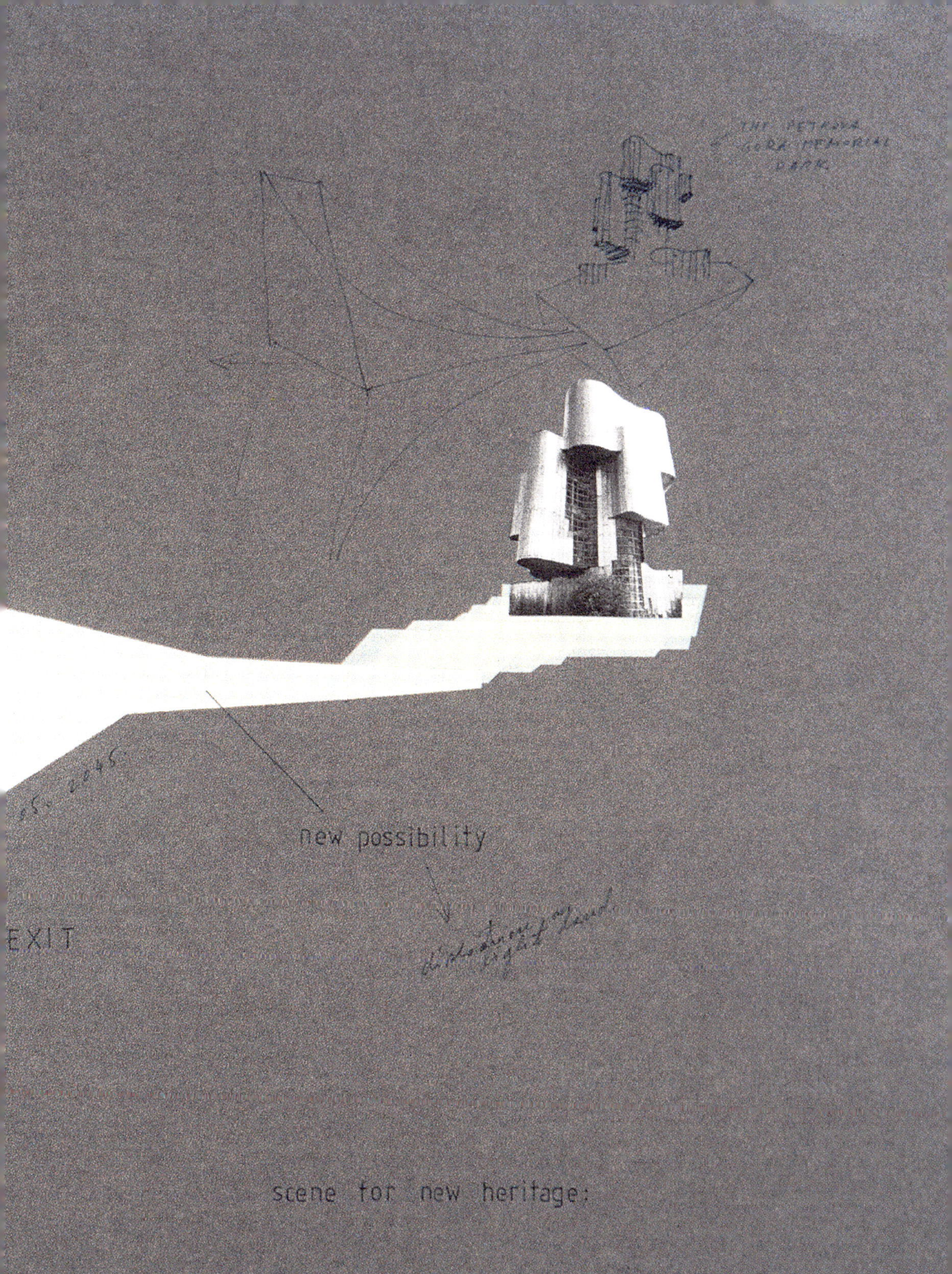


*Scene for New Heritage – New Possibilities for the Petrova Gora Memorial Park: Attempt to Dislocate the Monument on Light Land*, 2004, collage

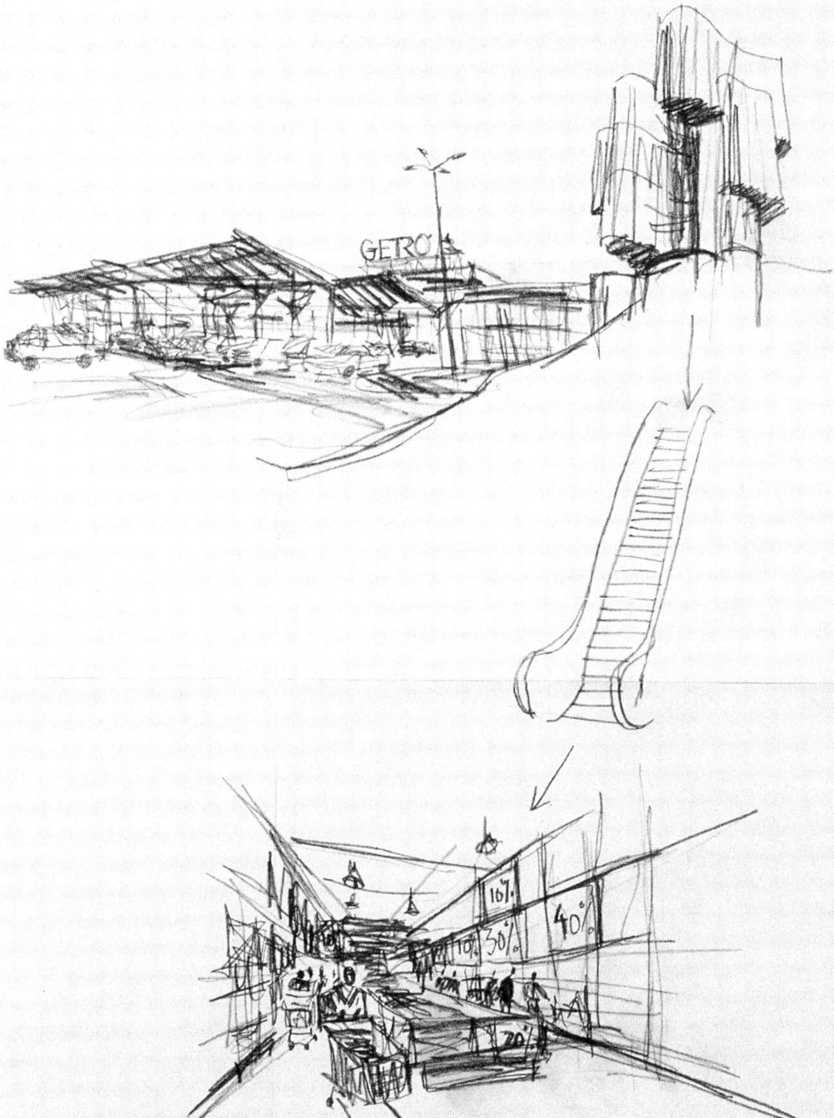
GERO
10%
30%
40%

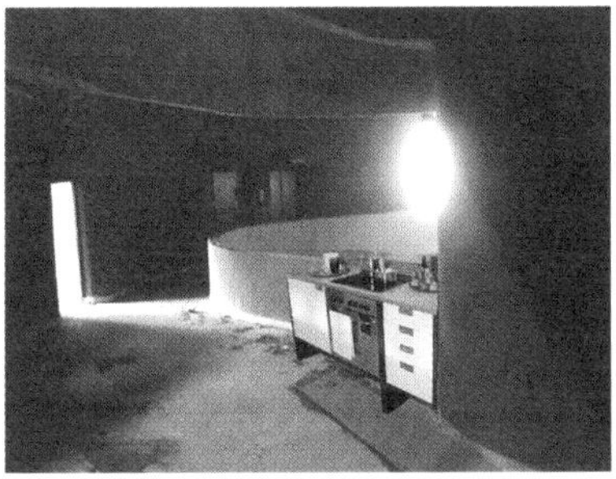

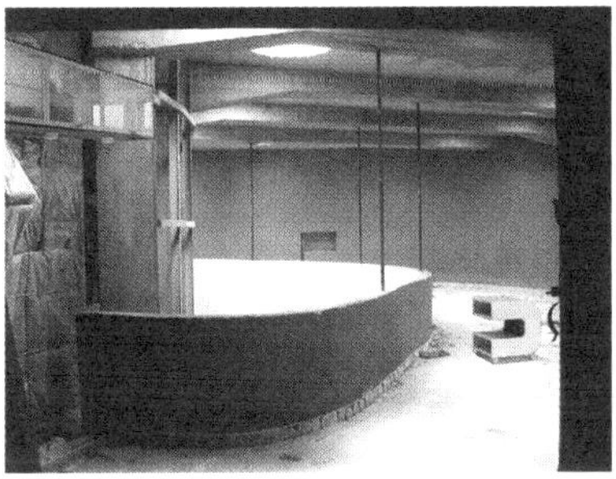

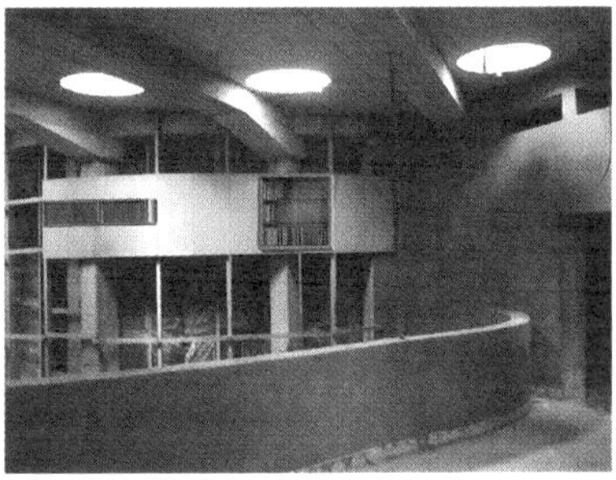

Above: *Scene for New Heritage – New Possibilities for the Petrova Gora Memorial Park: Interior Options*, 2004, collages

Opposite: *Scene for New Heritage – New Possibilities for the Petrova Gora Memorial Park*, 2004, drawing

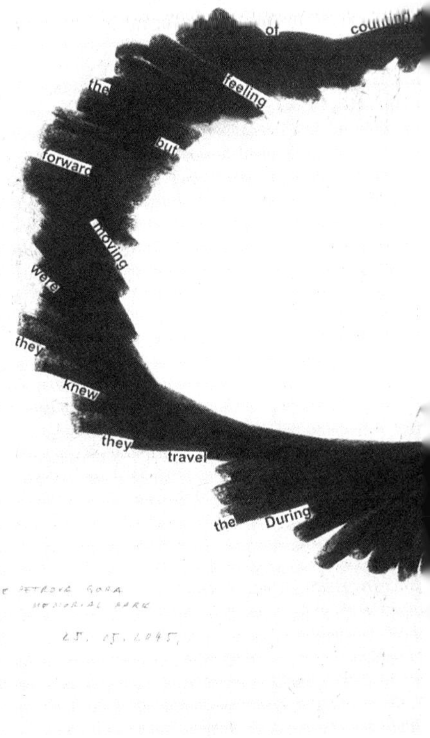
of
counting
the
feeling
but
forward
moving
were
they
knew
they
travel
the
During
THE PETROVA GORA
MEMORIAL PARK
25. 05. 2045.

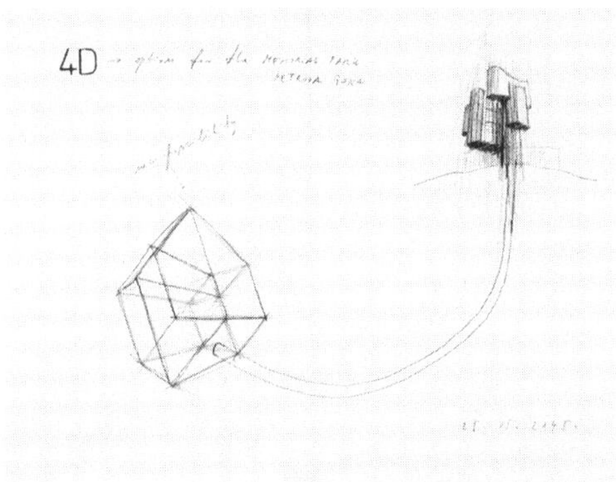
4D

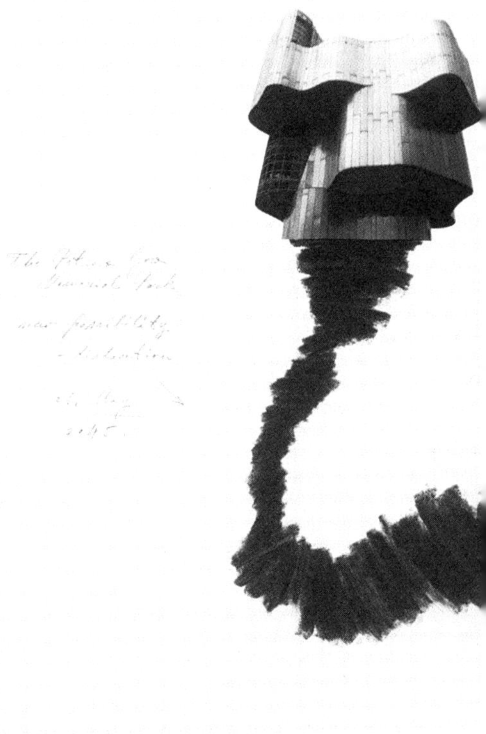

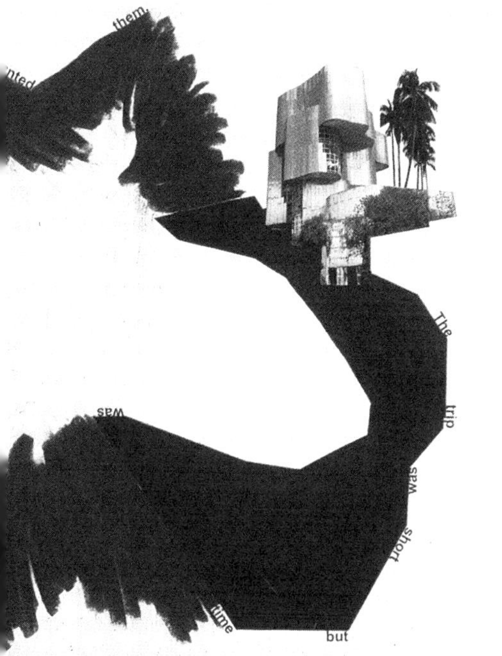


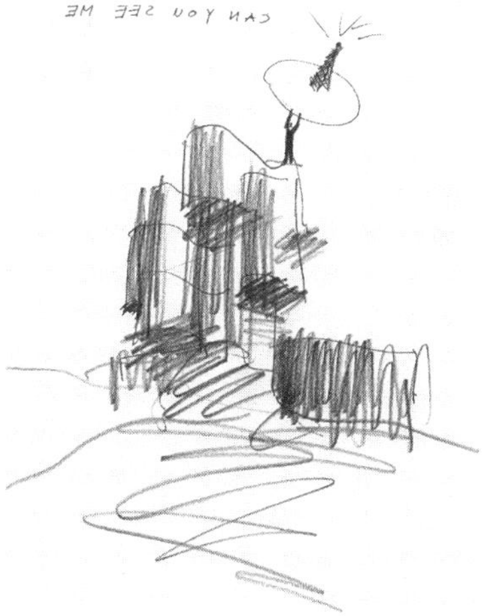

Above: *Scene for New Heritage*, 2004, drawing

Centre top: *Scene for New Heritage – New Possibilities for the Petrova Gora Memorial Park: Attempt to Set Up the Monument Inside a Closed Circle*, 2004, collage

Centre below: *Scene for New Heritage – New Possibilities for the Petrova Gora Memorial Park: Land 2*, 2004, collage

Opposite: *Scene for New Heritage – New Possibilities for the Petrova Gora Memorial Park: 4D Option*, 2004, drawing

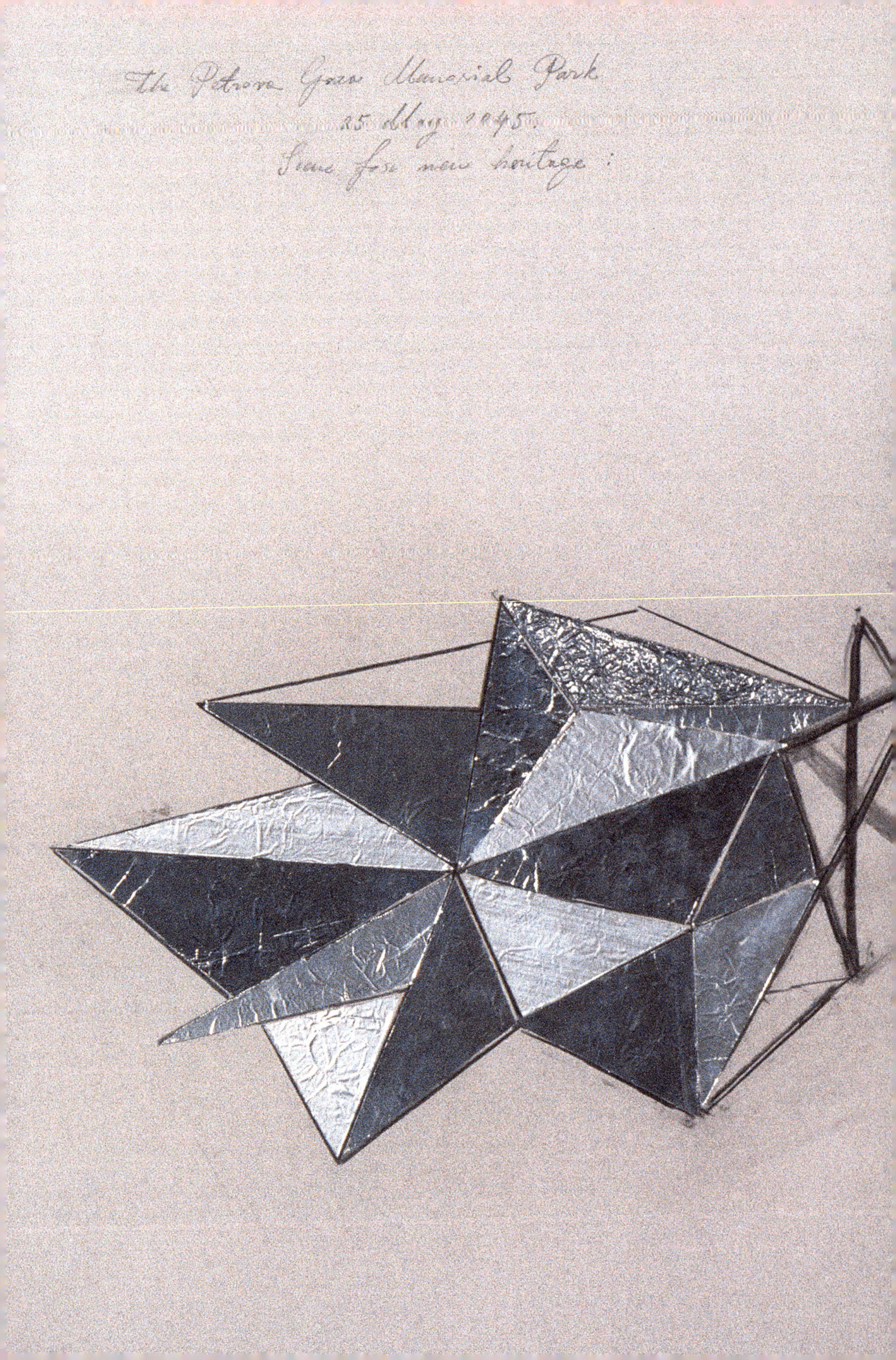
The Petrova Gora Memorial Park
25 May 1945.
Scene for new heritage :

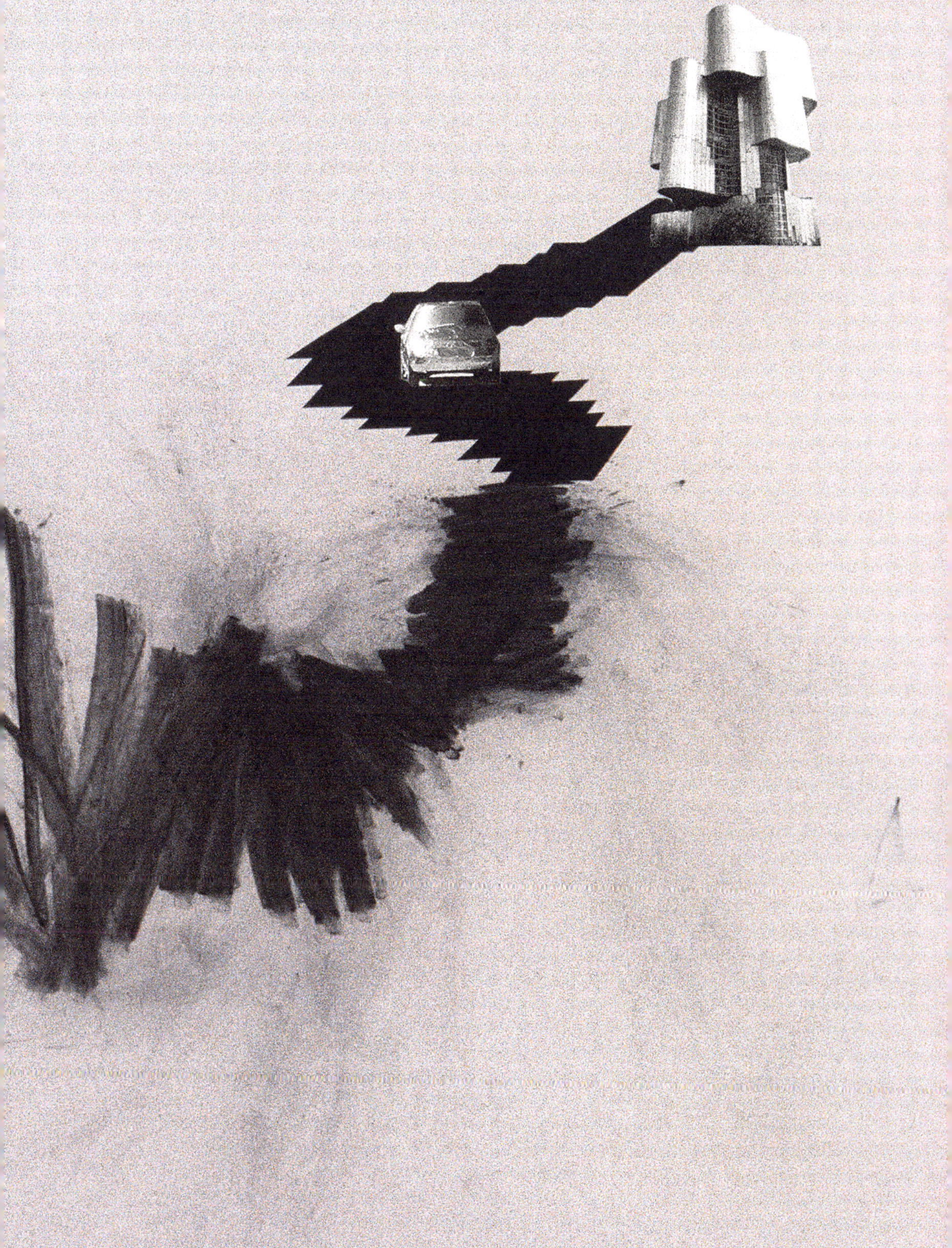

*Scene for New Heritage – New Possibilities for the Petrova Gora Memorial Park: New Ground*, 2004, collage

# AGAIN FOR

Cetinje

Nataša and René invited me to come to Cetinje. It was a big challenge for me; I was afraid of how my machine *Again for Tomorrow* would work outside the studio, and it was also my first exhibition after a long break. I felt that everything was in a way essential. It seemed that it was about time for me to go out. *Again for Tomorrow* triggered *Scene for New Heritage*, even before Cetinje. That summer *Again for Tomorrow* chose parallel journeys leading to real places in the future and the past. Understandably, it was annoyed by the tedious process of creating an illusion that the vision still existed, but it was not going to quit under any circumstances. Anyway, I think that a dead end is a good beginning.

I went to the Grand Hotel which stood intact, frozen in time: the reception, the lounge, the glasses – they all preserved the time of Yugoslavia. I met with Nataša and René in Atelier Djurić in a discussion about whether *Again for Tomorrow* would be set in the deserted factory Obod or in the Blue Castle. We opted for the Blue Castle. I was one of the first to arrive on the set. I was the only one who installed everything on the spot. Eventually it turned out well; things were going slowly; I had no qualms that I wouldn't make it on time, and neither did my two scene assistants, Neno and Vesko. The atmosphere before the exhibition was good, the thematic strand was the Balkans, although nobody actually talked about it. Perhaps because it took place in the Balkans.

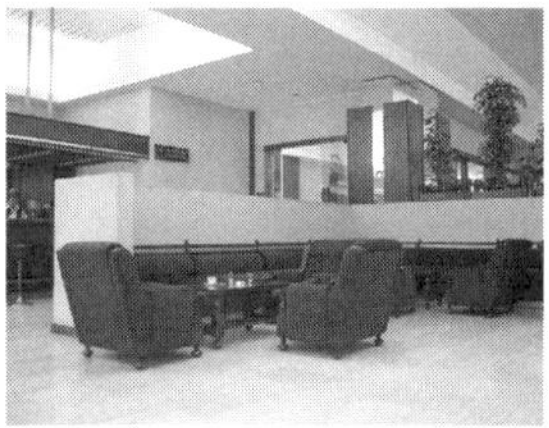

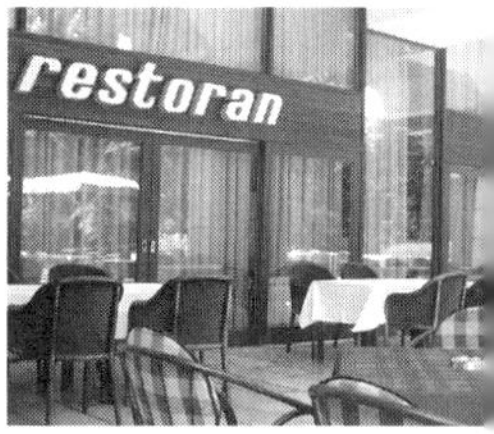


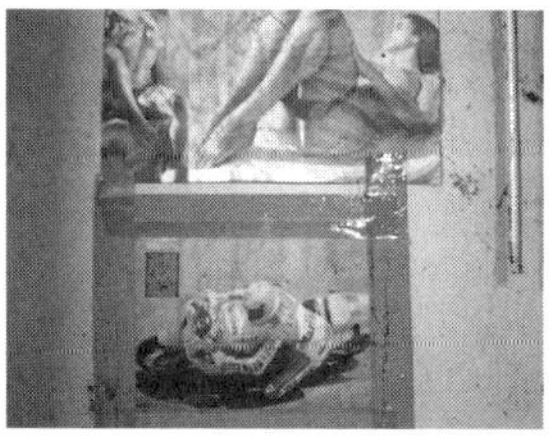

# TOMORROW 2

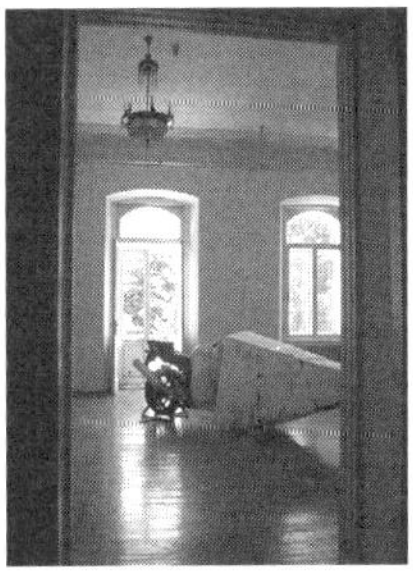

As I have already said, I was the first one to arrive and things were going slowly. I had time to devote myself to Cetinje. I didn't feel the social depression. Cetinje radiated a particularly strong energy, erotic energy; it encouraged my optimism. It started – the scene assistants were having fun constructing the installation and I started to feel more and more strange. It looked so bare and empty; I missed my sketches and the energy I left back in the studio. I was told that this was the place where the last meeting of the Presidium of Yugoslavia had been held. It had nothing to do with my work but I couldn't exclude it as a fact. After some time I stopped feeling the emptiness. The place and people filled *Again for Tomorrow*, and two Turkish artists, Aydan Murtezaoğlu and Halil Altindere, watched my back.

The monitor displayed the video of my last trip in search of a vision and everything was set in that real context while I still felt strange. It was, as Nataša said, 'the apex of the innocent modernism of the fifties, when post-war reconstruction and the building of a new world expressed their short-lived optimism'. However, the installation was there, maybe not in an ideal form, but charged with positive energy, which was important, and it gave me the strength to allow myself the luxury of being stunned. It seems that by going out, the static energy was triggered and was ready for some real travels.

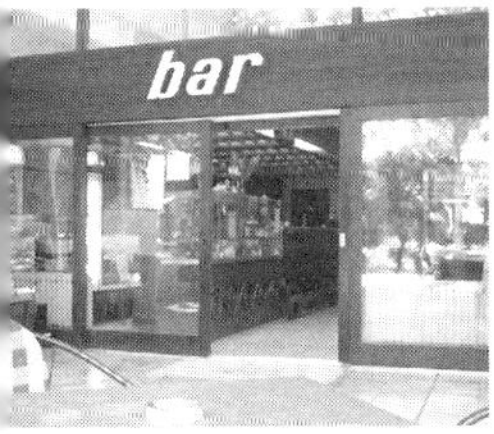


P.S.
I drank a lot of red Vranac with Ana and Renata that last evening.
It all ended at the reception.

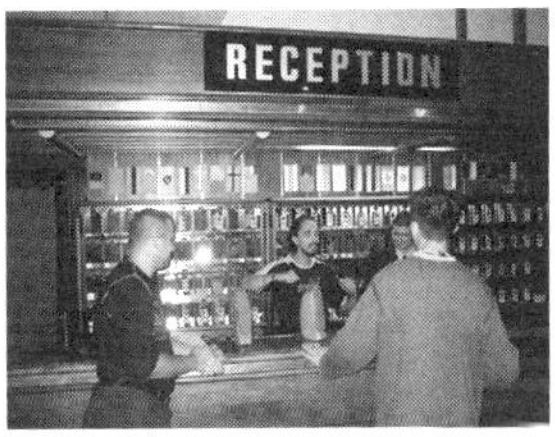


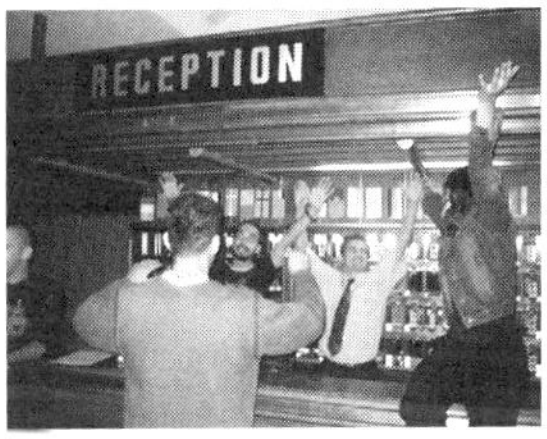

# AGAIN FOR

## Before Prague

*Again for Tomorrow* doesn't stand still. After a couple of months I got an e-mail from Branko in which he suggested that we apply for the Prague Biennial and that, if I was interested, it would be best to send them an offer. I insisted that *Again for Tomorrow* and *Scene for New Heritage* be presented together. I did not decide this way because the two projects were so alike but because they were in a causal relationship. *Again for Tomorrow* was a father and a guide who took me to Petrova Gora, reminding me that the visions were held within memories of the past. I heard from Branko, that he was happy with my proposal; he said that the application had been successful, and so I was happy too.

I didn't think about Prague for a while. The winter came. I was walking through Zagreb and I saw 'A GREAT OFFER: 3 days / 2 nights in Prague or Amsterdam', a budget offer for the period after New Year's Day. I took the poster off the display window of a closed store that had not been able to survive the age of transition. It was interesting that the poster advertised the two destinations *Again for Tomorrow* was going to: Prague and, again, Amsterdam. But let's stick to Prague. Although the deadline was in six-months' time, *Again for Tomorrow* wandered off to Prague for a short while, to be prepared better. It was 5 October 1920 and it arrived in Café Union to meet some of the founders of the Devětsil Artistic Union and its initiator Karel Teige. It was interested in what the young artists were doing. '... like Dada artists, the young artists of Devětsil entirely rejected Western technological civilization and with it, modern art as well. Unlike the Dada rebellion and the negation of all values, they sought refuge in obedience and tradition, in the simple things of life, in elementary values of human living, in the "gospel of the simple". Their works were not created as a vehicle for a political struggle, but as a symbol of the idyllic world of the future.'

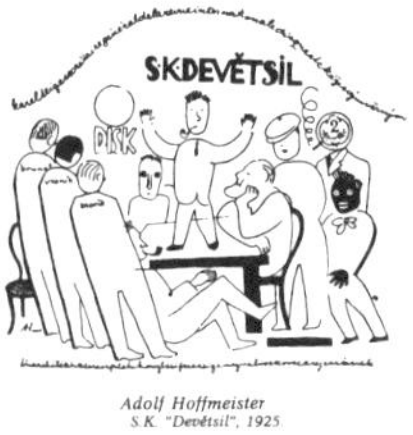


Adolf Hoffmeister, S.K. 'Devětsil', 1925

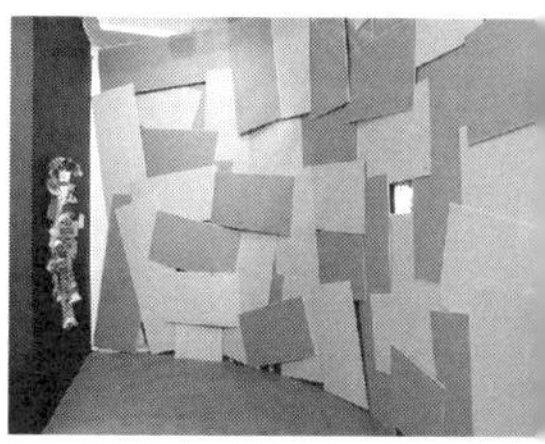

Installation at Annet Gelink Gallery, Amsterdam, 2005

# TOMORROW 3

*Again for Tomorrow* had to leave the café, be patient and wait for its turn, although it noticed that the problems between the regional and the global were still present. *Again for Tomorrow* wasn't the same after Cetinje and it understood that the grandfathers had not done their job and that again it was on the road to integration in the Western system. It seems that the divide is something constant. It was not without reason that Karel Teige was crying out, 'Our basis and our way!' in Prague in 1922. We, too, cried out in Zagreb, with our eyes turned toward the West. It looked as though the time of integration had arrived again, or at least new attempts at integration. *Again for Tomorrow* grew more aware of the fact that it should get out of that phenomenological travel, for otherwise it might be sent back to the beginning, once the circus act was over.

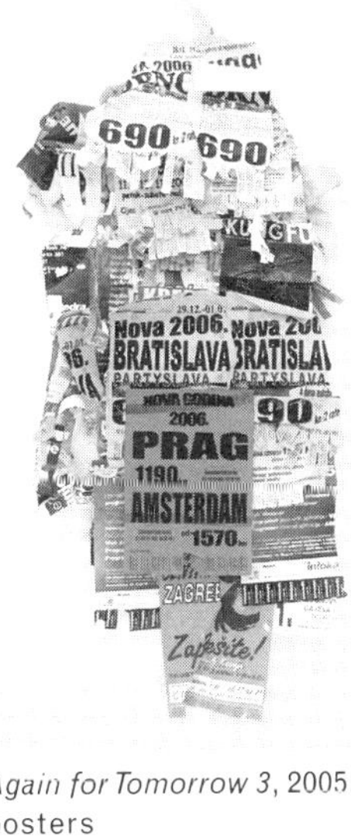


*Again for Tomorrow 3*, 2005, posters

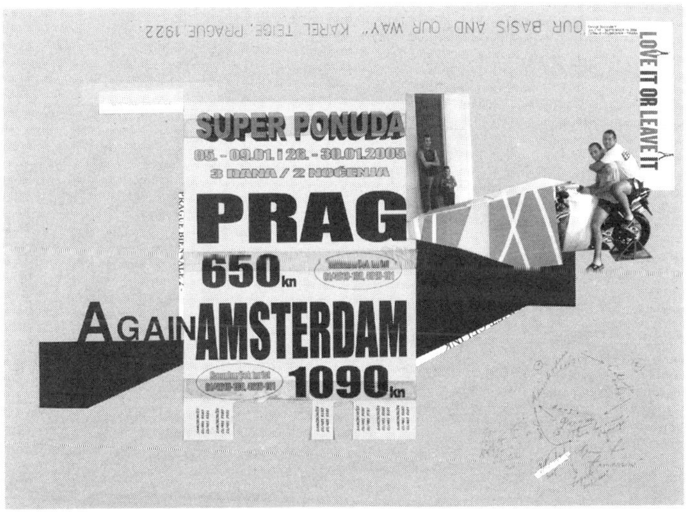


*Again for Tomorrow 3*, 2005, collage

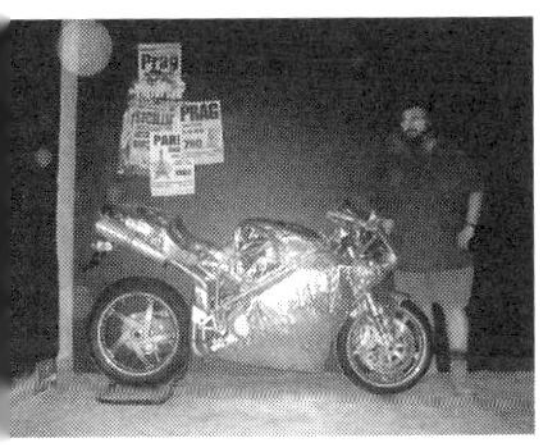

nternational Biennal of
Contemporary Art, Prague,
2005

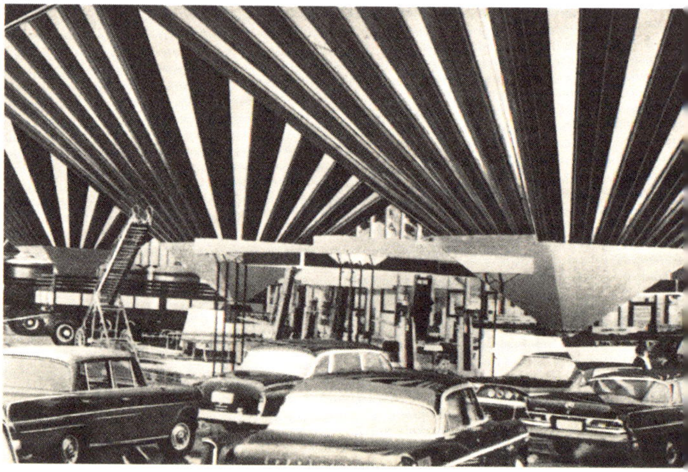

Italian Pavilion at the Zagreb Fair in the 1960s

# THESE DAYS

*These Days* takes place on the grounds of the Zagreb Fair, more precisely, in front of the former Italian pavilion which saw its heyday in the 1960s and 1970s that were the Zagreb Fair's golden age. The Zagreb Fair was quite important for social, political and economical growth. It was a major link, in an economic sense, between East and West, and with its national pavilions was a 'small scale world' and one of the most important bearers of optimism. Today this is a tired place that has given shelter to a tired generation which, with long preparations, has been waiting for a 'better tomorrow' – the year 2009 is the potential year for going West to the so called EU.

Tired dialogues in slow-motion are actually collages of the well known lessons from Easy English textbooks, i.e. absurd and long preparations for tomorrow in a fixed present of today. The mood projected is one of loss, of physical and emotional weariness of a lost generation. Yet it is also a promise of new beginnings.

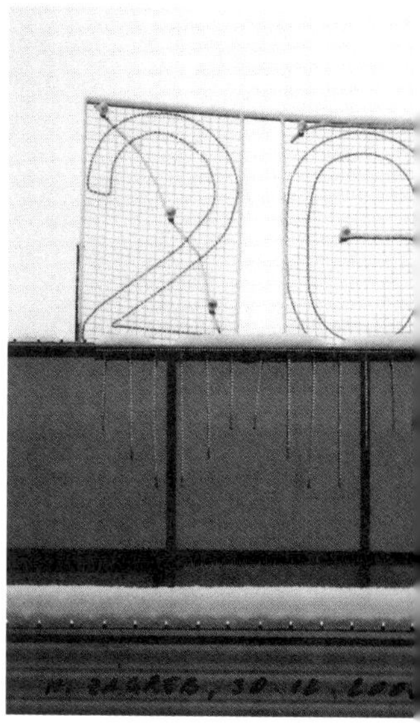

*These Days*, 2005, collage

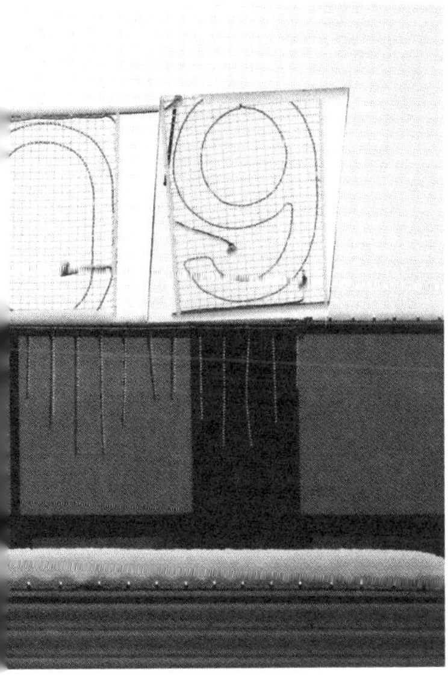

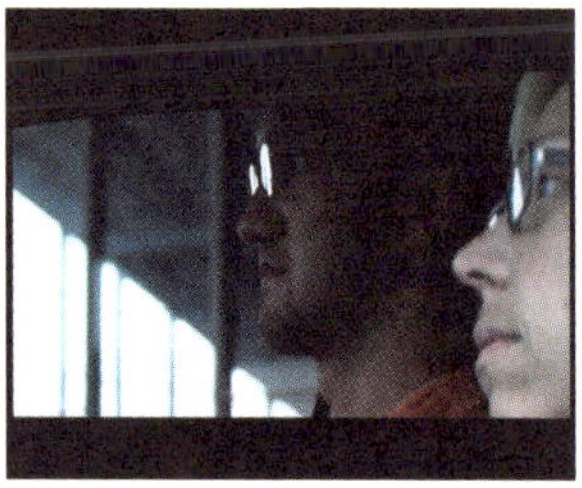

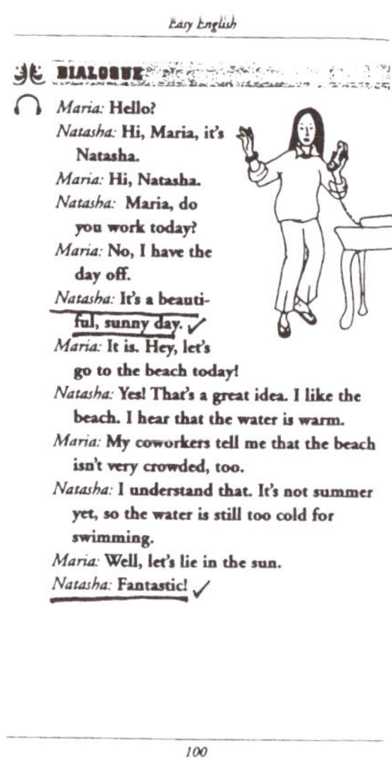

Easy English

DIALOGUE

*Maria:* Hello?
*Natasha:* Hi, Maria, it's Natasha.
*Maria:* Hi, Natasha.
*Natasha:* Maria, do you work today?
*Maria:* No, I have the day off.
*Natasha:* It's a beautiful, sunny day.
*Maria:* It is. Hey, let's go to the beach today!
*Natasha:* Yes! That's a great idea. I like the beach. I hear that the water is warm.
*Maria:* My coworkers tell me that the beach isn't very crowded, too.
*Natasha:* I understand that. It's not summer yet, so the water is still too cold for swimming.
*Maria:* Well, let's lie in the sun.
*Natasha:* Fantastic!

100

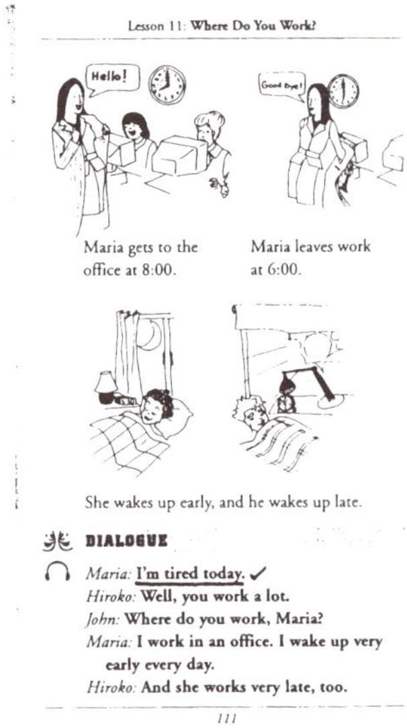

Lesson 11: Where Do You Work?

Hello!

Good bye!

Maria gets to the office at 8:00.

Maria leaves work at 6:00.

She wakes up early, and he wakes up late.

DIALOGUE

*Maria:* I'm tired today.
*Hiroko:* Well, you work a lot.
*John:* Where do you work, Maria?
*Maria:* I work in an office. I wake up very early every day.
*Hiroko:* And she works very late, too.

111

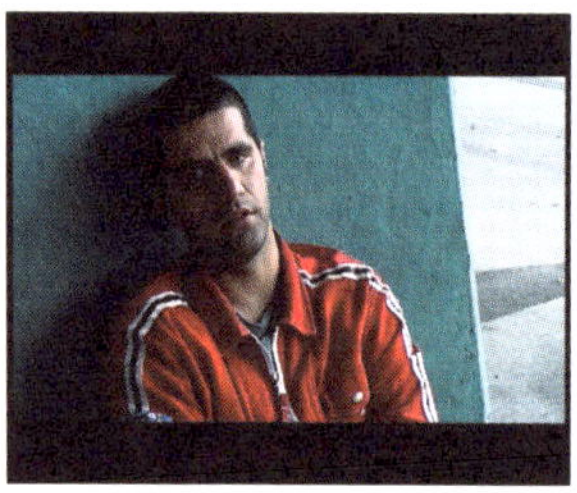

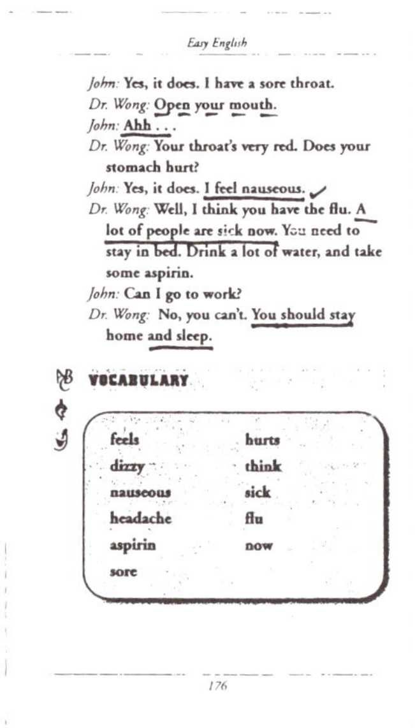

Easy English

*John:* Yes, it does. I have a sore throat.
*Dr. Wong:* Open your mouth.
*John:* Ahh . . .
*Dr. Wong:* Your throat's very red. Does your stomach hurt?
*John:* Yes, it does. I feel nauseous.
*Dr. Wong:* Well, I think you have the flu. A lot of people are sick now. You need to stay in bed. Drink a lot of water, and take some aspirin.
*John:* Can I go to work?
*Dr. Wong:* No, you can't. You should stay home and sleep.

VOCABULARY

| | |
|---|---|
| feels | hurts |
| dizzy | think |
| nauseous | sick |
| headache | flu |
| aspirin | now |
| sore | |

176

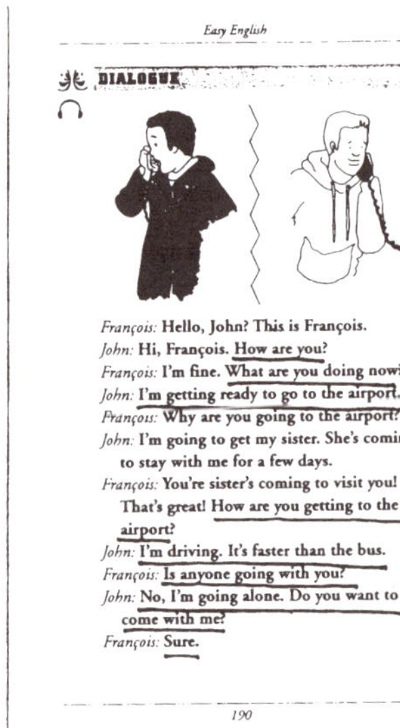

Easy English

DIALOGUE

*François:* Hello, John? This is François.
*John:* Hi, François. How are you?
*François:* I'm fine. What are you doing now?
*John:* I'm getting ready to go to the airport.
*François:* Why are you going to the airport?
*John:* I'm going to get my sister. She's comin[g] to stay with me for a few days.
*François:* You're sister's coming to visit you! That's great! How are you getting to the airport?
*John:* I'm driving. It's faster than the bus.
*François:* Is anyone going with you?
*John:* No, I'm going alone. Do you want to come with me?
*François:* Sure.

190

Video stills from *These Days*, 2005 and dialogue extracts from *Easy English* by Living Language

Lesson 13: **How Much Does This Shirt Cost?**

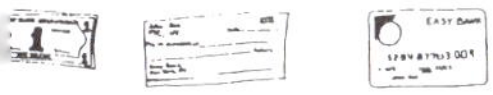

cash check credit card

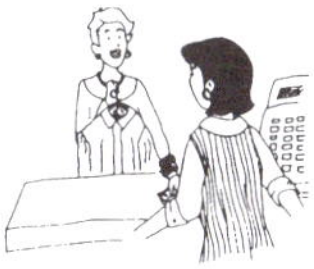

Natasha buys a shirt.
The saleswoman sells the shirt.

Natasha pays for the shirt.
She pays cash.

Natasha gives the cash to the saleswoman.
The saleswoman takes the cash.

**DIALOGUE**

*Maria:* **Hiroko, look at this blue shirt!**
*Hiroko:* **It's beautiful. Is it your size?**
*Maria:* **Yes, it is. It's a medium. But I don't see the price.**
*Hiroko:* **Ask the salesperson.**
*Maria:* **Excuse me, how much does this shirt cost?**
*Salesperson:* **That shirt costs $25.00, but it's on sale for $15.00. Do you like it?**

*135*

Lesson 16: **I Don't Feel Good Today!**

It's 6:30 now. It's 3:00 now. It's 8:45 now.

**DIALOGUE**

*John:* **Dr. Wong, I don't feel good today. I feel sick.**
*Dr. Wong:* **Do you have a headache?**
*John:* **Yes, I have a headache, and I feel dizzy.**
*Dr. Wong:* **Does your throat hurt?**

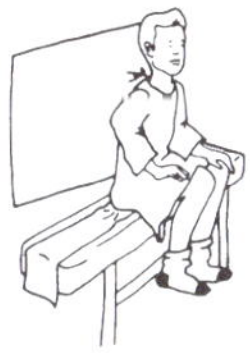

*175*

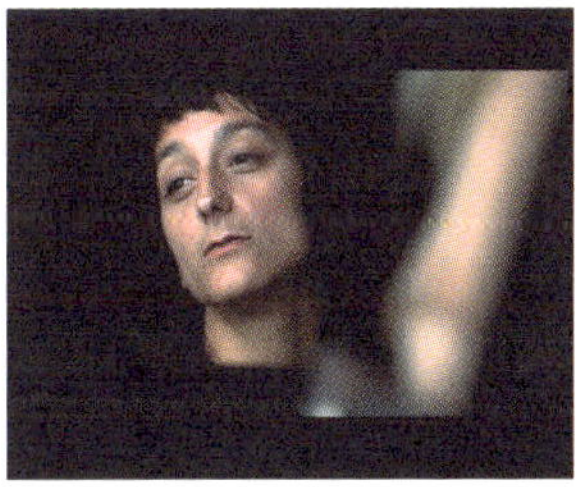

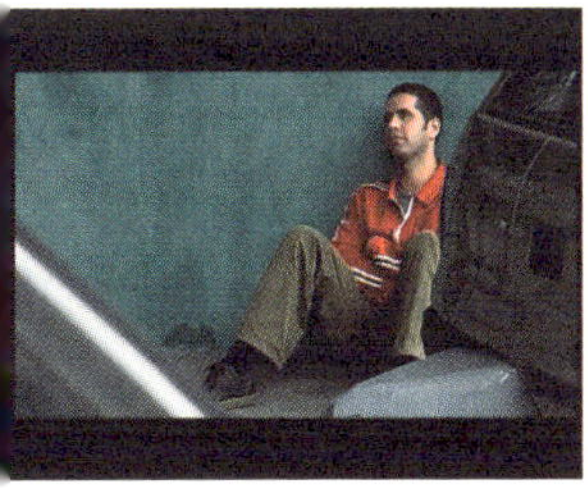

Lesson 18: **We're Going to Take a Trip This Weekend.**

Ram reads every day.

He is reading now.

He's going to read tonight.

He will read tonight.

**DIALOGUE**

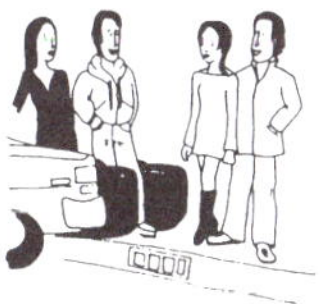

*Ram:* **Maria, Jose, are you going somewhere?**
*Maria:* **Yes, we're going to take a trip this weekend. We're going to drive to the country to visit my sister and her family.**
*Amrita:* **How nice! Where does your sister live?**
*Maria:* **She lives in a very little town about five hours away.**

*207*

*Easy English*

**DIALOGUE**

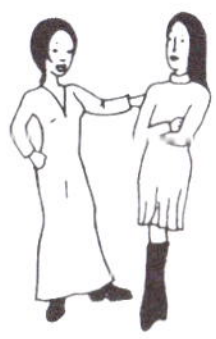

*Maria:* **Hi, Amrita!**
*Amrita:* **Hello, Maria. Where were you this weekend? I called you, but no one answered the phone.**
*Maria:* **Oh, Jose and I were in the country. We went to visit my sister for a few days.**
*Amrita:* **How was your trip? Did you have a good time?**
*Maria:* **It was great. We had a very good time.**
*Amrita:* **Did you and Jose stay with your sister and her family?**
*Maria:* **Yes, we did. They have a big house, so we stayed there.**
*Amrita:* **What did you do?**
*Maria:* **Well, I talked a lot with my sister. We looked at old photos, we walked next to a beautiful river, we drove to a little town and ate dinner in a restaurant.**
*Amrita:* **That's great. Welcome back!**

*222*

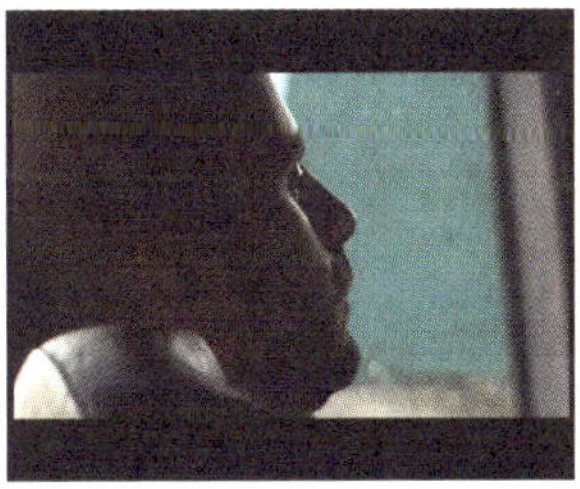

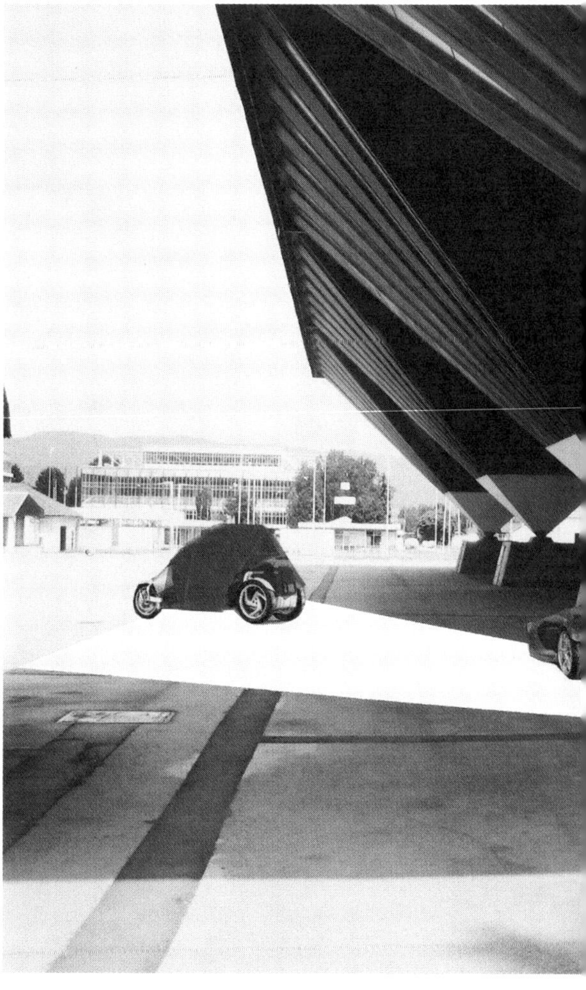



*These Days: Lost Pavilion*, 2005, collage

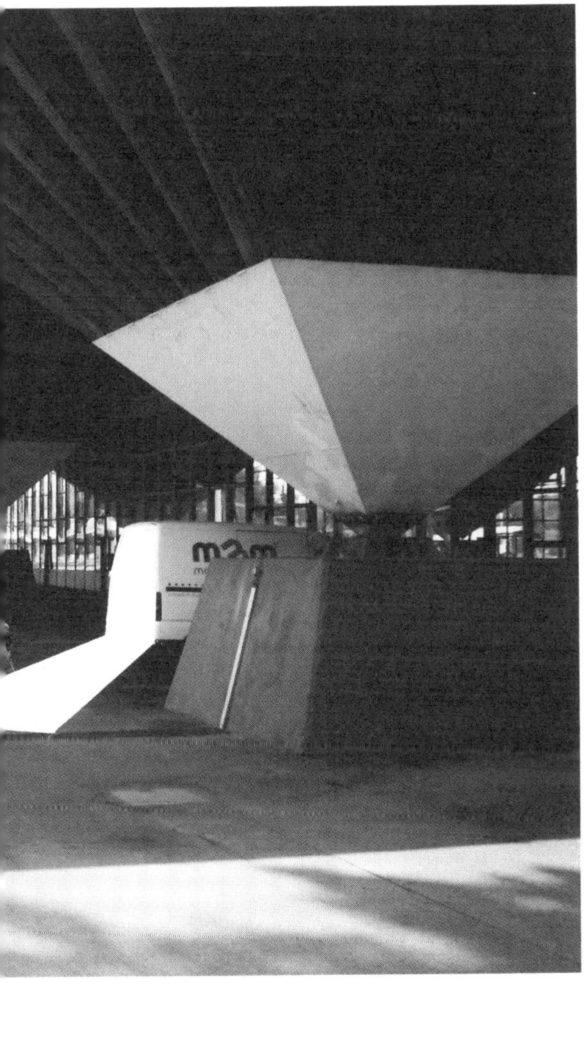

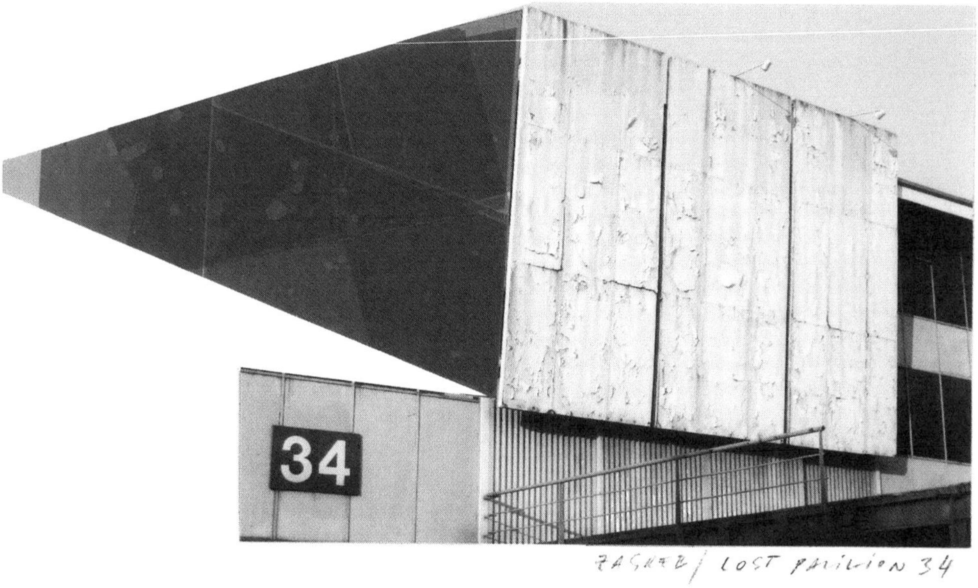




*These Days*: *Lost Pavilions*, 2005, collages

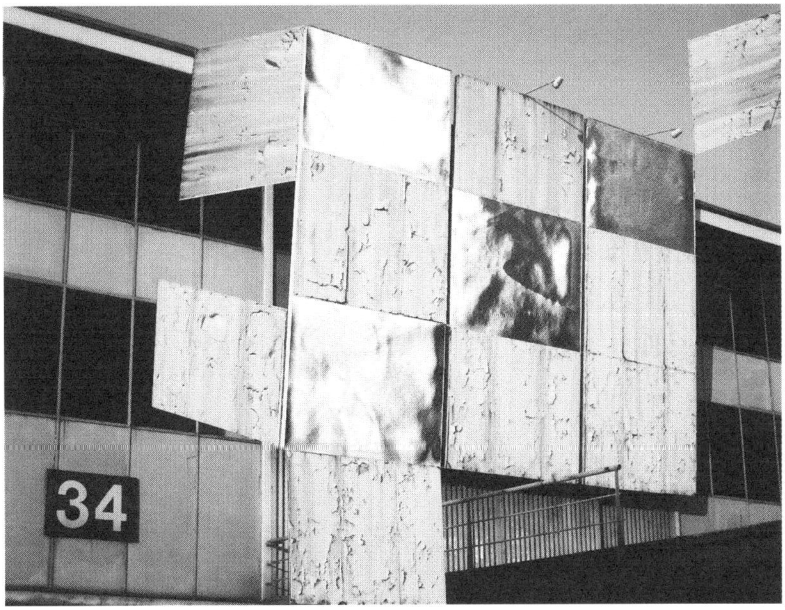
34

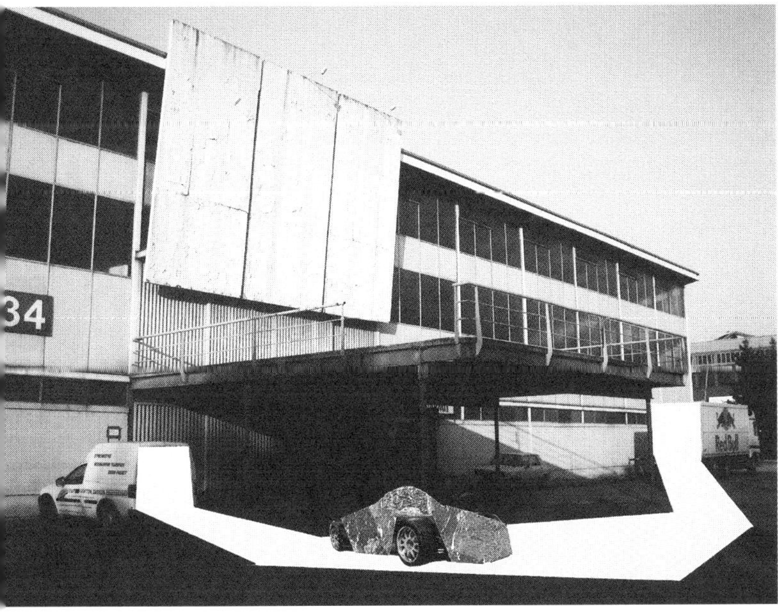
34

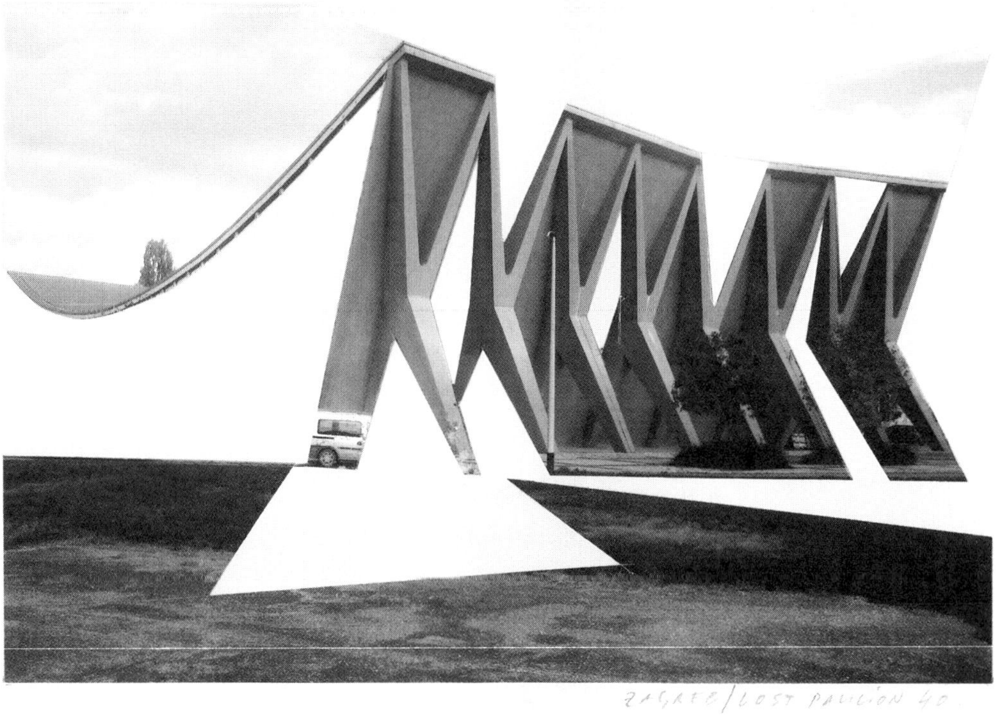


Above and opposite: *These Days: Lost Pavilions*, 2005, collages

Overleaf: *These Days*, 2005, collage

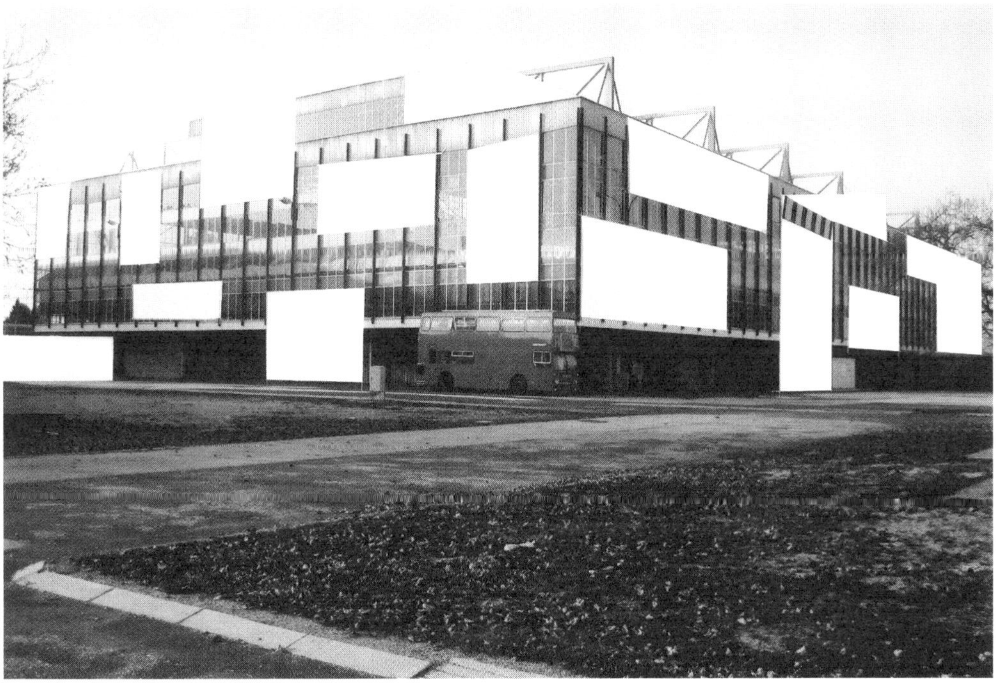

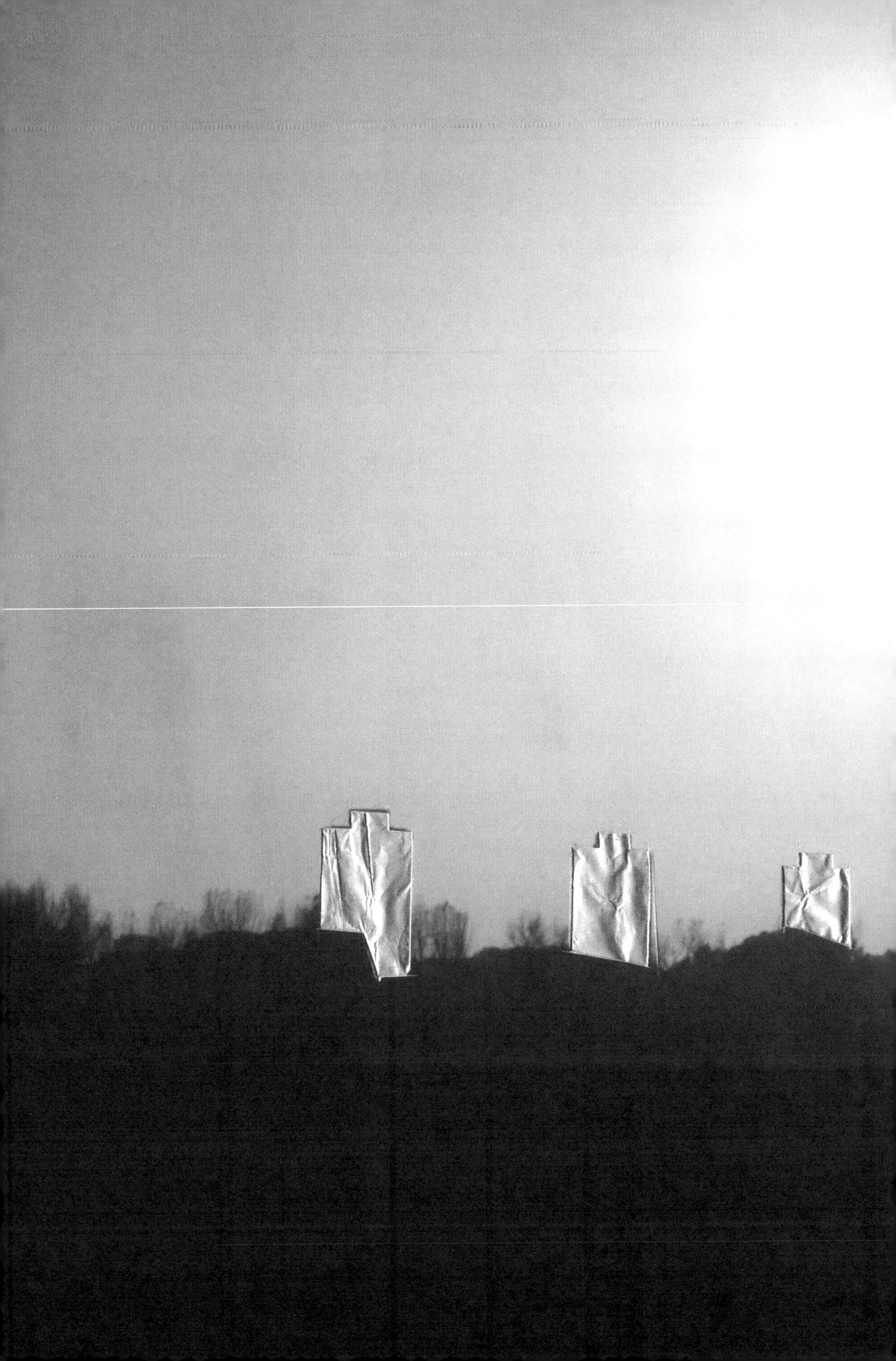

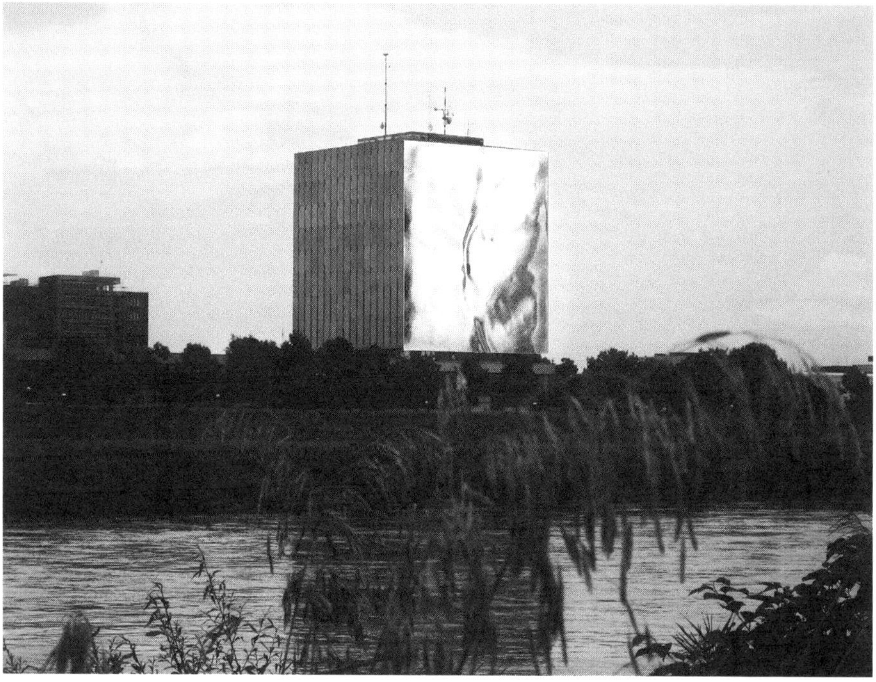

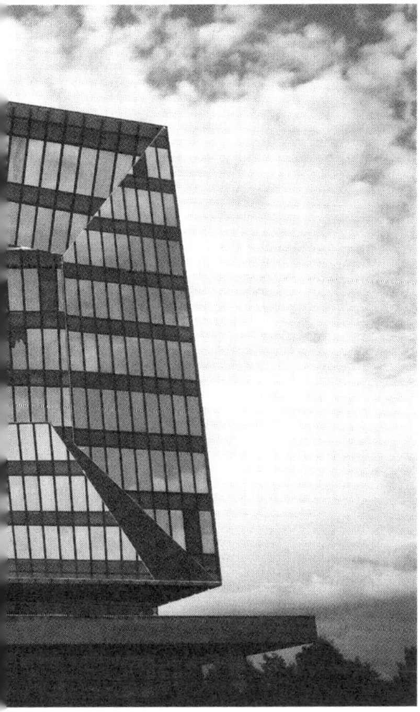

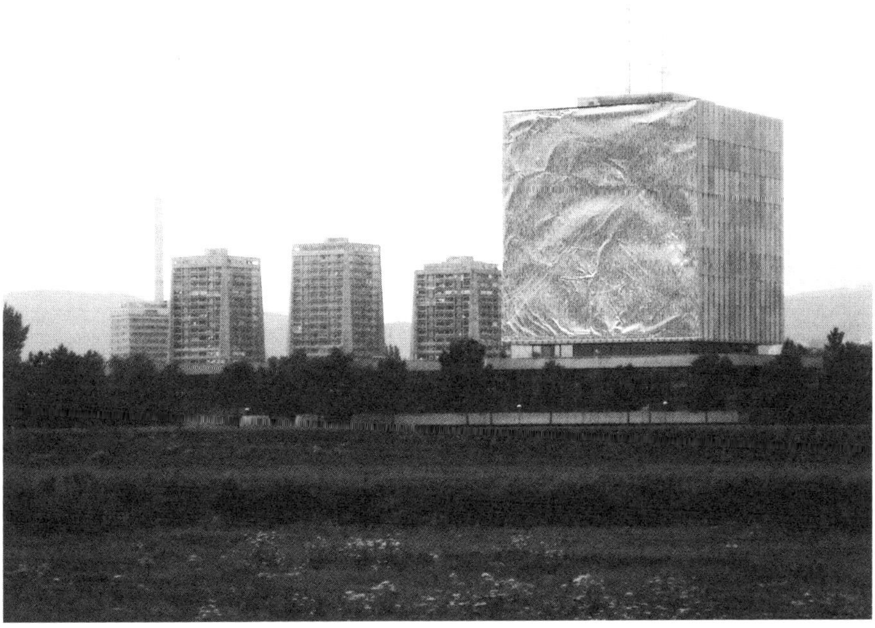



*These Days*, 2005, collages

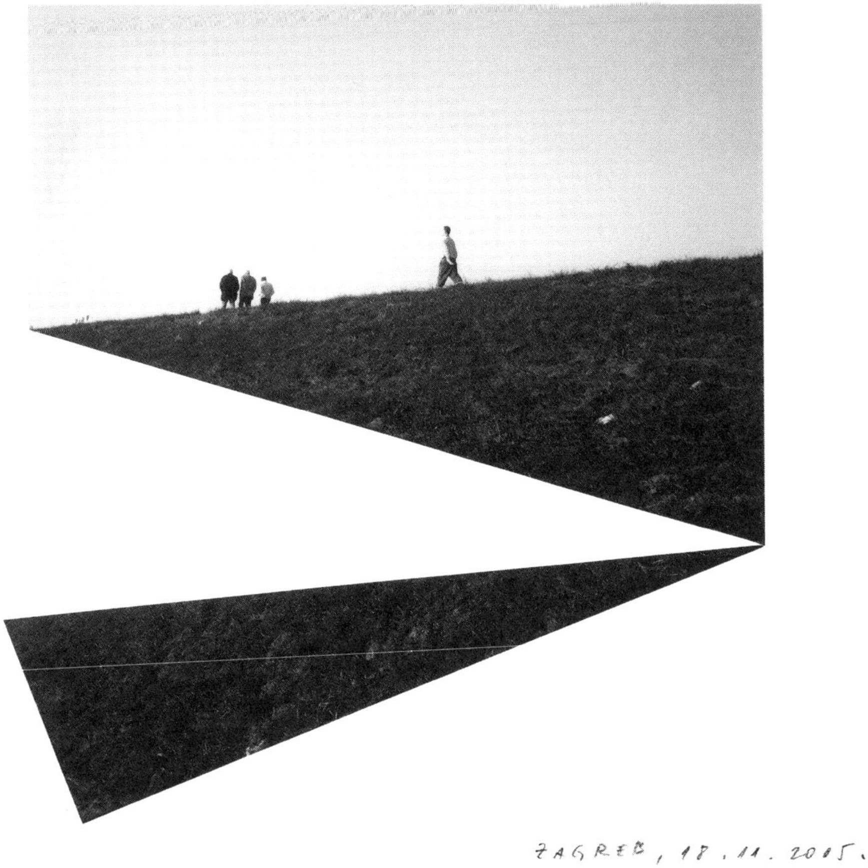




*These Days*, 2005, collages

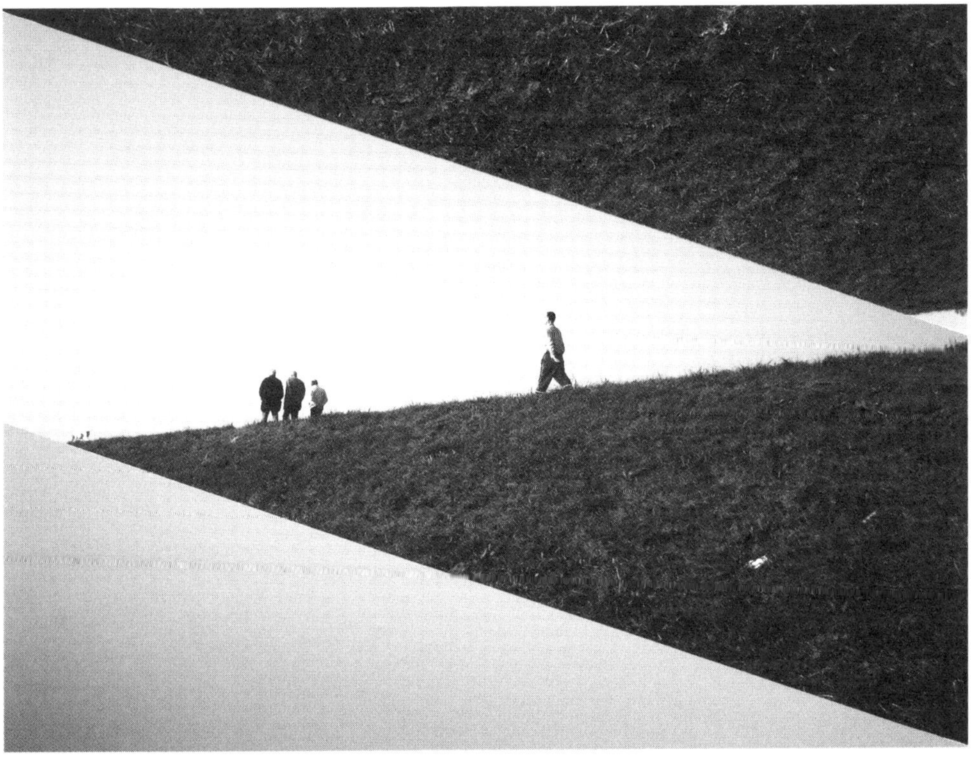

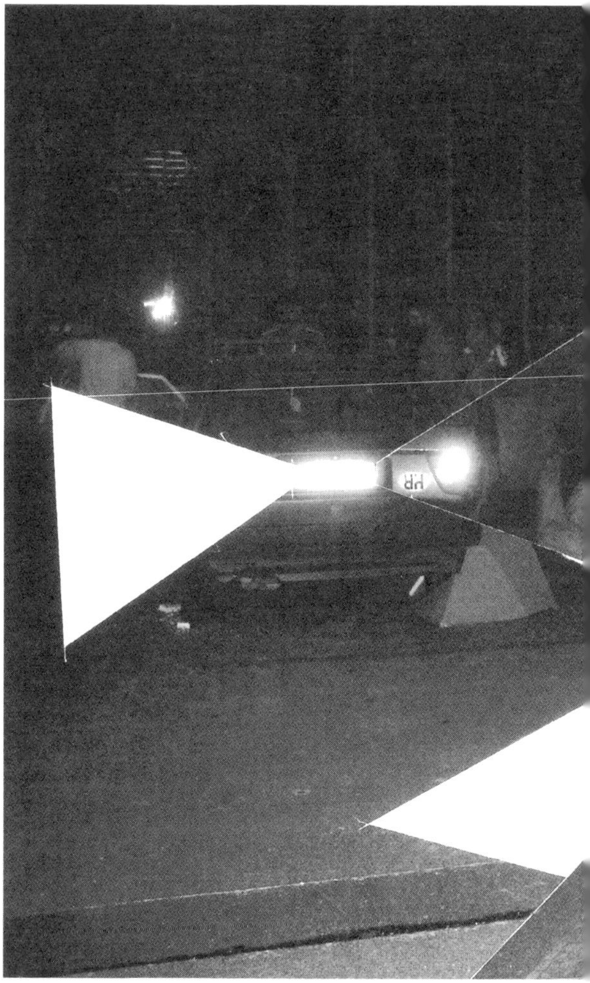



*These Days*, 2005, collage

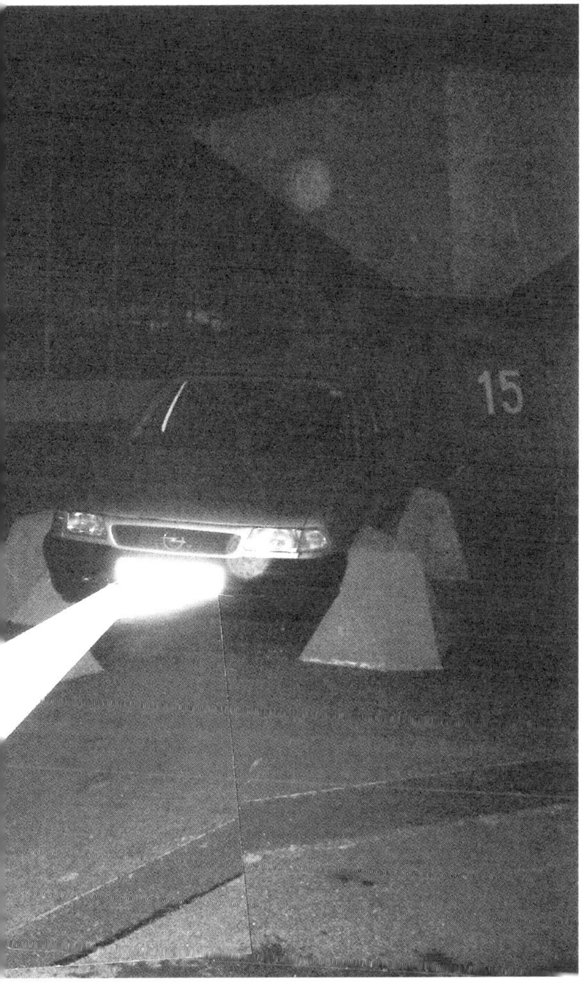
15

# THE ILLNESS OF TIME OR WHY THE CONDITIONS OF THE TRIP HAVE CHANGED

ANSELM FRANKE

This text is the rewritten version of a lecture I prepared for Galerija Nova in Zagreb following an invitation by David Maljković extended to me in connection with his exhibition there in spring 2006. The lecture was not about David's work as such; rather I decided to respond to the work with a set of ideas which I hoped bear the potential of being a different, associative kind of context for his work, confronting it with speculations on the contemporary condition of aesthetic experience. The immediate background to the invitation was that David's work *Again for Tomorrow 4 (Before 3)* has been shown in a group exhibition in Berlin under the title *The Imaginary Number* which I co-developed.[1] One implicit motif that ran through the exhibition was that of the 'trip', and I saw *Again for Tomorrow 4 (Before 3)* in that light, as a trip exploring the connection between memory and the imaginary. The exhibition began with Rodney Graham's famous Berlin re-enactment of Albert Hofmann's first LSD experiment, next to a work by Omer Fast based on historical museum-towns in the US, where history is played live, everyday anew, by the staff of the museum who are professional actors of sorts. Both works were involved with re-enactments, at a time when the notion of the re-enactment had already gained (a somewhat tiresome) popularity in contemporary art. In the past few years the idea of the 're-enactment' has provided the ground for discussions on the relation between fiction, simulacra and reality, and, more interestingly, on repetition and difference, all in the context of exhibitions of contemporary art. Yet the general interest in re-enactments not only relates to the performative aspect. The interest itself is a symptom of a peculiar relation to the past, to heritage and continuity. Of course the interest of artists in re-enactment has to be distinguished from that of the participants in historical re-enactments and their enthusiasm for role-play, identity and specific historical events. It seems to me that often works portraying or employing re-enactment strategies aim at registering a sense of disturbance, a sense of reality being no longer identical with itself, of a present that can no longer be distinguished from its other (the non-present, the absent, etc.). In that sense, the re-enactment is a ghostly scenario, even if lacking any sense of the uncanny, simply because it is a past that returns, and the return disturbs the order and unity of the present. It expresses a sense of being caught in limbo between the times, a sense of being damned to repeat and to return, and a sense of confusion, of threshold. But both Graham's as well as Fast's work, together with some other pieces in the exhibition, with their various references and editing methods, moved a step beyond the re-enactment, from the introspective to the projective. The trip back to the past is also a trip into the conditioning of our imagination. And it was this idea of moving one step further that united most of the works, each bringing about a specific historical context in which the relation of aesthetics and politics in connection with the possibility of a future was at stake.

Unlike many re-enactment works (and the exploration of the various genres of memorials that preceded them in art history), David Maljković's work is not primarily about the past as such, or more precisely, about commemoration. Rather, David Maljković lets the protagonists in his trips become *media* for the relationship between the present and the past. This mediality is not a recording of the past *as it was*. The motif of the need for translation, of an incomprehensible language plays a significant role in his work. We often tend to forget the difference between hearing (pure stream of data) and understanding (imagination, intelligibility, empathy). *Scene for New Heritage* is a series of works reacting to a historical condition in which the latter has been lost. In order to make sense of the discrete data of history, we need reconstruction, and that means projection. Seen in comparison to practices of archaeology, his work would expand the gap that separates pure data from synthesis, where, in order to make sense of the bits and shreds of a buried past, inevitably imagination and narrativization need to come into play, filling the empty space *between* the different parts or evidence, like narrative bridges, or the glue of the imaginary. In everyday life, the difference between hearing and understanding hardly exists. Rather, normality *is* the special condition of undoing, of closing this gap. It is only in aesthetic experience, in relation to the past or when common sense is being transgressed, as in madness or under the influence of psychoactive substances, that the projective imagination, fantasy and fiction that are at play in our relations and making sense of the world are peeled off the visible surfaces and proofs to have a life of their own (as do the objects which are consequently no longer held together by a meaningful frame). But while a certain critique of archaeology takes this as proof that archaeology has to abandon narrativization and imagination altogether because it produces the past only as a projective image of ourselves (this radically anti-essentialist and anti-anthropomorphic critique fails to explain how it is able to *speak* about the discrete data it then assembles), what shall be of interest in our context is to see how imagination and projection are not only active in our reconstructive relation to the narrative of history, but what role they play in the construction of what is to come.[2] Are we able to project a future and make it real? As soon as this question is asked in the plural, referring to a collective dimension, we are ultimately facing the heritage of modernism, its political Utopias and the aesthetic means which were thought to be the appropriate tools for making the new world come true. *Scene for New Heritage* as well as other works by David Maljković are set against the backdrop of an architecture that both symbolizes and embodies the modern (we may call it literally the *constructivist*) belief in the ability to master, produce and invent the future. Today, this future lies in ruins; it has become mere data, and we stand before it without being able to revive, to reanimate it. Insofar as its ability to project has failed, so does our own ability to projectively reconstruct, to imaginatively appropriate; our capability to imagine fails when confronted with it. What I am aiming at is an attempt to analyze a situation in which the impossibility of remembering the past (empathetically, beyond mere data) results in an impossibility to imagine the future.

David Maljković's work, like a significant amount of other contemporary artists' work engaging with the heritage of modern Utopias like archaeologists, explores this aftermath, the disruption and continuity with the modernist project insofar as this heritage is realizing itself *in* and *through* us. It is not important at this stage to specify the historical circumstances and the momentum of the rupture; rather, we shall look at its metaphysical structure, that is, our relation to imagination, projection and the magic of signification. The evocative language of modernism, attempting to call into being what it represents, failed in multiple ways. But while today this sense of failure dominates (and provides the grounds for endless reactionary revisions), it also succeeded in many ways, but in ways that seem irretrievable, still unpredictable, and which therefore don't provide us with any tools. It is as if the history of modernism has been written as a history of collateral effects, or of a text behind the text, as a text that remained unspoken and implicit, and that has to be distinguished from the propagandistic surfaces, from everything that has been said. The task is to recover the history of desires behind the surface text. For while the explicit text and the promises of the modernist Utopias still echo through the corridors of history, they do not speak to us anymore. We are caught in a modernist non-place, paralyzed by the unspeakability of the history of spectral disappointments which modernism has left behind. This is how I would see the condition exposed in *Scene for New Heritage*, confronting a heritage which doesn't speak to us anymore, whose language we have to split open in order to relearn and understand anew, understand differently, to both undo and master its magic and the magic we have long lost, and to learn what it didn't know about itself. What is at stake is the very ability to imagine. And because the ability to imagine is bound up with the ability to move and to be moved, I have come to suggest the use of the trip as a metaphor and method for talking about mental mobility. The inability to change, to make a difference, is rooted in the inability to imagine a difference.

In the context of *Scene for New Heritage* and *These Days*, the lost world of modern Utopias manifest in the visionary designs of the Petrova Gora Memorial Park and the Zagreb International Fair are actual ruins, ruins of the collective imaginary, signifiers of a broken relationship with the past. Since their meaning has been lost, they stand before us as 'dead metaphors', metaphors that don't take us anywhere anymore. In that sense, especially in the case of *These Days*, we are already at the end of the trip, and what is at stake is the ability to move away again. Their language from this world has been lost, which is still ours (for we still speak as moderns, without alternative). And words are powerless if things don't respond to them. If the petrified figures in the video *These Days*, shot at the former Italian pavilion of the Zagreb International Fair, recite isolated sentences from a guide to Easy English, we are confronted precisely with such an expression of a language which has lost its capabilities to affect, and of the conditions under which we yearn for a reappropriation of its emotional, significatory and creative capacity. But how can we give back these buildings, and with them the inhabitants of the lost world, their history?

I began the lecture at Galerija Nova with the question 'What trip is possible?' It is another way of asking: 'What can we imagine?' This was in part a rhetorical question. Not just since the so-called psychedelic era has the trip become a synonym for exploring possibility, like in the slogan 'expanding consciousness'. And indeed, the Italian art historian Carlo Ginzburg referred to the predecessor of the modern trip, the shamanistic journey, as the 'matrix of all possible narratives'. Stories are trips insofar as they tell us 'what happens to our desires in the world' (Sigmund Freud). The question thus goes like this: What (hi)story can we imagine? And what follows is: What story can be told? What is meant is not *any* old story, but the possibility of cohesion, and that is the possibility of successful projection, collectivization in the medium of an autonomous language, and of 'making the world anew'. To ask 'What trip is possible?' was meant to sound tautological at first, only in order to hint at significant transformations of possibility itself, and at the history of the faculty of imagination. The global aspect of this transformation is the history of modernity as a history of expansion, of mobilizations, which first covered the globe and went on to mobilize the human interior, the psyche. The trip is the last possible mobilization, but it also bears the possibility within it of responding to the internalization by turning upside down. The trip, like the hallucinating body in general, is a collectivized self cast into privatization.

To come closer to an understanding of the historical transformation of possibility, it is necessary to turn to the conditions under which nothing at all is possible: depression. The French sociologist Alain Ehrenberg has written a very influential study about the rise of depression under the name *The Exhausted Self*, in which he claims that in the past four decades we have been witnessing a general transformation of subjectivity and its relation to the objective world.[3] It is important to keep in mind throughout the following that, although the scenery of these thoughts is the subject, what is at stake is the subject's relationship to the world, its capability and position therein. Ehrenberg uses historical categories introduced by Michel Foucault and Gilles Deleuze, namely the *disciplinary society* which Foucault speaks of in his works on clinics, prisons and the emergence of biopower; and the *society of control* introduced by Gilles Deleuze to signify that in neo-liberalism the disciplinary institutions have been internalized, consequently have also become a matter of the subject's self-management.[4] Ehrenberg complements these categories with the history of psychopathology. According to Ehrenberg, the subject of disciplinary society was organized along the lines of what was forbidden and what was allowed. This regime is enforced by the institutions of discipline and finds its counterpart in the human psyche in the concept of guilt. The symptomatic psychopathologies of disciplinary society are hysteria and neurosis – the latter also having been called the disease of narration. Neurosis and hysteria are based on traumatic experiences and feelings of guilt produced by the subject's desires transgressing the rules and laws that determine what is forbidden and what is allowed.

As a result of emancipation, individualization and the transformation of repressive capitalism into the self-governing subject of neo-liberalism, subjectivity's dual organizing principle *forbidden/allowed* has changed into *possible/impossible*, and the symptomatic mental pathologies have consequently changed, too. It is this regime of internalized self-governance that has been called society of control. According to Ehrenberg, neurosis and hysteria, the mass diseases of desire, have been replaced by depression in the course of this transformation, the mass disease of possibility. Ehrenberg argues that while neurosis draws upon guilt, depression draws upon failure, the failures of the subject confronted with the need to take an initiative, to be responsible, to reinvent itself and to use its possibilities as an autonomous and yet flexible self. Ehrenberg shows how since the 1970s numerous and diverse clinical symptoms have been brought together under the umbrella term 'depression', all of them having in common that the patient suffers from fundamental deficits, from a weakness and inability to fulfil the requirements of what it means today to be an individual. As far as the psychedelic figure 'trip' is concerned, the main part of Ehrenberg's path-breaking study focuses on the social and political significance of anti-depressive, psychoactive medications like Prozac, this other kind of drug implying altered states of consciousness, which, in total opposition to the trip invoked by psychedelic drugs, is meant to reintegrate the subject into a functioning normality, not to push it beyond. This sheds another light on the question of 'What trip is possible', since the matrix of the trip, together with the structure of madness, has changed, and tripping has become a necessary ability of the flexible self. If the normality of depression is the inability to achieve normality, depression involves a longing for the ability of closing the gap between imagination and the objective world, that precondition of the subject/object relation in normality I have mentioned above. If, in the history of art, it was the surrealists who made tripping an epistemological methodology of transgression tailored to turning normality on its head and exposing it to the powers of transformation, it is this normality that has itself become surreal, yet deprived of the power of transformation, and consequently, the condition and direction of transgression has changed, too. It is as if the subject is enveloped by its imaginary projections, but these projections don't find any grip on the world of real objects outside. The impossibility of communicating meaningfully with the objective world has indeed been identified elsewhere as another key feature of depression, which has been identified as a condition of 'objectless longing'.[5] If depression is a surreal condition deprived of the powers of transformation, it must be said that is not really because in depression nothing can be imagined. In fact, in depression, all trips seem possible, but non-desirable, and it is because one's desires are deprived of the ability of interacting with the world, which consequently renders the possible impossible. It is this rendering of the possible impossible that is exploited by capitalist culture, which answers the fear of 'objectless longing' with desirable objects and their emotional and identificatory promise, a promise to become. It is no surprise that under these circumstances, the three key terms of the 'trip' are to be found among the commercial mantras and key-words, too: possibility, imagination, movement/mobility. If depression is not only an exceptional abnormality, but a mass phenomenon symptomatic of a cultural condition, of the normality of culture in neo-liberalism today, then we come to see that 'objectless longing' is the dialectical counterpart of the expansion of the 'phantom objectivity' of capitalist commodification into the sphere of life. Perhaps one out of many recent campaigns stands out, that is, that of the sportswear maker, Adidas, with its slogan '*Impossible is Nothing*',[6] which reverses the usual promise of expanded possibility and can actually be read as the real threat, the neo-liberal counterpart to the disciplinary threat of internment and punishment. '*Make it real*', or you will be cast into nothingness. And of course the rest of this text could go on to be written in commercial quotes.

*Again for Tomorrow*, *Scene for New Heritage*, *These Days*: the titles of these 'trips' refer to yet another dimension of depression, namely, depression as the 'illness of time'.[7] Subjects thrown into an 'irretrievable past and an unimaginable future': The sociologist Avery Gordon has written a study on haunting, on uncanny returns, and their significance for the American public and political sphere. In her book, entitled *Ghostly Matters*, she describes contemporary collective psychopathology through an analysis of American consumer culture (exemplified in Don DeLillo's novel *White Noise*), and its inability to relate to what it excludes, to its own ghosts. 'No shadows, no ghosts', a world forced into the visibility of phantom objectivity, in which nothing that is said or thought really matters any longer and counts.[8] This is the deprivation of mobility, of access to the powers of change. Are not re-enactments like the parading ghosts of history, but a history which already has been lost? Are they not, rather then reanimations, registrations of the loss, illustrations of a condition of time that became ill, a time we can no longer talk with and relate to? 'Depression is a disorder in which the temporalities of psychic life – to remember, to represent, to desire and to project – have been immobilized. Such a suspension means that the depressed individual is unable to situate itself, neither in relation to the future (to hope, dream, anticipate, make plans, decide tomorrow's actions) nor to the past (to give mobility to memories, to activate remembrance)'.[9] The world of depression, ultimately, is a spectral world, a world shred into discontinuous pieces in which the subject is unable to reconnect, to synthesize again. This is the failure Ehrenberg speaks of, ultimately linking what is 'possible' for the subject to its ability to synthesize, that is, to historicize, narrativize, and leaping from there, its power to metaphorize, mobilize and rename.

The reference to a broken continuity (or a broken resistance, broken claims to continuity, muted stories creating a rightful place in the world) is structurally reminiscent of the traumatic experience, and makes us think of reanimation of the broken connection as a process of healing, of winning back one's relative autonomy, one's ability to imagine, speak and to act. And all forms of curing traumatic experiences are mediated by narrativization, by giving back an experience its history. I like to think of the buildings in David Maljković's work in that sense. The silence, their formal language which has become strange, calls for reanimation, for learning to speak once again. What better image could be found for the attempt at reanimating a lost common language than singing before the destroyed futuristic monument? The scenery of David Maljković's trips, as it comes to embody the 'failure' of its collective aspirations, also comes to embody a new possible history, ultimately resisting commodification, standing for the ability to again imagine things as different ones. In a world of capitalist 'phantom objectivity', this heritage has become an 'objective phantom', a phantom whose presence will not vanish until its languages are once again appropriated, practised, and understood.

Notes

1 *The Imaginary Number*, curated by Anselm Franke and Hila Peleg, KW Berlin, 5.6–11.9.2005, see: <www.kw-berlin.de/english/program_theimaginerynumber.htm> (13.08.2007).
2 See: Wolfgang Ernst, *Das Rumoren der Archive. Ordnung aus Unordnung*, Merve, Berlin, 2002.
3 Alain Ehrenberg, *La Fatigue d'être soi. Dépression et société*, Collection Poches Odile Jacob, Paris, 2000.
4 Gilles Deleuze's text *Society of Control*, originally published in French in *L'autre journal*, Nr. 1, May 1990, can be read online at <http://www.nadir.org/nadir/archiv/netzkritik/societyofcontrol.html> (13.8.2007).
5 Jennifer Church, *Depression, Depth and the Imagination*, in: *Imagination and Its Pathologies*, ed. James Phillips and James Morley, Cambridge: Massachusetts, 2003, p. 181.
6 see: <http://www.adidas.com/campaign/iin/content/index/asp?adidas_cc=com> (13.8.2007).

7 Pierre Fédida, *Des bienfaits de la dépression. Eloge de la psychothérapie*, Collection Poches Odile Jacob, Paris, 2003.

8 Avery F. Gordon, *Ghostly Matters – Haunting and the Sociological Imagination*, University of Minnesota Press, 1997, p. 13.

9 Christine Ross, *Depression and video art at the turn of the millennium: the work of Diana Thater,* in: *Affective Encounters,* see: <http://media.utu.fi/affective/index.html> (13.08.2007).

# DIE KRANKHEIT DER ZEIT ODER WARUM SICH DIE BEDINGUNGEN DES TRIPS VERÄNDERT HABEN

ANSELM FRANKE

Dieser Text ist die überarbeitete Fassung eines Vortrags, den ich auf Einladung von David Maljković anlässlich seiner Ausstellung im Frühjahr 2006 in der Galerija Nova in Zagreb gehalten habe. Der Vortrag handelte nicht von David Maljkovićs Werk als solchem, sondern präsentierte eine Reihe von Ideen, von denen ich hoffte, dass sie das Potential eines anderen, assoziativen Kontexts für sein Werk bereitstellen, indem sie dieses mit Spekulationen über die zeitgenössische Lage der ästhetischen Erfahrungen konfrontieren. Der unmittelbare Hintergrund der Einladung war, dass David Maljkovićs Werk *Again for Tomorrow 4 (Before 3)* in Berlin in der von mir mitentwickelten Gruppenausstellung *The Imaginary Number* gezeigt wurde.[1] Ein implizites Motiv, das die Ausstellung durchzog, war dasjenige des ›Trips‹, und ich sah *Again for Tomorrow 4 (Before 3)* vor diesem Hintergrund als einen Trip, der den Zusammenhang zwischen Erinnerung und Imaginärem untersucht. Die Ausstellung begann mit Rodney Grahams berühmtem Berliner Re-enactment (Wiederaufführung/Neuinszenierung) von Albert Hofmanns erstem LSD-Experiment, neben einem Werk von Omer Fast, das auf historischen Museumsstädten in den USA basierte, wo Geschichte von den Angestellten des Museums, die eine Art Berufsschauspieler sind, jeden Tag neu in Szene gesetzt wird. Beide Werke waren selbst eine Art Re-enactment und dies zu einem Zeitpunkt, da dieser Begriff bereits eine leicht notorische Popularität in der zeitgenössischen Kunst erlangt hatte. In den letzten Jahren bildete die Idee des Re-enactment im Umfeld von Ausstellungen zeitgenössischer Kunst die Grundlage für Diskussionen über die Beziehung zwischen Fiktion, Simulakren und Realität sowie, und dies ist besonders interessant, über die Beziehung von Wiederholung und Differenz. Doch das allgemeine Interesse an Re-enactments bezieht sich nicht nur auf das performative Element, sondern ist selbst ein Symptom für eine bestimmte Beziehung zur Vergangenheit, zum Erbe und zur Kontinuität. Natürlich muss man das Interesse von Künstlern am Re-enactment von dem der Teilnehmer an historischen Re-enactments und ihrer Begeisterung für Rollenspiel, Identität und spezifische historische Ereignisse unterscheiden. Ich habe den Eindruck, dass Werke, die Strategien des Re-enactment darstellen oder verwenden, häufig die Absicht haben, das Gefühl einer Störung festzuhalten, das Gefühl, dass die Realität nicht mehr mit sich selbst identisch ist, das Gefühl, dass sich die Gegenwart nicht mehr von ihrem anderen – der Nicht-Gegenwart, dem Abwesenden usw. – unterscheiden lässt. In diesem Sinne ist das Re-enactment ein gespenstisches Szenario, selbst wenn es nichts Unheimliches an sich hat, einfach, weil es eine Vergangenheit ist, die wiederkehrt, und weil diese Wiederkehr die Ordnung und Einheit der Gegenwart stört. Es bringt das Gefühl zum Ausdruck, in einem Übergangsstadium zwischen den Zeiten gefangen zu sein, ein Gefühl, zur Wiederholung und Wiederkehr verdammt zu sein, ein Gefühl der Verwirrung, der Schwellenhaftigkeit. Doch sowohl Grahams als auch Fasts Arbeiten, ebenso wie einige andere in der Ausstellung mit ihren verschiedenen Verweisen und Bearbeitungsmethoden, gingen einen Schritt über das Re-enactment hinaus: von der Introspektion zur Projektion. Der Trip zurück in die Vergangenheit ist auch ein Trip in die Bedingtheit unserer Imagination. Und diese Idee, noch einen Schritt weiter zu gehen, war es, welche die meisten Werke, von denen jedes einen spezifischen historischen Kontext bewirkte, in dem die Beziehung von Ästhetik und Politik in Verbindung mit der Möglichkeit einer Zukunft auf dem Spiel stand, miteinander verband.

Im Gegensatz zu vielen Re-enactment-Werken und den Untersuchungen der verschiedenen Gattungen von Denkmälern, die ihnen in der Kunstgeschichte vorausgingen – geht es in David Maljkovićs Werk weder primär um die Vergangenheit als solche und erst Recht nicht um das Gedenken. Vielmehr lässt es die Protagonisten seiner Trips zu *Medien* der Beziehung der Gegenwart zur Vergangenheit werden. Diese Medialität ist keine Aufzeichnung der Vergangenheit *so wie sie war*. Das Motiv des Übersetzungsbedürfnisses, das Motiv einer unverständlichen Sprache spielt eine wesentliche Rolle in seinem Werk. Häufig neigen wir dazu, den Unterschied zwischen Hören (reiner Datenstrom) und Verstehen (Imagination, Fassbarkeit, Einfühlungsvermögen) zu vergessen. Bei *Scene for New Heritage* handelt es sich um eine Serie von Werken, die auf eine historische Situation reagieren, in der letzteres verloren gegangen ist. Um sich einen Reim auf einzelne Daten der Geschichte zu machen, bedarf es der Rekonstruktion und damit der Projektion. Im Vergleich zur Vorgehensweise der Archäologie erweitert David Maljkovićs Werk die Lücke, die reine Daten von der Synthese trennt, bei der unweigerlich Imagination und Narrativierung auf den Plan treten müssen, um sich einen Reim auf die verstreuten Fetzen einer begrabenen Vergangenheit zu machen und den leeren Raum *zwischen* den verschiedenen Beweisstücken mit narrativen Brücken oder dem Leim des Imaginären zu füllen. Im Alltag gibt es praktisch keinen Unterschied zwischen Hören und Verstehen. Vielmehr *ist* die Normalität die Aufhebung, die Schließung dieser Lücke. Nur in der ästhetischen Erfahrung, im Verhältnis zur Vergangenheit oder dann, wenn der gesunde Menschenverstand überschritten wird, etwa im Zustand des Wahnsinns oder unter dem Einfluss psychoaktiver Substanzen, wird die projektive Imagination, die Phantasie und Fiktion, die in unserer Beziehung zur Welt und der Art, wie wir uns einen Reim auf sie machen, im Spiel ist, von den sichtbaren Oberflächen abgelöst und beweist, dass sie ein Eigenleben führt (wie dies auch die Objekte tun, die folglich nicht mehr durch einen sinnvollen Rahmen zusammengehalten werden). Doch während eine bestimmte Kritik der Archäologie in diesem Phänomen den Beweis dafür sieht, dass die Archäologie von der Narrativisierung und Imagination insgesamt Abstand nehmen sollte, da sie die Vergangenheit nur als projektives Bild unserer selbst produziert (diese radikal anti-essentialistische und anti-anthropomorphe Kritik vermag nicht zu erklären, wie sie unter diesen Umständen im Stande ist, über die einzelnen Daten zu sprechen), soll uns in unserem Kontext nicht nur interessieren, wie sich Imagination und Projektion bei unserer rekonstruktiven

Beziehung zur Geschichte der Historie auswirken, sondern auch welche Rolle sie bei der Konstruktion des Zustandegekommenen spielen.[2] Sind wir in der Lage, eine Zukunft zu projizieren und sie Wirklichkeit werden zu lassen? Sobald diese Frage im Plural gestellt wird und sich auf eine kollektive Dimension bezieht, sind wir letztlich mit dem Erbe des Modernismus konfrontiert, seiner politischen Utopien und den ästhetischen Mitteln, von denen man annahm, sie seien die angemessenen Werkzeuge, um die neue Welt wahr werden zu lassen. *Scene for New Heritage* und andere Werke David Maljkovićs sind vor der Kulisse einer Architektur angesiedelt, die den modernen, man könnte auch buchstäblich sagen, den *konstruktivistischen* Glauben an die Fähigkeit, die Zukunft zu beherrschen, zu produzieren und zu erfinden, sowohl versinnbildlichen als auch verkörpern. Heute liegt diese Zukunft in Trümmern da, ist zu bloßen Daten geworden, und wir stehen vor ihr, außerstande, sie wiederzubeleben, sie zu re-animieren. Ebenso sehr wie ihre Fähigkeit zu projizieren gescheitert ist, scheitert auch unsere eigene Fähigkeit zur projektiven Rekonstruktion, zur imaginativen Appropriation. Mir geht es um den Versuch, eine Situation zu analysieren, in der die Unmöglichkeit, die Vergangenheit zu erinnern (emphatisch, nicht bloß die Daten), in der Unmöglichkeit resultiert, die Zukunft zu imaginieren.

David Maljkovićs Werk ebenso wie dasjenige einer bemerkenswerten Anzahl anderer zeitgenössischer Künstler, die sich wie Archäologen mit dem Erbe moderner Utopien auseinandersetzen, untersucht diese Folgen, den Bruch mit dem, und das Festhalten am Projekt der Moderne insofern sich dieses Erbe *in* und durch *uns* realisiert. Es geht an dieser Stelle nicht darum, die historischen Umstände und die Wucht des Bruchs zu spezifizieren, sondern wir sollten uns vielmehr seine metaphysische Struktur ansehen, das heißt, unsere Beziehung zur Imagination, zur Projektion und Magie der Signifizierung. Die evokative Sprache des Modernismus, die versucht, das von ihr Repräsentierte zum Leben zu erwecken, ist in vieler Hinsicht gescheitert. Doch auch wenn heute dieses Gefühl des Scheiterns vorherrscht (und die Grundlage für endlose reaktionäre Revisionen bietet), war diese Sprache auch in vieler Hinsicht erfolgreich, allerdings auf eine Weise, die unwiederbringlich erscheint, immer noch unberechenbar ist und die uns daher auch keinerlei Werkzeuge an die Hand gibt. Es ist so, als habe man die Geschichte des Modernismus als eine Geschichte der Kollateraleffekte geschrieben, oder als Text hinter dem Text, als unausgesprochener und impliziter Text. Denn auch wenn der explizite Text und die Verheißungen der modernistischen Utopien nach wie vor in den Gängen der Geschichte widerhallen, spricht er doch nicht mehr mit uns. Wir sind in einem modernistischen Nicht-Ort gefangen, paralysiert von der Unaussprechbarkeit der Geschichte gespenstischer Enttäuschungen, die der Modernismus hinterlassen hat. So würde ich die Lage sehen, die in *Scene for New Heritage* geschildert wird, die Konfrontation mit einem Erbe, das uns nichts mehr sagt, dessen Sprache wir aufspalten müssen, um wieder zu lernen und neu zu begreifen, anders zu begreifen, ihre Magie und die Magie, die wir verloren haben, sowohl ungeschehen zu machen als auch zu bemeistern und das zu lernen, was sie von sich selbst nicht wusste. Auf dem Spiel steht nichts Geringeres als die Fähigkeit zu imaginieren. Und da diese Fähigkeit mit derjenigen, sich zu bewegen und bewegt zu werden, zusammenhängt, schlage ich den Trip als eine Metapher und Methode vor, um über geistige Beweglichkeit zu sprechen. Die Unfähigkeit zur Veränderung, zur Differenz, wurzelt in der Unfähigkeit, sich eine Differenz vorzustellen.

Im Kontext von *Scene for New Heritage* und *These Days* sind die verlorene Welt der modernen Utopien, die sich in den visionären Entwürfen des Petrova Gora Memorial Park und der Zagreb International Fair manifestieren, tatsächliche Ruinen, Ruinen des kollektiven Imaginären, Signifikanten einer zerbrochenen Beziehung zur Vergangenheit. Da ihre Bedeutung verloren gegangen ist, stehen sie als ›tote Metaphern‹ vor uns, als Metaphern, die uns heute nirgendwo mehr hinführen. In diesem Sinne sind wir vor allem im Fall von *These Days* bereits am Ende des Trips angekommen, und was auf dem Spiel steht, ist die Fähigkeit, sich wieder davon zu entfernen. Ihre Sprache dieser Welt ist verloren gegangen, die nach wie vor unsere ist (denn wir sprechen nach wie vor als Menschen der Moderne, ohne Alternative). Und Worte sind machtlos, wenn die Dinge nicht auf sie reagieren. Wenn die versteinerten Figuren in dem Video *These Days*, das im ehemaligen italienischen Pavillon der Zagreb International Fair aufgenommen wurden, einzelne Sätze aus einem Sprachführer zu Leichtem Englisch rezitieren, dann werden wir genau mit einem solchen Ausdruck einer Sprache konfrontiert, die ihre affektiven Eigenschaften eingebüßt hat, und dem Ausdruck der Bedingungen, unter denen wir uns nach einer Wieder-Aneignung ihrer emotionalen, bedeutungsgenerierenden und kreativen Eigenschaften sehnen. Doch wie können wir diesen Gebäuden und mit ihnen den Bewohnern der verlorenen Welt ihre Geschichte zurückgeben?

Zu Beginn des Vortrags in der Galerija Nova stellte ich die Frage: ›Welcher Trip ist möglich?‹ Genauso gut hätte die Frage aber auch lauten können: ›Was können wir imaginieren?‹ Das war zumindest teilweise eine rhetorische Frage. Nicht nur, weil der Trip seit dem so genannten psychedelischen Zeitalter ein Synonym für das Erkunden von Möglichkeiten geworden ist, was etwa im Schlagwort der ›Bewusstseinserweiterung‹ zum Ausdruck kommt. Und tatsächlich bezeichnete der italienische Kunsthistoriker Carlo Ginzburg den Vorläufer des modernen Trips, die schamanistische Reise, als ›Matrix aller möglichen Narrative‹. Geschichten sind Trips, insofern sie uns erzählen, was mit unseren Wünschen und Begierden in der Welt geschieht (Sigmund Freud). Die Frage lautet daher, welche *(historische)* Geschichte können wir imaginieren? Und was folgt ist die Frage: Welche *(fiktive)* Geschichte lässt sich erzählen? Gemeint ist nicht irgendeine *(fiktive)* Geschichte, sondern die Möglichkeit eines Zusammenhangs, und das heißt, die Möglichkeit einer erfolgreichen Projektion, Kollektivierung im Medium der souveränen Sprache und des ›die Welt-neu-Machens‹. Die Frage ›Welcher Trip ist möglich?‹ sollte zunächst tautologisch klingen, um auf die bezeichnenden Verwandlungen der Möglichkeit selbst und auf die *(historische)* Geschichte des Imaginationsvermögens selbst hinzudeuten. Der globale Aspekt dieser Verwandlung ist die Geschichte der Neuzeit als einer Geschichte der Expansion, der Mobilisationen, die zunächst die Erde überzogen und anschließend auch noch das Innere des Menschen, die Psyche mobilisiert haben. Der Trip ist die letzte mögliche Mobilisierung, aber er bringt auch die Möglichkeit mit sich, auf die Internalisierung zu reagieren, indem er sie auf ihren Kopf stellt. Der Trip, ebenso wie der halluzinierende Körper allgemein, ist ein kollektiviertes Selbst, das in die Privatisierung gestürzt wurde.

Um sich einem Verständnis der historischen Verwandlung der Möglichkeit anzunähern, ist es erforderlich, sich jenem Zustand zuzuwenden, in dem überhaupt nichts möglich ist: der Depression. Unter dem Titel *Das erschöpfte Selbst* verfasste der französische Soziologe Alain Ehrenberg eine sehr einflussreiche Untersuchung über die Zunahme der Depression, in der er die These vertritt, wir seien in den letzten vier Jahrzehnten Zeugen einer allgemeinen Verwandlung der

Subjektivität und ihrer Beziehung zur Objekt-Welt geworden.[3] Im Folgenden ist es wichtig, sich vor Augen zu halten, dass das Subjekt zwar die Szenerie dieser Gedanken ist, tatsächlich jedoch die Beziehung des Subjekts zur Welt auf dem Spiel steht, seine/ihre Fähigkeit und Position in dieser. Ehrenberg bedient sich historischer, von Michel Foucault und Gilles Deleuze eingeführter Kategorien, nämlich der *Disziplinargesellschaft*, über die Foucault in seinen Arbeiten über die Klinik, Gefängnisse und das Entstehen der Biomacht spricht, sowie der von Gilles Deleuze beschriebenen *Kontrollgesellschaft*, in der die Disziplinareinrichtungen verinnerlicht wurden und damit ebenfalls zu einer Angelegenheit des Eigenmanagements des Subjekts geworden sind.[4] Ehrenberg ergänzt diese Kategorien um eine Geschichte der Psychopathologie. Laut Ehrenberg wurde das Subjekt der Disziplinargesellschaft nach Maßgabe des Verbotenen und des Erlaubten organisiert. Dieses Regime wird durch die Disziplinierungsinstitution durchgesetzt und findet sein Pendant in der menschlichen Seele im Begriff der Schuld. Die symptomatischen Psychopathologien der Disziplinargesellschaft sind Hysterie und Neurose; letztere wurde übrigens auch als Krankheit der Narration bezeichnet. Neurose und Hysterie beruhen auf traumatischen Erfahrungen und Schuldgefühlen, die dadurch hervorgerufen werden, dass die Begierden des Subjekts die Regeln und Gesetze dessen überschreiten, was verboten und was erlaubt ist.

Als eine Folge der Emanzipation, Individualisierung und Verwandlung vom repressiven Kapitalismus zum sich selbst regierenden Subjekt des Neoliberalismus hat sich das duale Organisationsprinzip der Subjektivität *verboten/erlaubt* in *möglich/unmöglich* verwandelt, und die symptomatischen mentalen Pathologien haben sich dementsprechend verändert. Dieses Regime der verinnerlichten Selbstregierung wurde Kontrollgesellschaft genannt. Ehrenberg zufolge trat im Verlauf dieser Verwandlung an die Stelle der Massenkrankheiten des Begehrens – Neurose und Hysterie – die Massenkrankheit der Möglichkeit: Depression. Ehrenberg vertritt die These, während die Neurose sich auf die Schuld stütze, stütze sich die Depression auf das Scheitern, das Scheitern des Subjekts in Anbetracht der Notwendigkeit, die Initiative zu ergreifen, verantwortlich zu handeln, sich selbst neu zu erfinden und seine/ihre eigenen Möglichkeiten als souveränes und dennoch flexibles Selbst zu nutzen. Ehrenberg zeigt, dass seit den 1970ern zahlreiche unterschiedliche klinische Symptome unter dem Kollektivbegriff ›Depression‹ zusammengefasst wurden, deren Gemeinsamkeit darin besteht, dass die Patienten an fundamentalen Mängeln leiden, an einer Schwäche und Unfähigkeit, den Erfordernissen dessen gerecht zu werden, was es heute bedeutet, ein Individuum zu sein. Hinsichtlich der psychedelischen Figur ›Trip‹ konzentriert sich der Hauptteil von Ehrenbergs bahnbrechender Studie auf die soziale und politische Bedeutung von das seelische Befinden beeinflussenden Antidepressiva wie Prozak, jener anderen Art von Drogen, die zu veränderten Bewusstseinszuständen führt, welche in völligem Gegensatz zu einem durch psychedelische Drogen ausgelöstem Trip dazu beitragen sollen, das Subjekt wieder in eine funktionstüchtige Normalität zu integrieren, statt ihm/ihr über diese hinwegzuhelfen. Dies wirft ein anderes Licht auf die Frage ›welcher Trip möglich ist‹, da sich die Matrix des Trips gemeinsam mit der Struktur des Wahnsinns verändert hat, und das ›Tripping‹ eine notwendige Fähigkeit des flexiblen Selbst geworden ist. Wenn die Normalität der Depression in der Unfähigkeit besteht, einen Zustand des Normalseins zu erreichen, dann geht die Depression mit der Sehnsucht nach der Fähigkeit einher, die Lücke zwischen der Imagination und der Objektwelt, jener oben erwähnten Vorbedingung der Subjekt/Objekt-Beziehung in der Normalität, zu schließen. Wenn es in der Kunstgeschichte die Surrealisten waren, die den Trip zu einer epistemologischen Methodologie der Überschreitung gemacht haben, welche darauf angelegt war, die Normalität auf den Kopf zu stellen und sie den Mächten der Verwandlung auszusetzen, dann ist inzwischen diese Normalität selbst surreal geworden, wurde dabei jedoch ihres Verwandlungsvermögens beraubt, so dass sich folglich auch der Zustand und die Richtung der Verwandlung verändert haben. Es ist so, als sei das Subjekt von seinen/ihren imaginären Projektionen eingehüllt, ohne dass diese Projektionen einen Halt in der Welt der realen Objekte außerhalb fänden. Die Unmöglichkeit, auf sinnvolle Weise mit der Objektwelt zu kommunizieren, wurde in der Tat andernorts als ein weiteres Schlüsselmerkmal der Depression und diese damit als ein Zustand ›objektlosen Sich-Sehnens‹ identifiziert.[5] Doch tatsächlich lässt sich die Depression nicht wirklich als ein surrealer, des Verwandlungsvermögens beraubter Zustand bezeichnen, da Depression und Imagination einander ausschließen. De facto scheinen in einem depressiven Zustand alle Trips möglich, doch keiner von ihnen wünschenswert zu sein; da die eigenen Wünsche und Begierden der Fähigkeit beraubt sind, mit der Welt zu interagieren, wird das Mögliche folglich zu etwas Unmöglichem. Diese Verwandlung von Möglichem in Unmögliches wird von der kapitalistischen Kultur ausgebeutet, welche die Furcht des ›objektlosen Sich-Sehnens‹ mit wünschenswerten Objekten und ihrer emotionalen und identifikatorischen Versprechen beantwortet, einem Versprechen zu werden. Es überrascht nicht, dass sich unter diesen Umständen auch die drei Schlüsselbegriffe des ›Trips‹ unter den kommerziellen Mantras und Schlüsselworten finden: Möglichkeit, Imagination, Bewegung/Mobilität. Wenn die Depression nicht nur eine außergewöhnliche Anormalität ist, sondern ein Massenphänomen, das für einen kulturellen Zustand symptomatisch ist, für die Normalität der Kultur im Neoliberalismus heute, dann erkennt man, dass das ›objektlose Sich-Sehnen‹ das dialektische Gegenstück zur Ausdehnung der ›Phantom-Objektivität‹ der kapitalistischen Kommodifizierung in die Sphäre des Lebens ist. Unter den zahlreichen Werbekampagnen der letzten Zeit, ragt dabei vielleicht eine besonders heraus, nämlich diejenige des Sportartikelherstellers Adidas und seines Slogans ›Impossible is Nothing‹[6], der das übliche Versprechen erweiterter Möglichkeiten umkehrt, ja als regelrechte Drohung gelesen werden kann, als das neoliberale Gegenstück zu der disziplinarischen Drohung mit Internierung und Bestrafung. ›Make it real‹ – oder du wirst ins Nichts gestürzt werden. Und natürlich ließe sich der Rest dieses Textes mit Zitaten aus der Welt des Kommerzes bestreiten.

*Again for Tomorrow, Scene for New Heritage, These Days*: Die Titel dieser ›Trips‹ beziehen sich aber auch noch auf eine weitere Dimension der Depression, die Depression als ›Krankheit der Zeit‹[7]. Subjekte, die in eine ›unerinnerbare Vergangenheit und eine unvorstellbare Zukunft‹ gestürzt wurden. Die Soziologin Avery Gordon hat eine Untersuchung über das Heimgesuchtwerden, über Fälle unheimlicher Wiederkehr und ihrer Bedeutung für die öffentliche und politische Sphäre in Amerika verfasst. In ihrem Buch *Ghostly Matters* beschreibt sie die zeitgenössische kollektive Psychopathologie anhand einer Analyse der amerikanischen Konsumkultur (am Beispiel von Don DeLillos Roman *White Noise* [*Weißes Rauschen*]) und ihrer Unfähigkeit, mit dem in eine Beziehung zu treten, was sie ausschließt, nämlich mit ihren eigenen Gespenstern. ›Keine Schatten, keine Gespenster‹, eine Welt, die gewaltsam in die Sichtbarkeit der Phantom-Objektivität gedrängt wurde, in der nichts von dem, was gesagt und gedacht wird, wirklich noch eine Rolle spielt oder etwas zählt.[8] Dies ist die Mobilitätsberaubung, die Beraubung des oder etwas zählt.[8] Dies ist die Mobilitätsberaubung, die Beraubung des Zugangs zu den Mächten der Veränderung. Erinnern Re-enactments nicht an die vorbeimarschierenden Gespenster der Geschichte, doch einer Geschichte, die bereits verloren gegangen ist? Sind sie nicht eher Ausdruck eines Verlusts, Illustrationen eines aus dem Ruder gelaufenen Zeitzustands, einer Zeit, mit der wir nicht mehr kommunizieren und auf die wir uns nicht mehr beziehen können, statt Wieder-Belebungen zu sein? ›Die Depression ist eine Störung, in der die Temporalitäten des psychischen Lebens – erinnern, repräsentieren, begehren und projizieren – unbeweglich gemacht wurden. Eine solche Suspendierung bedeutet, dass das deprimierte Individuum außerstande ist, sich selbst zu situieren, weder in Bezug auf die Zukunft (hoffen, träumen, vorwegnehmen, Pläne machen, zu entscheiden, was morgen zu tun ist) noch auf die Vergangenheit (Erinnerungen Mobilität verleihen, das Erinnerungsvermögen aktivieren)‹[9]. Letztlich ist die Welt der Depression eine gespenstische Welt, eine in diskontinuierliche Teile zerschnittene Welt, die das Subjekt nicht mehr miteinander zu verbinden, zu synthetisieren vermag. Dies ist das Scheitern, von dem Ehrenberg spricht, womit er letztlich das, was dem Subjekt ›möglich‹ ist, mit seiner Fähigkeit zu synthetisieren, das heißt zu historisieren, Narrationen zu verfassen und, daraus entspringend, die Macht zu metaphorisieren, zu mobilisieren und neu- und umzubenennen, verknüpft.

Der Bezug auf eine zerbrochene Kontinuität (oder einen gebrochenen Widerstand, zerbrochene Ansprüche auf Kontinuität, zum Schweigen gebrachte Geschichten, die einen rechtmäßigen Platz in der Welt schaffen) erinnert strukturell an die traumatische Erfahrung und lässt uns an die Wieder-Belebung der zerbrochenen Verbindung als Heilungsprozess denken, an die Wiedererlangung der eigenen relativen Autonomie, der eigenen Fähigkeit zu imaginieren, zu sprechen und zu handeln. Und alle Formen der Heilung traumatischer Erfahrungen werden durch Narrativierung vermittelt, dadurch, dass man einer Erfahrung ihre Geschichte zurückgibt. In diesem Sinne begreife ich auch die Gebäude in Davids Werk. Die Stille, ihre formale, fremd gewordene Sprache fordert zur Wieder-Belebung auf, dazu zu lernen, einmal neu zu sprechen. Welches Bild könnte den Versuch, eine verloren gegangene gemeinsame Sprache wiederzubeleben, besser veranschaulichen als das von jemandem, der vor einem zerstörten futuristischen Denkmal singt? Die Szenerie von David Maljkovićs Trips, die nicht nur das ›Scheitern‹

seiner kollektiven Bestrebungen, sondern auch eine neue mögliche Geschichte verkörpert, widersetzt sich letztlich der Kommodifizierung, weil sie für die Fähigkeit steht, die Dinge einmal wieder anders zu imaginieren. In einer Welt kapitalistischer ›Phantom-Objektivität‹ ist dieses Erbe ein ›objektives Phantom‹ geworden, das nicht verschwinden wird, bis seine Sprachen endlich wieder appropriiert, praktiziert und verstanden werden.

Anmerkungen

1 *The Imaginary Number*, kuratiert von Anselm Franke und Hila Peleg, KW Berlin, 5.6.2005–11.9.2005.
2 Siehe Wolfgang Ernst, *Das Rumoren der Archive. Ordnung aus Unordnung*, Berlin 2002.
3 Alain Ehrenberg, *La Fatigue d'être soi. Dépression et société*, Paris 2000.
4 Gilles Deleuzes Text *Society of Control*, der ursprünglich auf Französisch in *L'autre journal*, Nr. 1, Mai 1990, erschienen ist, findet sich online unter <http://www.nadir.org/nadir/archiv/netzkritik/societyofcontrol.html> (13.8.2007).
5 Jennifer Church, *Depression, Depth and the Imagination*, in: James Phillips und James Morley (Hrsg.), *Imagination and Its Pathologies*, Cambridge, Massachussetts 2003, S. 181.
6 Siehe <http://www.adidas.com/campaigns/iin/content/index.asp?adidas_cc=com> (13.8.2007).
7 Pierre Fédida, *Des bienfaits de la dépression. Eloge de la psychothérapie*, Paris 2003.
8 Avery F. Gordon, *Ghostly Matters – Haunting and the Sociological Imagination*, Minneapolis 1997, S. 13.
9 Christine Ross, *Depression and video art at the turn of the millennium: the work of Diana Thater*, in: *Affective Encounters*, siehe <http://media.utu.fi/affective/index.html> (13.8.2007).

# SCENE FO

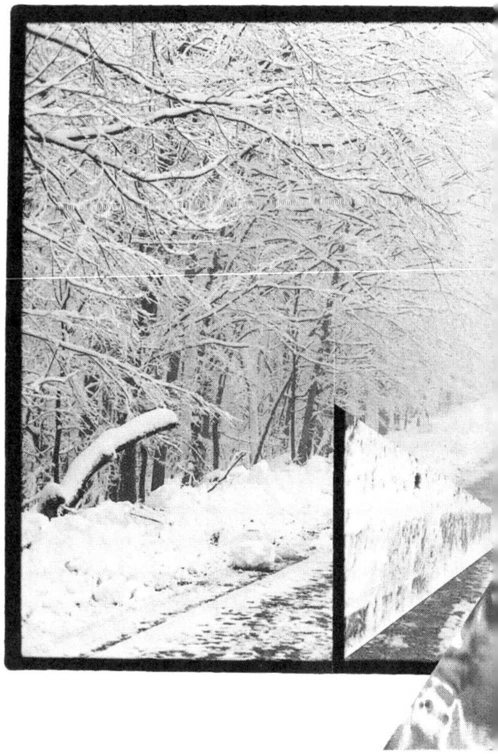

# IEW HERITAGE 2

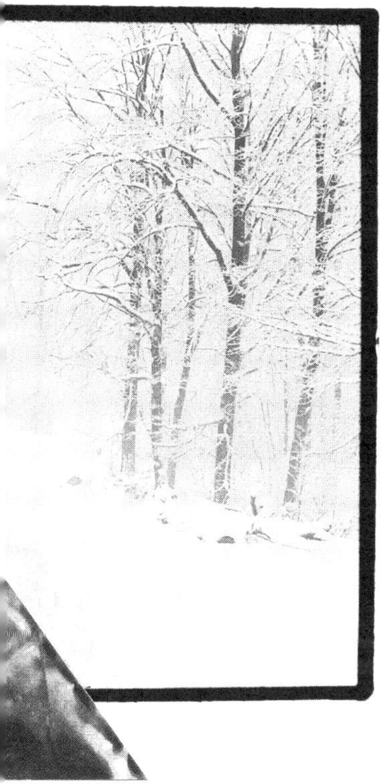

*Scene for New Heritage 2*, 2006, collage

Generation II: Second Coming

The arrival of the first generation of visitors to the Petrova Gora Memorial Park took place on 25 May 2045. It was led by a group of young people in search of their own heritage, suffering from collective amnesia created by the temporal distance which turned history into fiction. Let us recall that under Communist rule, the forgotten place was a memorial park dedicated to the victims of the Second World War or, to be more precise, it had been built on the site of the Central Partisans' Hospital. The monument's designer, Vojin Bakić, worked on it for 10 years, from 1970 to 1981.

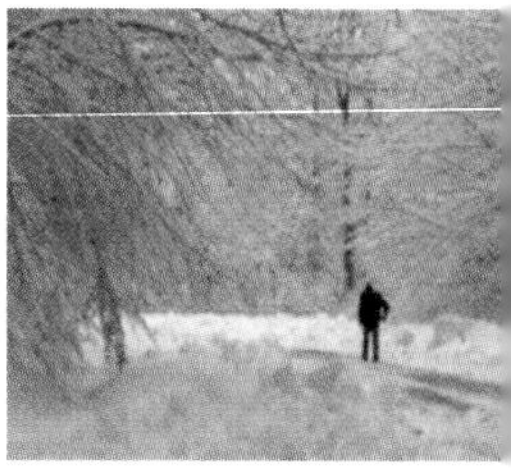



*Scene for New Heritage 2*, 2006, video stills and collage

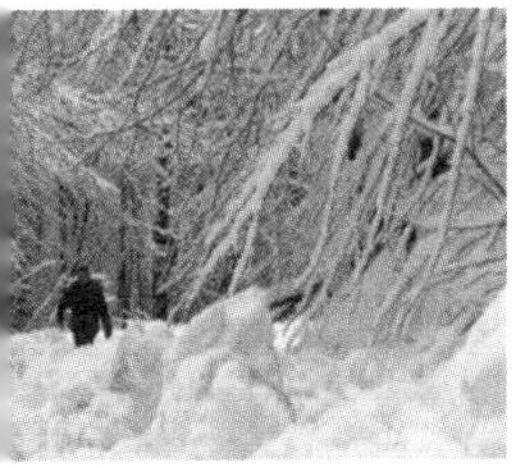

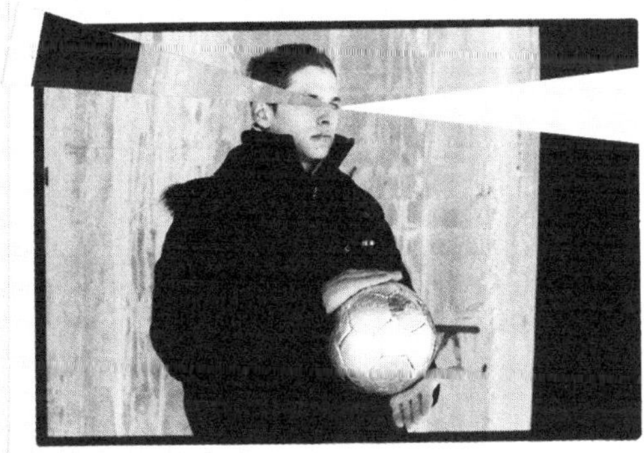

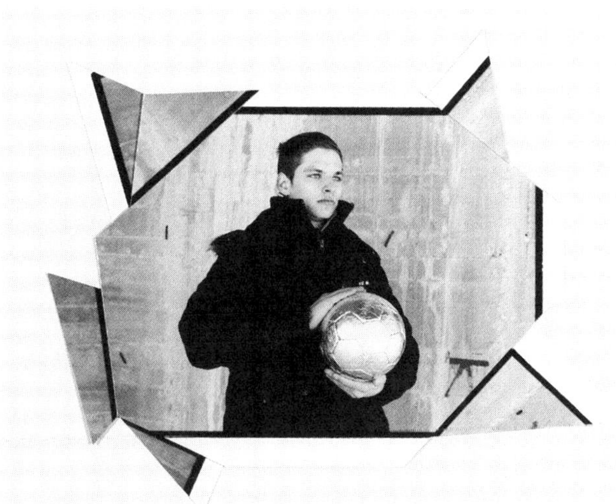



*Scene for New Heritage 2*, 2006, video stills and collage

In the period between September 1991 and August 1995, the memorial park was within the occupied area and was completely devastated at the time. Today it exists only as an artefact, a structure without function. Let us go back now to 2045 and to the generation perplexed by the monumentality of the site, so that the very recognition of the site has failed, just as the issue of their heritage has. This is followed by the arrival of a second generation, i.e. of its representative – the boy with the silver ball – who is aware of the fact that 'his moment in time is his heritage' but who nonetheless decides to establish contact with the site. He arrives on 29 November 2063. Unlike his predecessors, the boy decides to take a step further and enter the monument where the rooms of the museum used to be. Being more open and bolder, he is ready to play with the long forgotten and unknown place, but the absence of the interior does not allow it, so he wanders through the derelict rooms. The tension of the void engenders an inability to play.

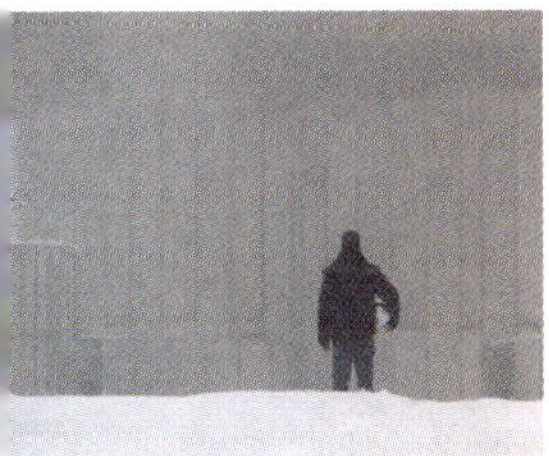

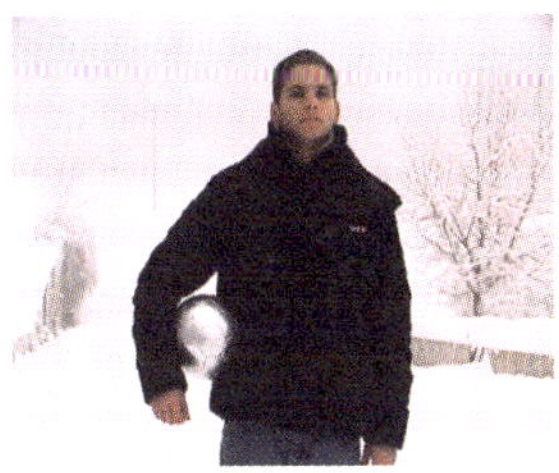

A new possibility of communication is opened by the discovery of a way out, leading through the monument's roof. It is followed by unintelligible – at least to us – message signals dissolving in the panorama. It is clear that the new generations cannot establish contact with the forgotten place and its historic structure but that every new visit, no matter how much it fails to be comprehended, will create new possibilities and relationships which are welcome in the formation of a rebirth of the monument.

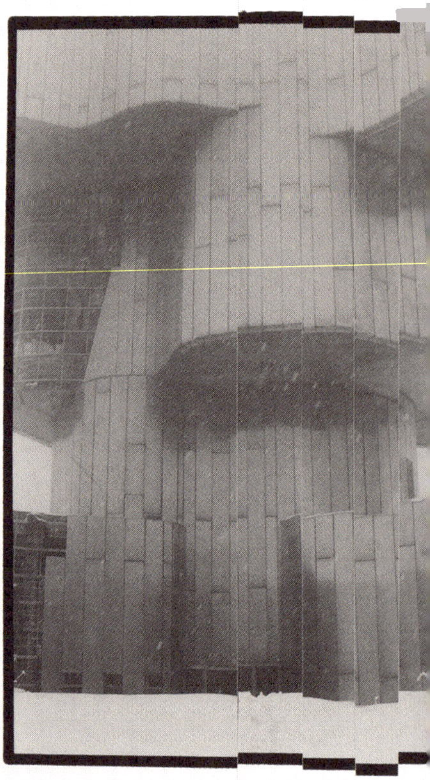

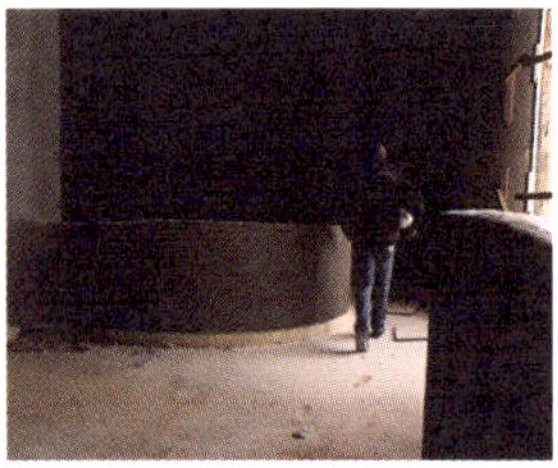

*Scene for New Heritage 2*, 2006, video still and collage

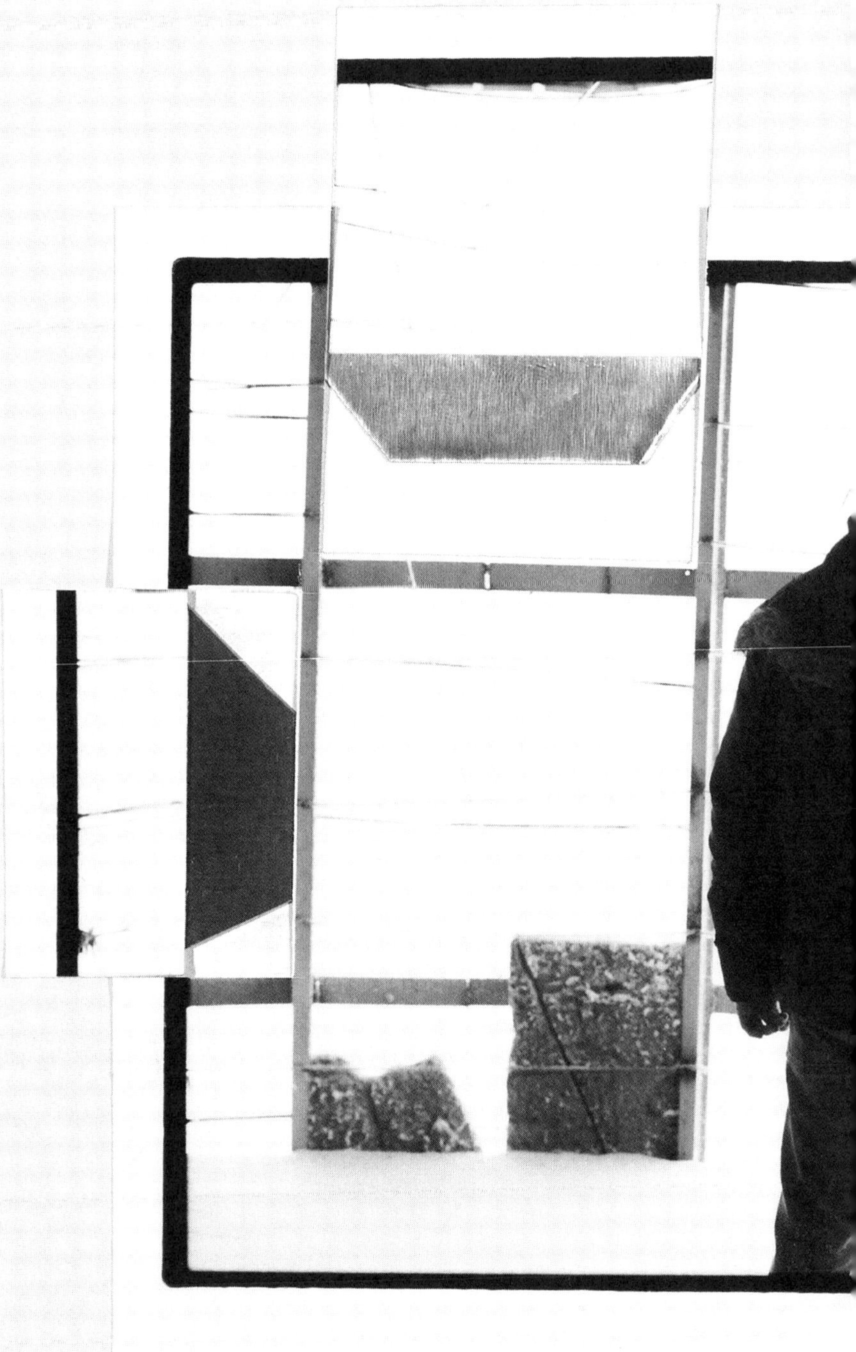

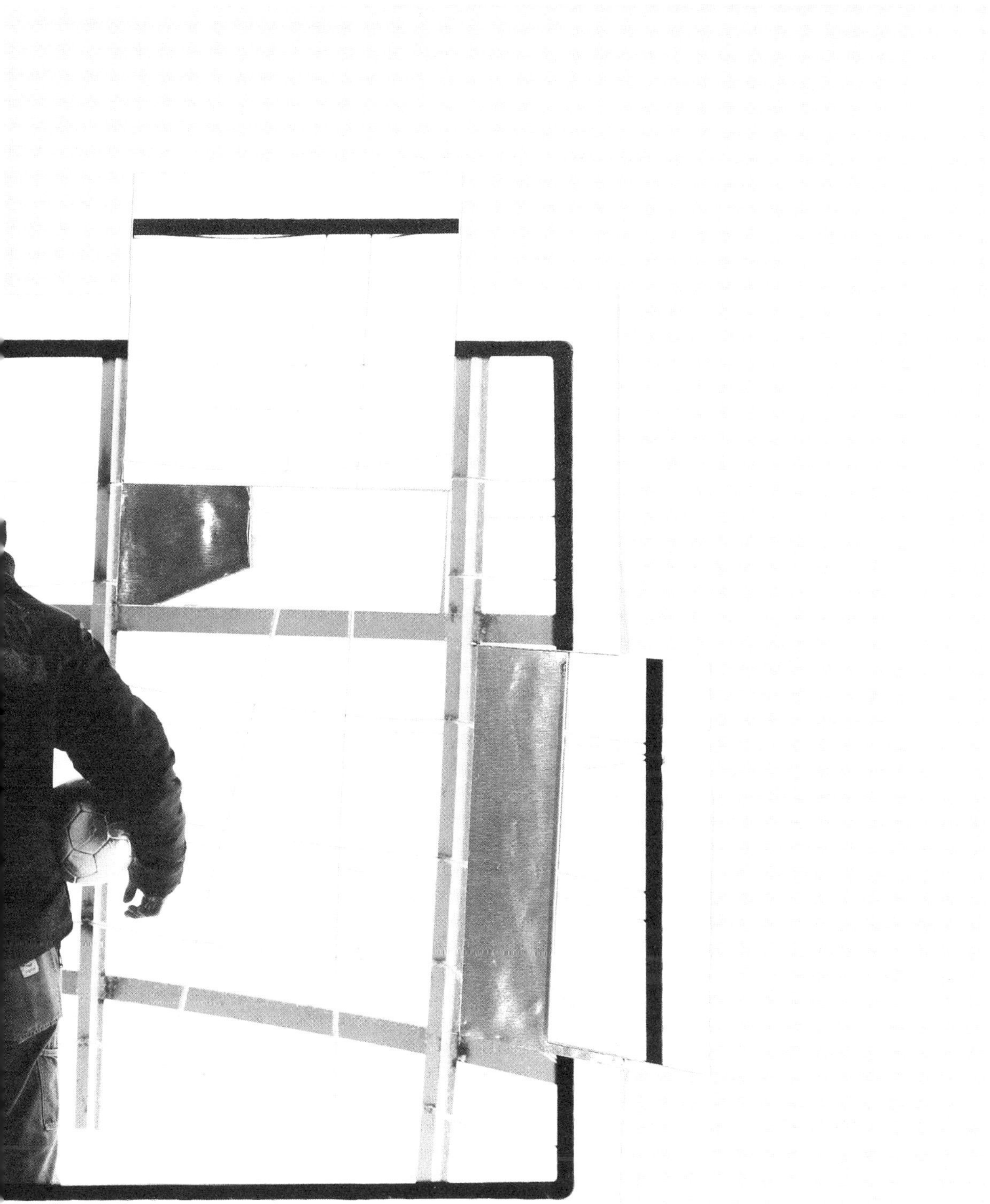

*Scene for New Heritage 2*, 2006, collage

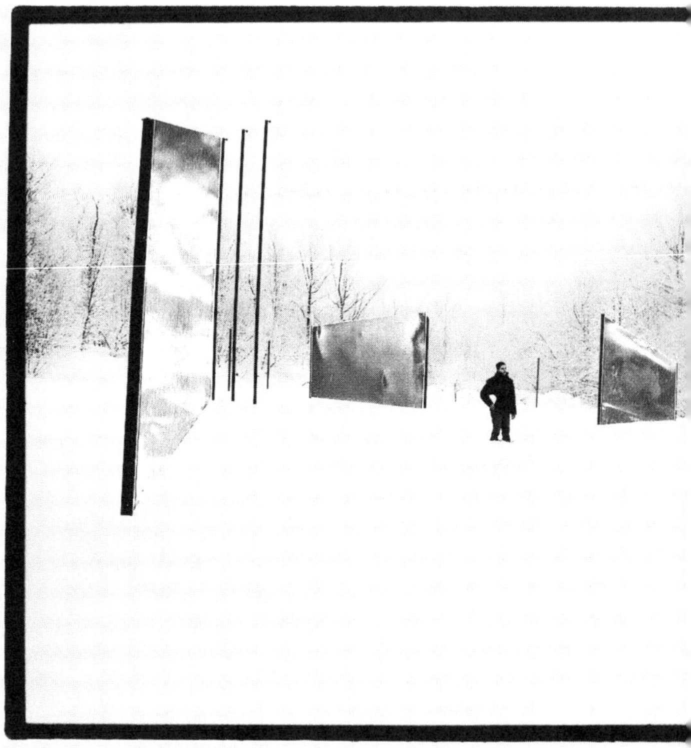



*Scene for New Heritage 2*, 2006, video stills and collage

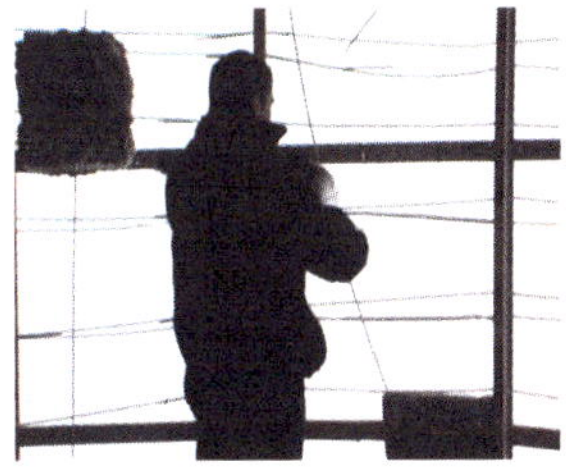

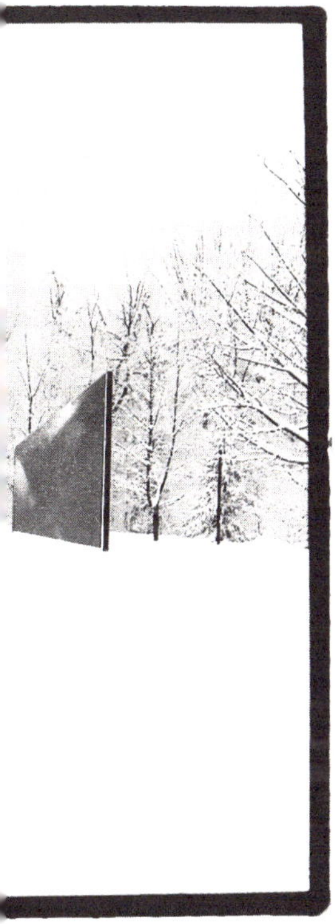

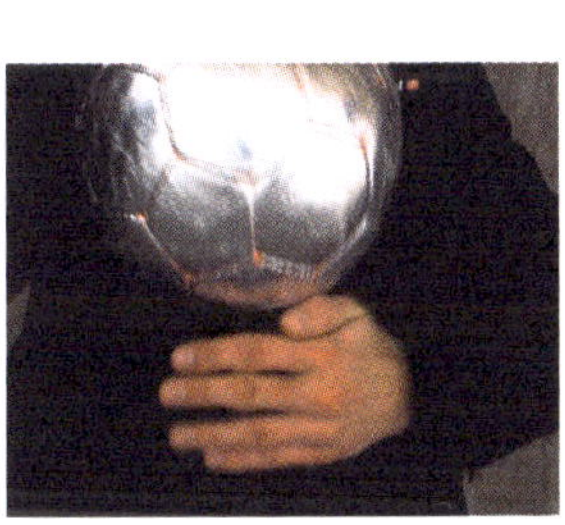

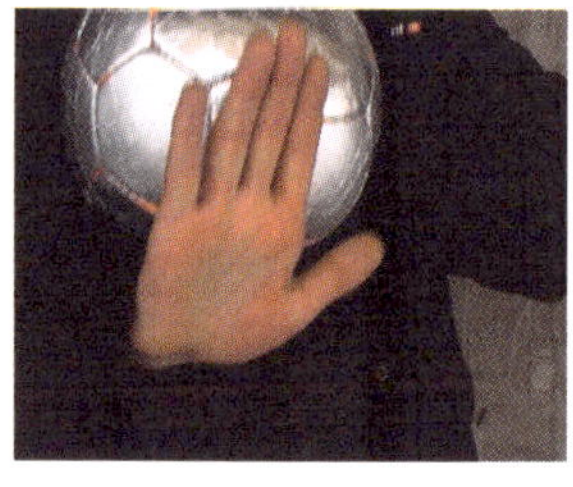

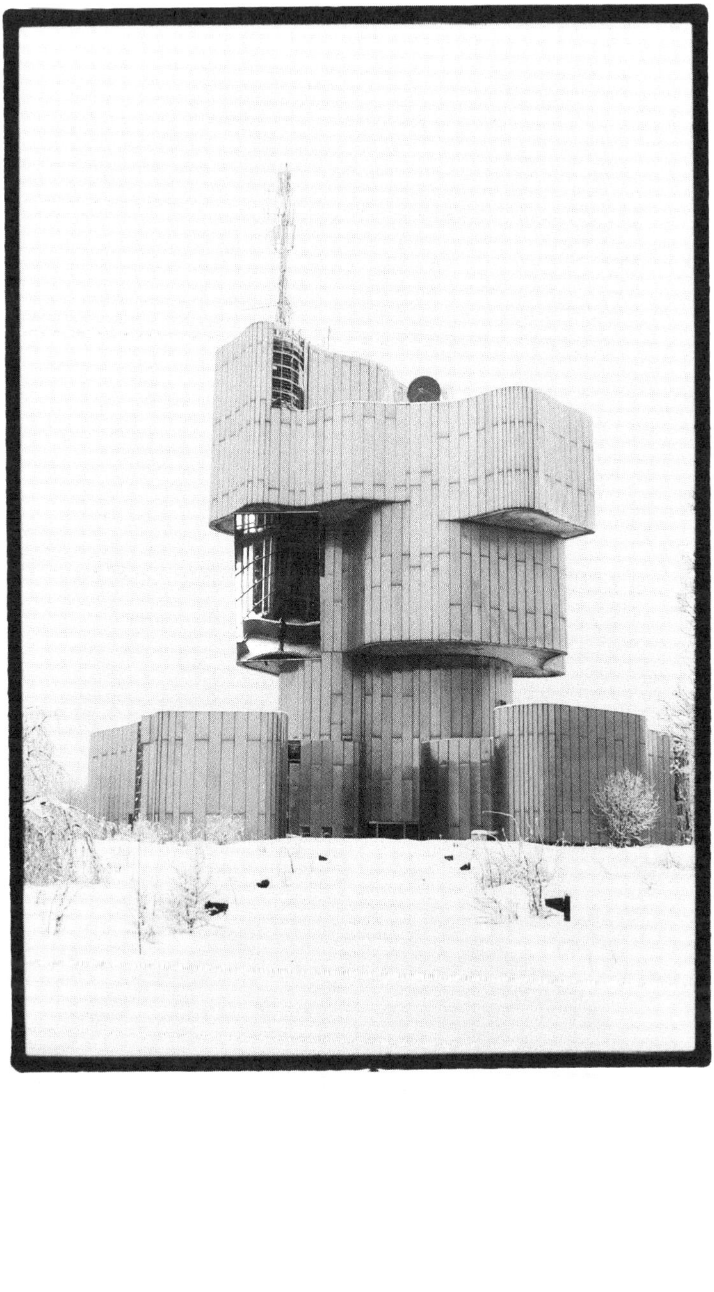



*Scene for New Heritage 2*, 2006, video still and collage

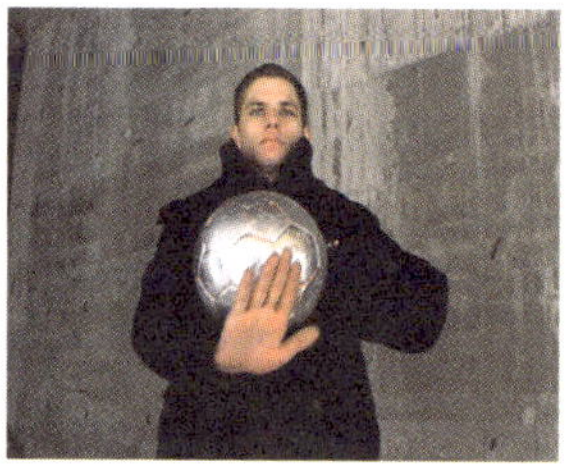

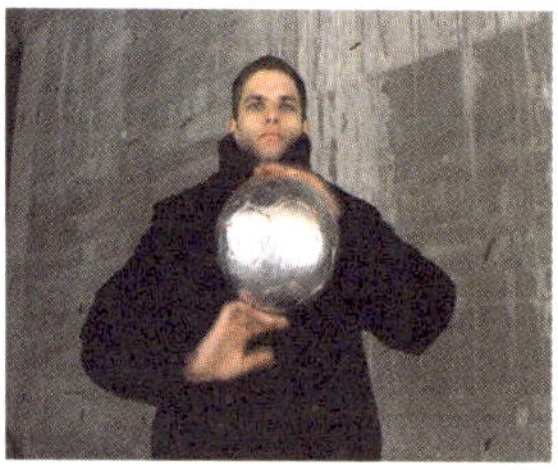

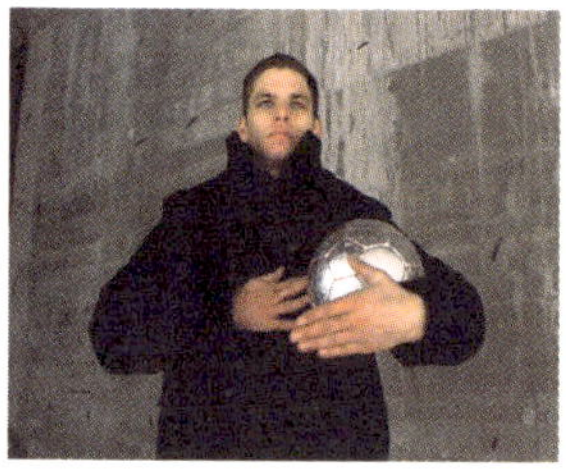

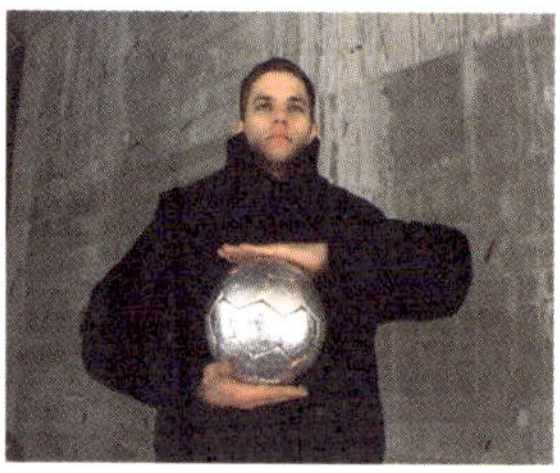

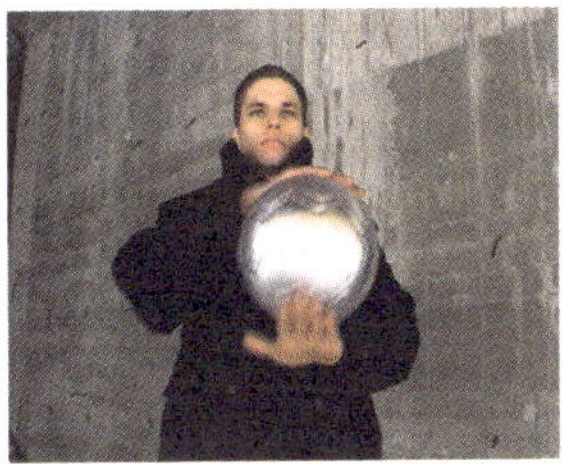

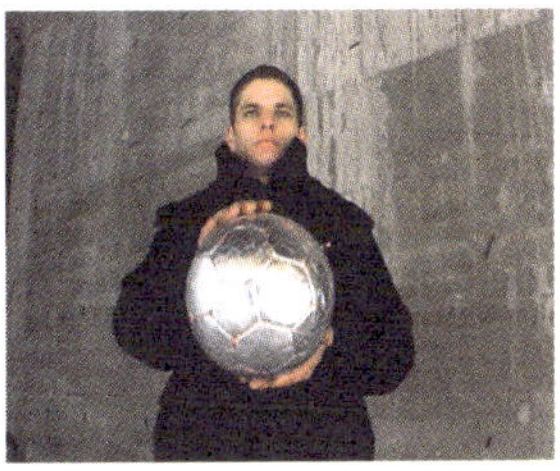

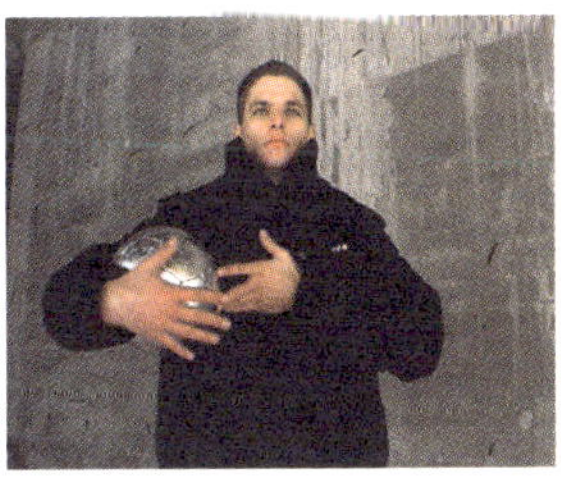

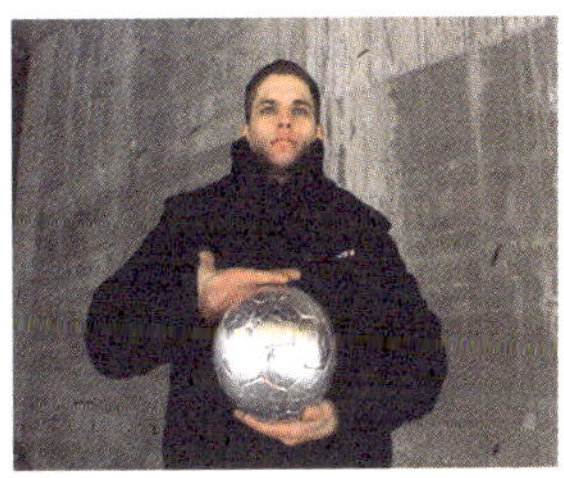



*Scene for New Heritage 2*, 2006, video stills

# LOST MEMORIES

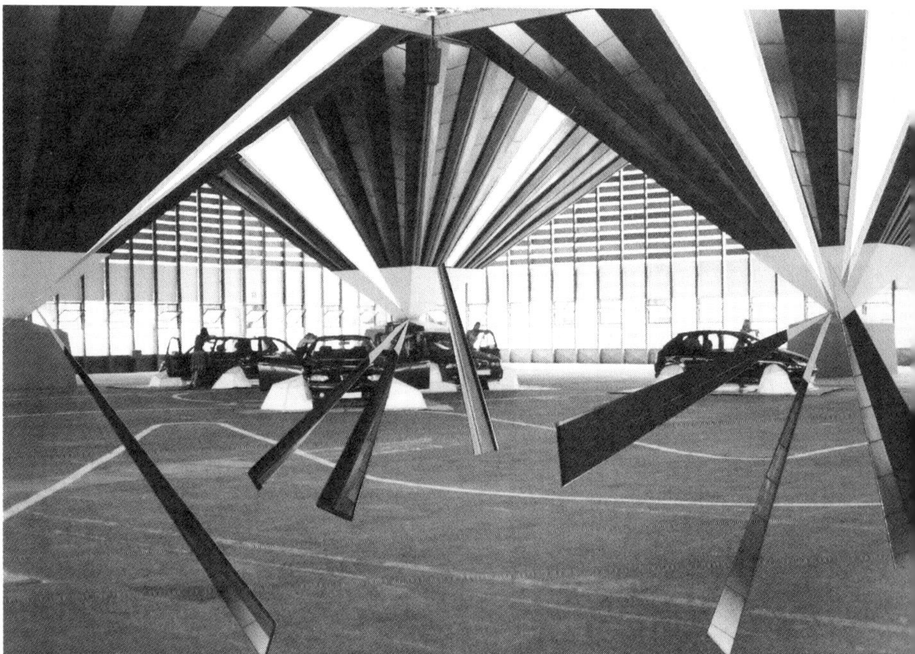

# FROM THESE DAYS

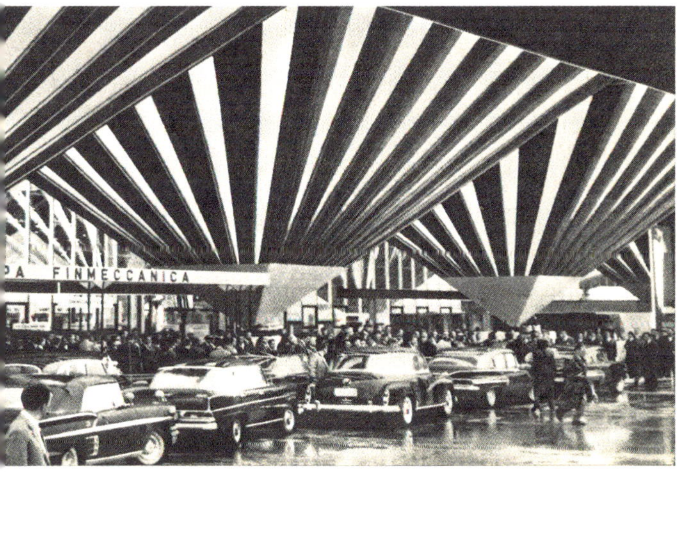


Above: Italian Pavilion at the Zagreb Fair in the 1960s
Opposite: *Lost Memories from These Days*, 2006, collage

The return to the site of the former Italian pavilion at the Zagreb Fair was not caused by the feeling that there were still some loose ends, but by the inability to escape the thoughts and feelings brought out during the shooting of its predecessor, *These Days*. This time I entered the pavilion. The feeling of emptiness was even stronger. I recalled a snap-shot from the 1960s – a vintage car sale – and the attempt to reanimate memory began. The reconstruction adopted its own pace; the cars were set up, the hostesses arrived and it looked like everything was going perfectly well until a strong feeling of the present kicked in. The absence of memory prevailed and at that point everything turned into a lost projection.

The anticipation was as great as that in the previous work, only this time it was reflected onto a younger generation. The smiling mode disappeared from the hostesses' faces the moment when the illusion of a better tomorrow vanished from the place that once had been built for that purpose.

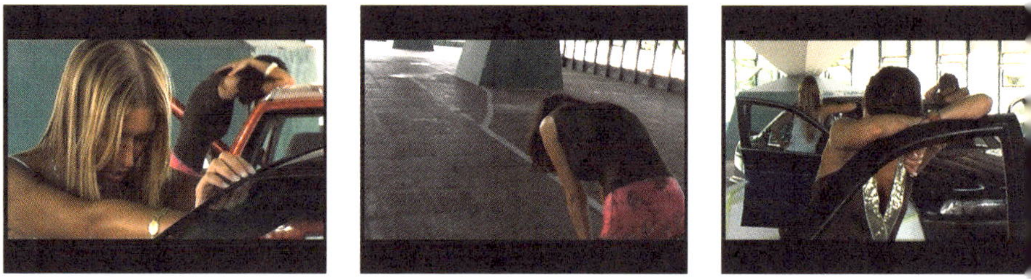



*Lost Memories from These Days*, 2006, video stills

There was no air in the pavilion; it had simply been sucked out by time, and we were there only for a short while, too short to bring it back. I shared a feeling of anxiety with the exhausted hostesses and reduced motion to a minimum. It seems that the new generation has been stuck in the immobile space between yesterday and tomorrow, and that history without continuity has produced a new standstill and its concealed part – the new victims.

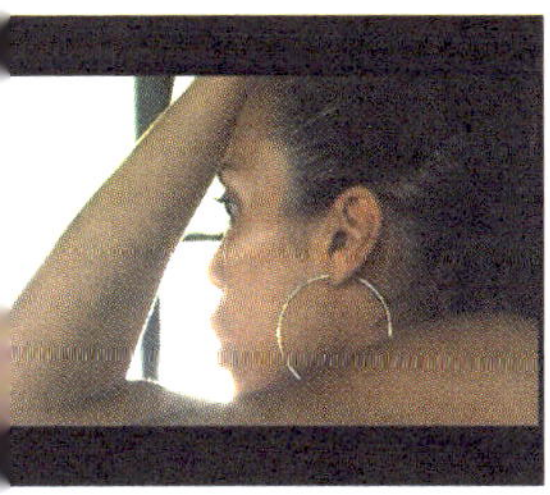
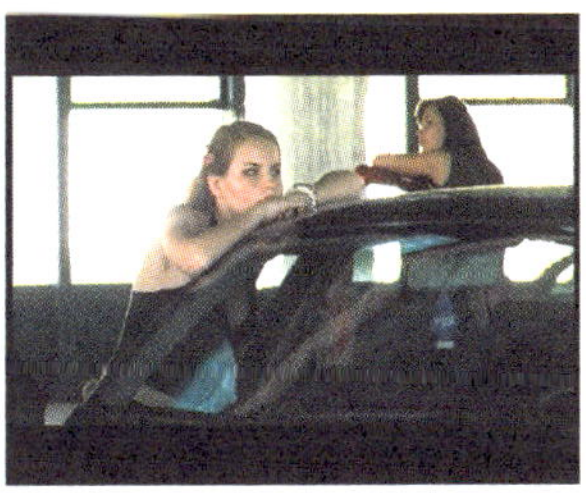
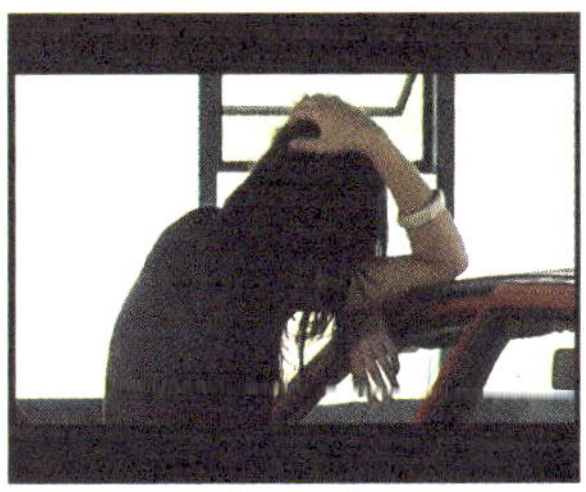

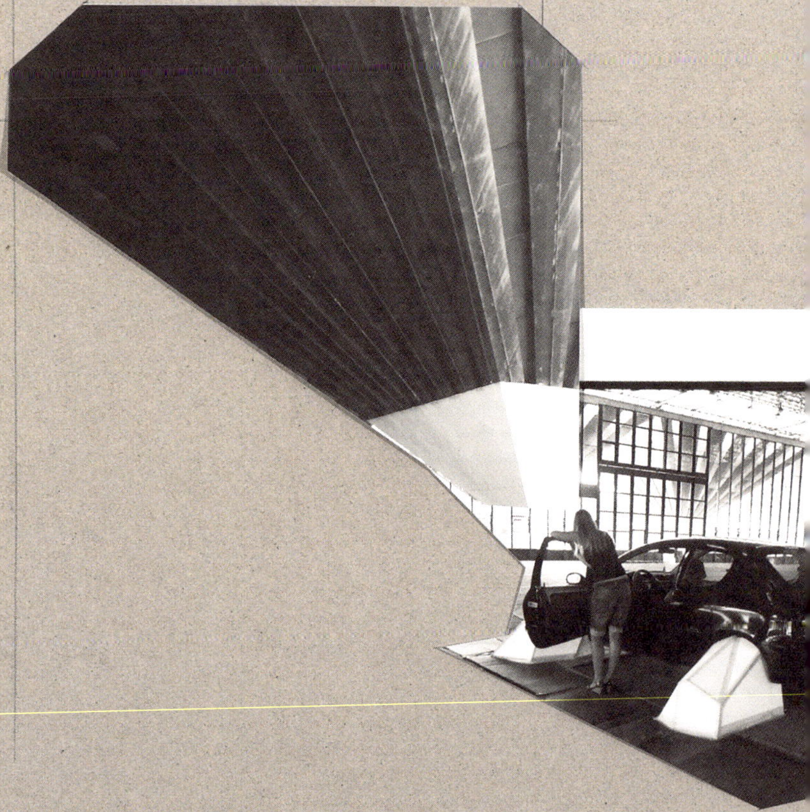

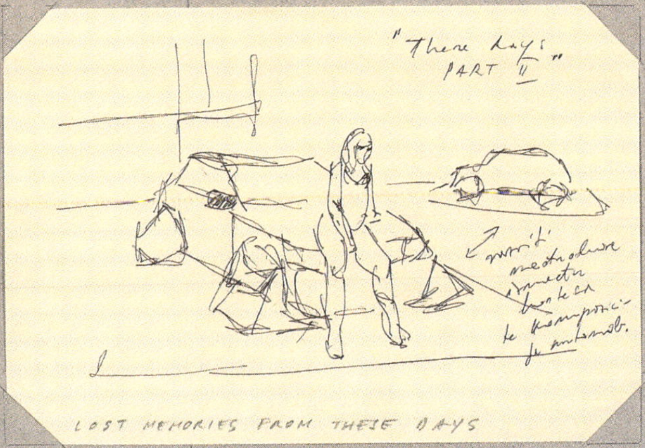
"These days PART II"
LOST MEMORIES FROM THESE DAYS

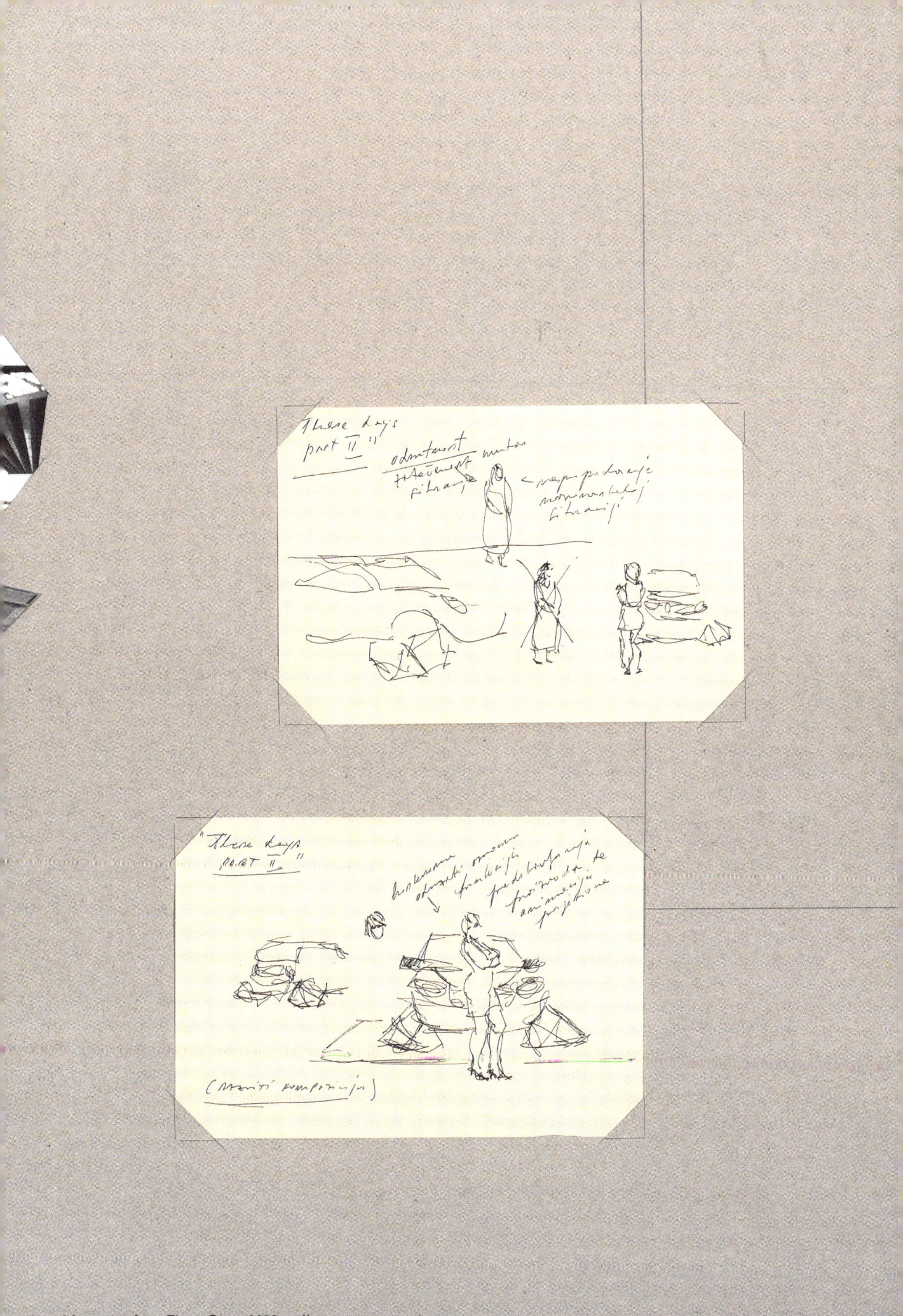


*Lost Memories from These Days*, 2006, collage

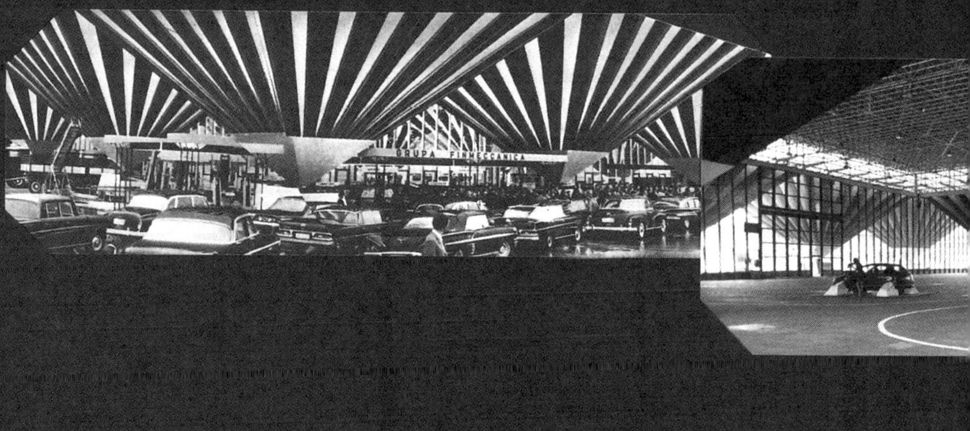
GRUPA FINMECCANICA

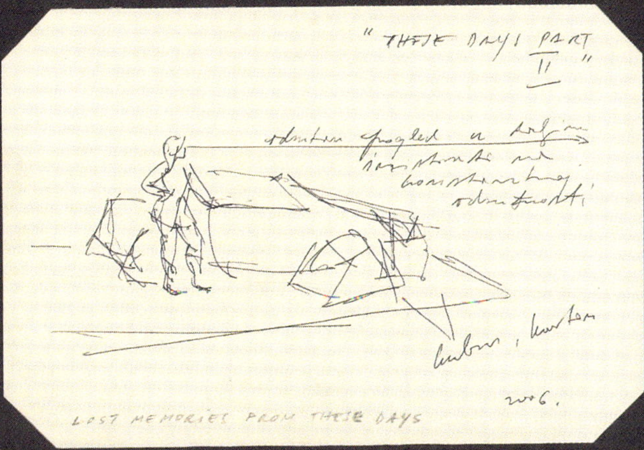


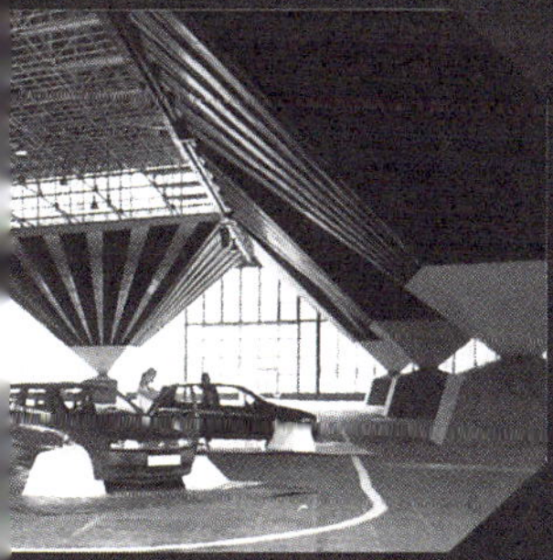

*Lost Memories from These Days*, 2006, collage

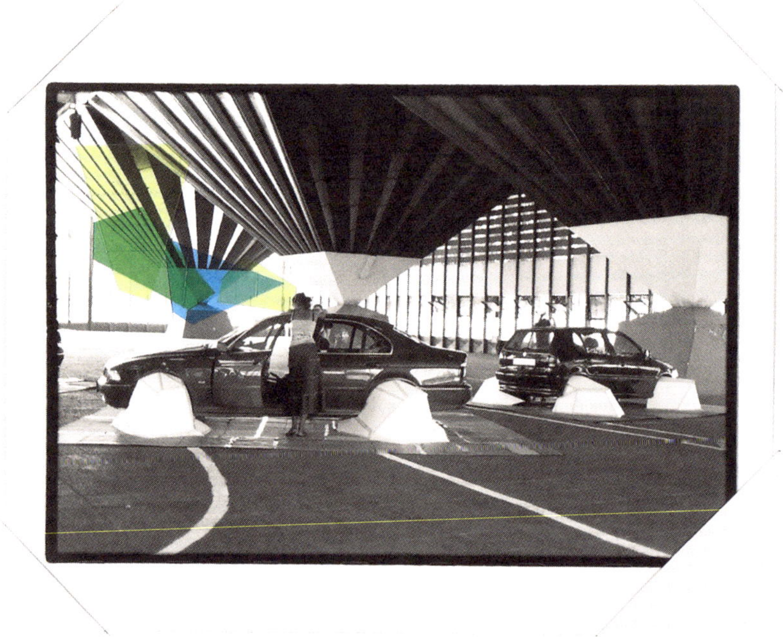

*Lost Memories from These Days*, 2006, collage

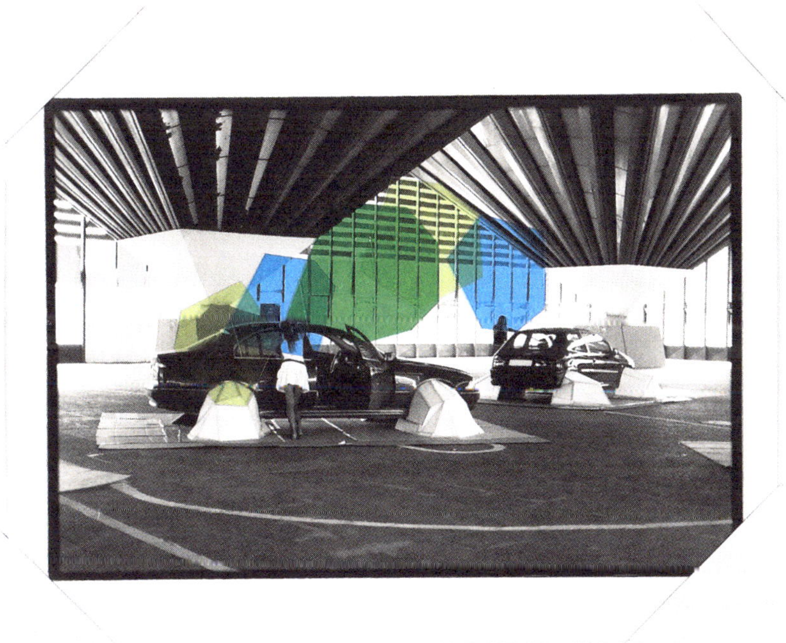

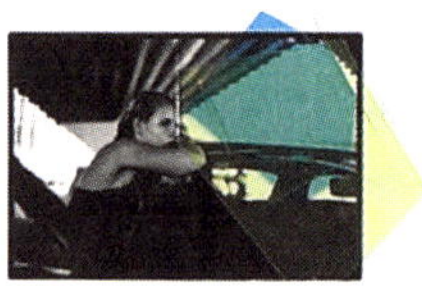

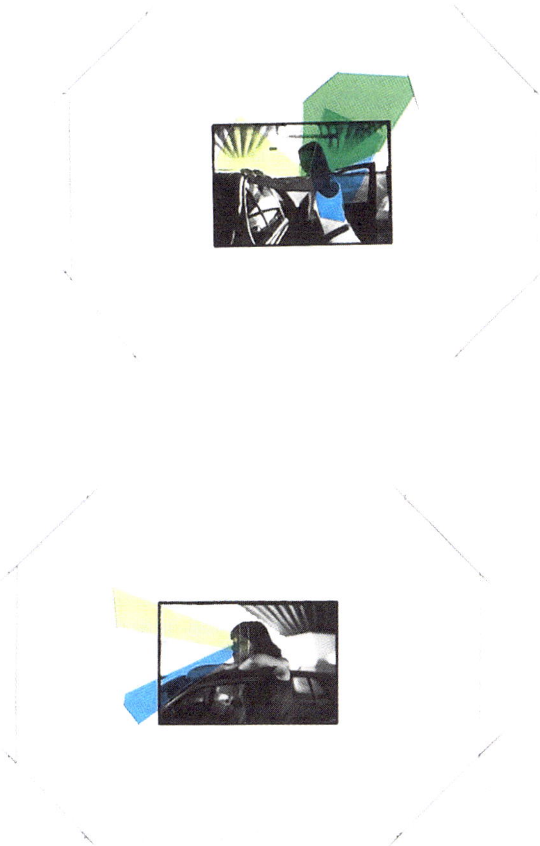

*Lost Memories from These Days*, 2006, collage

# SCENE FO

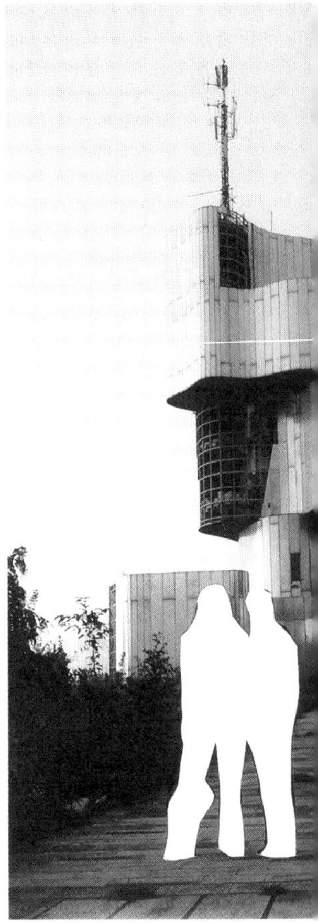

# NEW HERITAGE 3

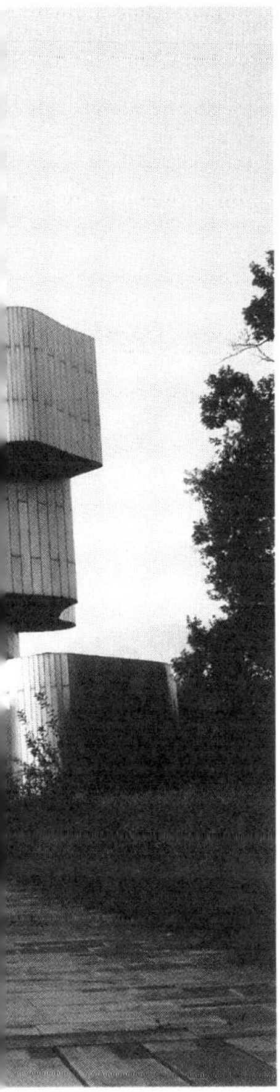

*Scene for New Heritage 3*, 2006, collage

## New Visitors – Visitors Forever

The smells were the same and only time disappeared, and they were not sure if it went through them or they through it. They could have been any generation; their absence from the place that had been existing, invisible to the eye, was the same. I started with time, following the experience of the first two parts and I dare say it was habit. Even in some initial sketches the year 2071 cropped up, but soon it turned out that the third part did not tolerate defining, especially not temporally. I was well prepared, or I thought I was. Somehow everything took a long time and the weather was also unstable; the rain, the clouds, then the sun and then again the clouds ... We set off to Petrova Gora rather early; the scene had been set up throughout the morning, and then the visitors arrived. I controlled them perfectly in the initial sketches, but suddenly they became subjects and everything seemed somehow real. I could say that at that moment reality beat fiction. I became nervous, no, serious anxiety came over me; I reached out for Xanax and decided to shoot the first frames from a panoramic viewing point on top of the monument.

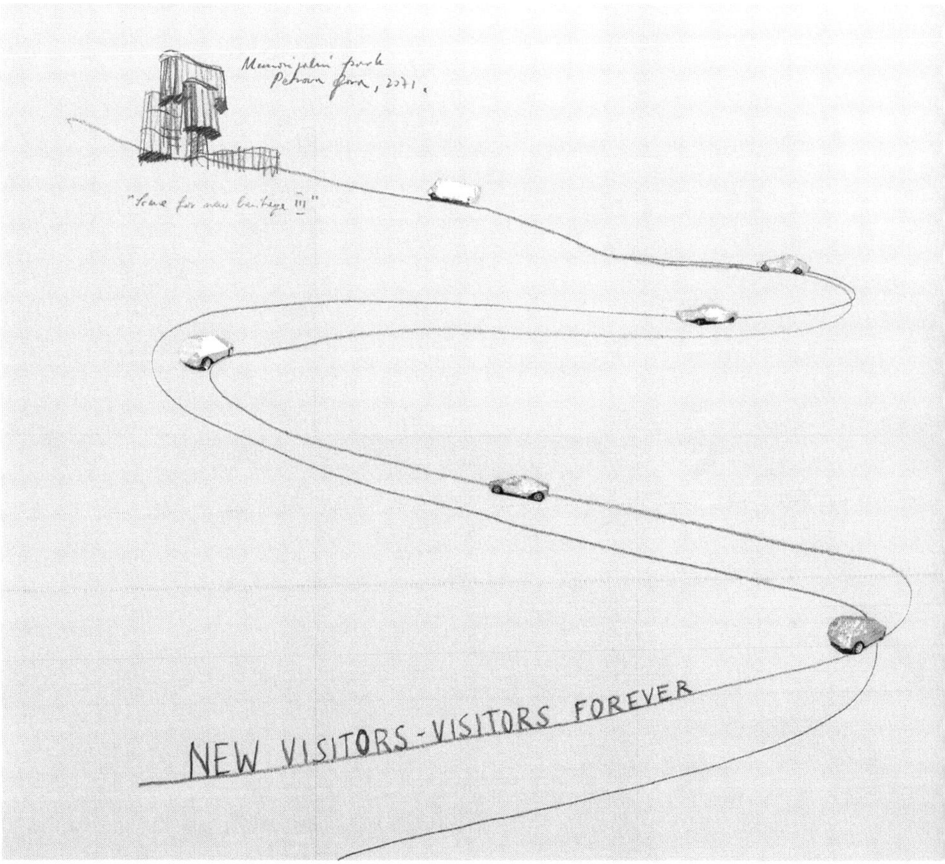

Immediately, one of the visitors approached me and started to talk about how he had been there during the war in the 1990s when he had fought in this area and how the place hadn't changed much since. I listened to him with interest and at the same time I had a feeling that reality was flooding over me with such intensity that I was losing control. Somehow I managed to concentrate and we started to shoot, and it seemed that the pill had started to kick in. We shot those first frames from that angle, but they turned out to be no good. Later on I started to control the situation and began calmly with static compositions as I had planned. That nervous beginning and the conversation with the visitor from the past as well as the experience of the place generated a regression of its own kind that reminded me just how much we have to behave gently with the changes that have happened to us.

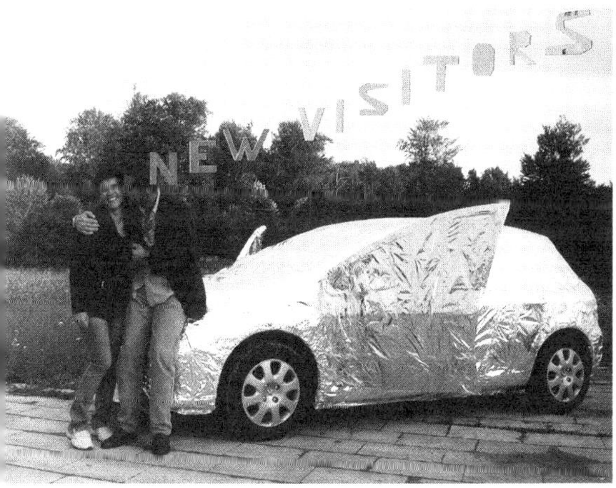


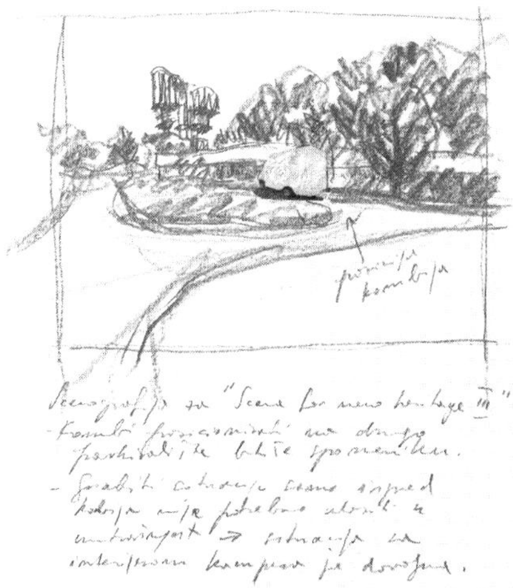

*Scene for New Heritage 3*, 2006, collages and sketch for video set

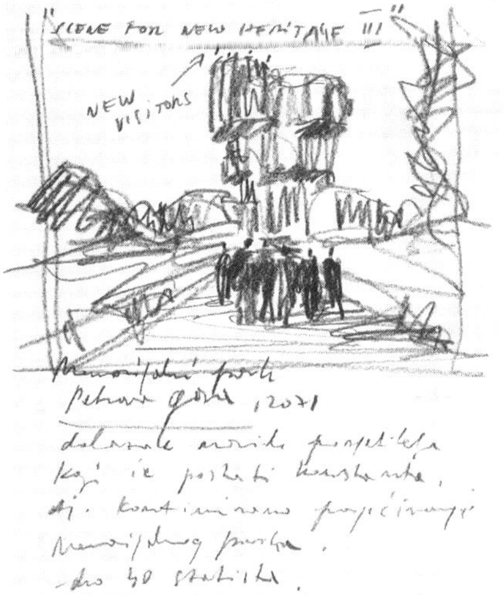


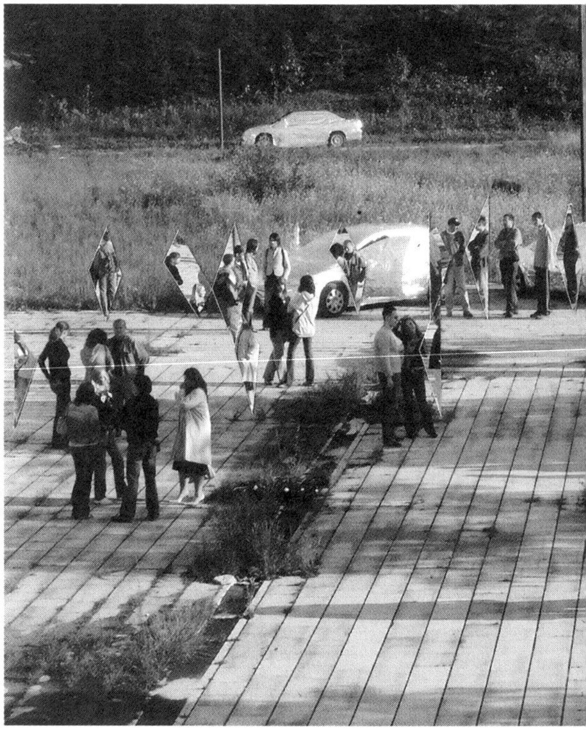

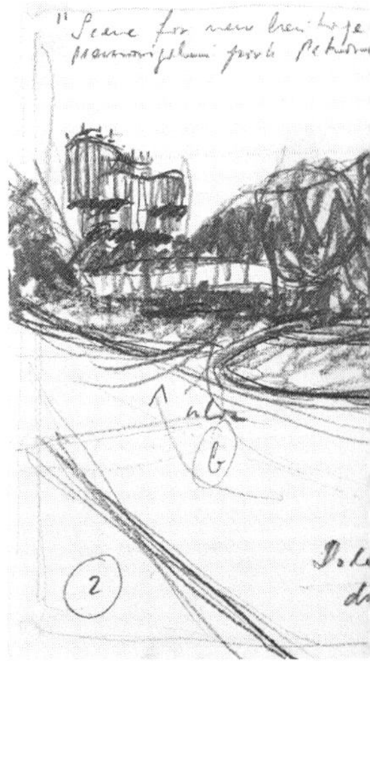


*Scene for New Heritage 3*, 2006, collage and sketches for video set

All the time I thought the visitors were not there, but when I visited Petrova Gora during preparations for the shooting, I noticed that somebody always pops by, a few of them, disorganized but of their own free will. They did not come to 'get in touch with the past' and it was no longer a 'place for gathering and planning the future' as it had been projected. However, the energy of the place and the monument generated primeval visitors, new visitors – visitors forever.

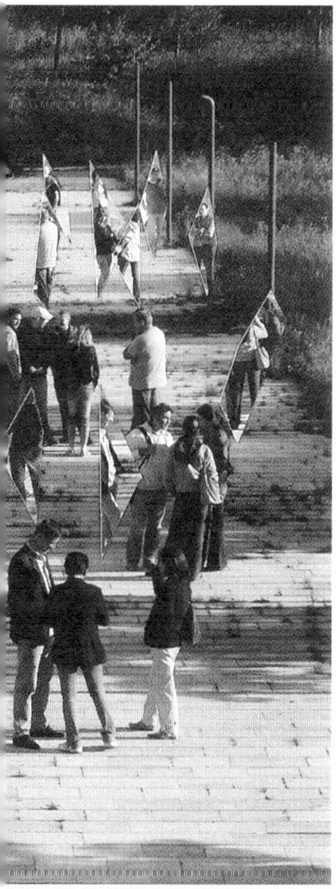

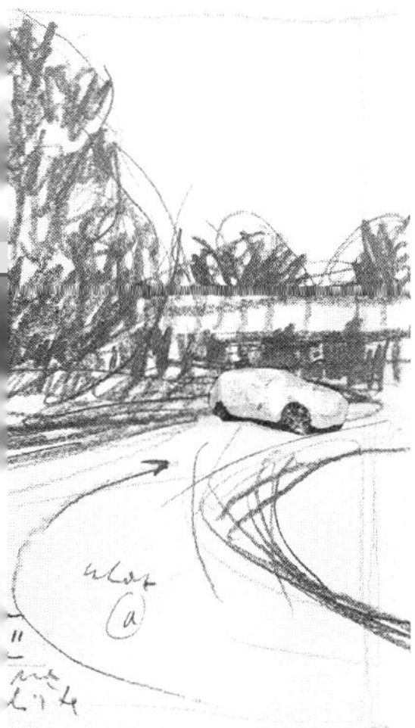

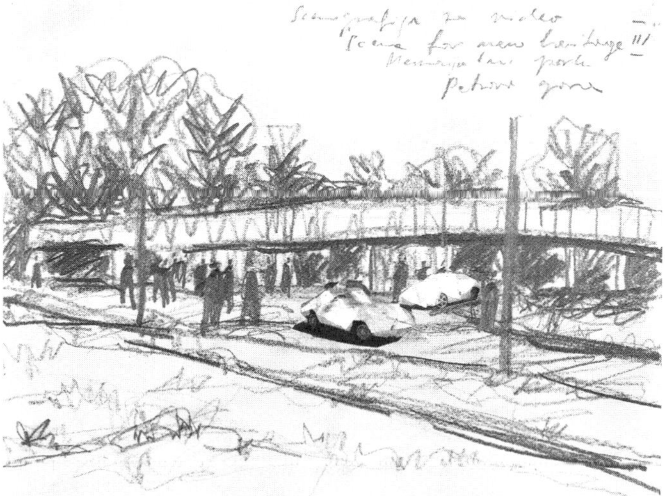

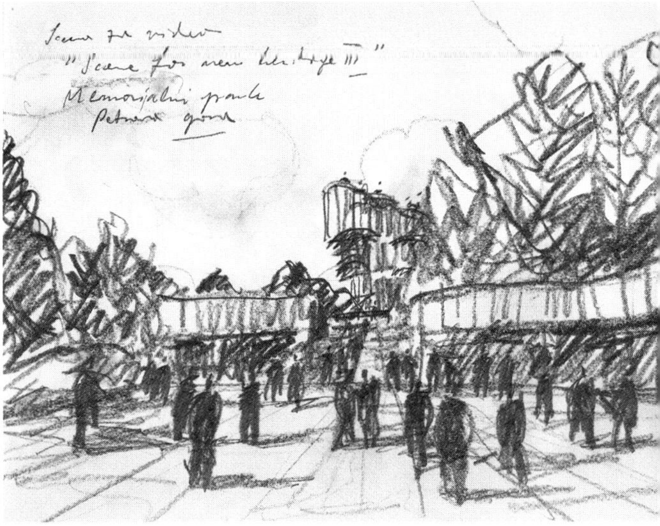

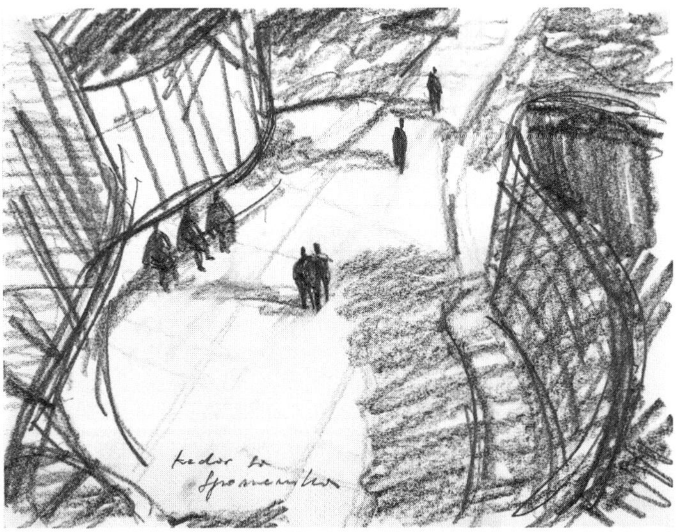

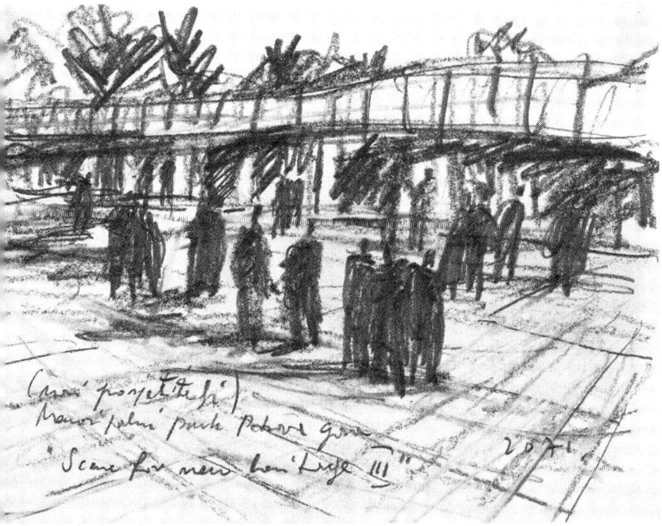



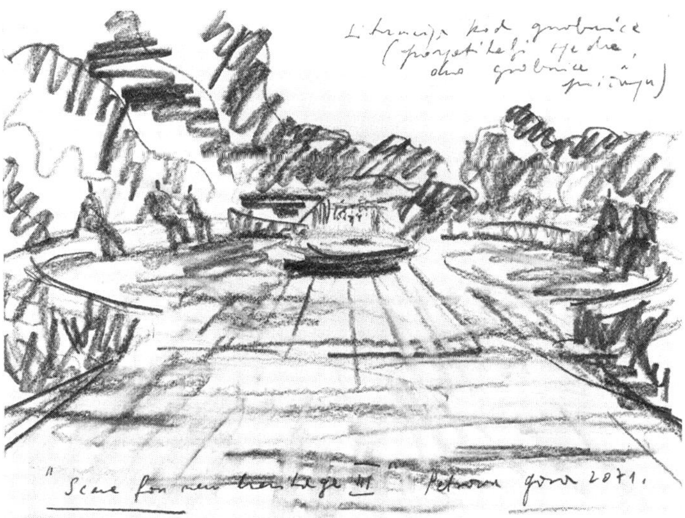



*Scene for New Heritage 3*, 2006, sketches for video set

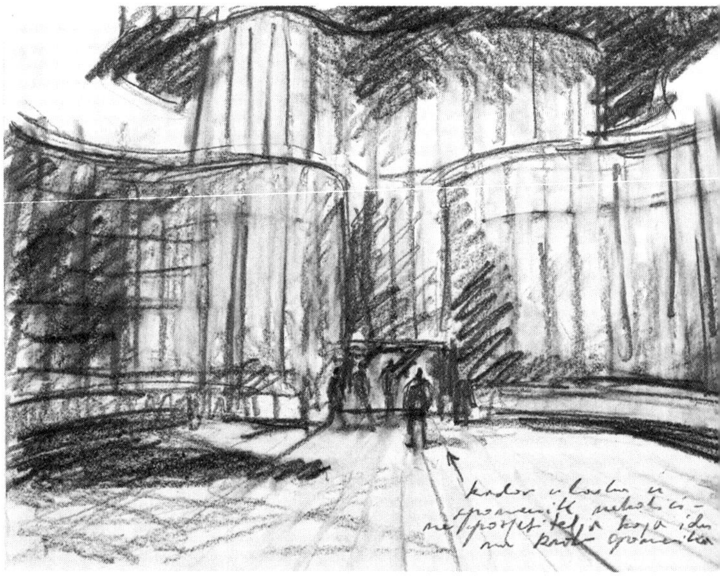

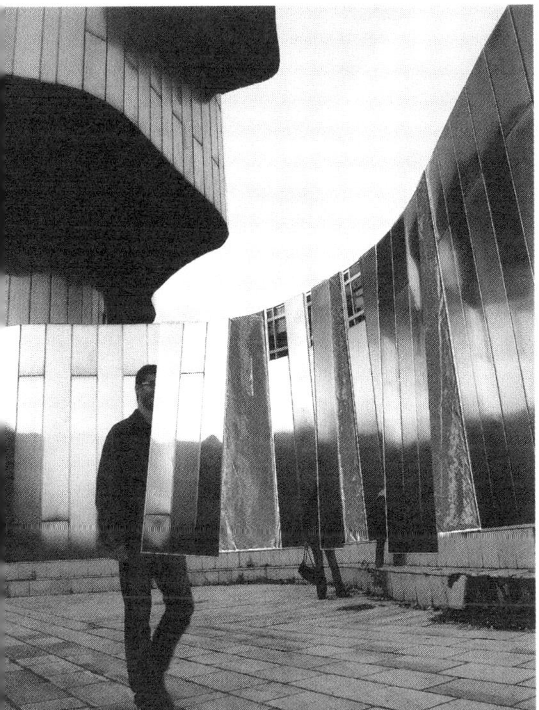

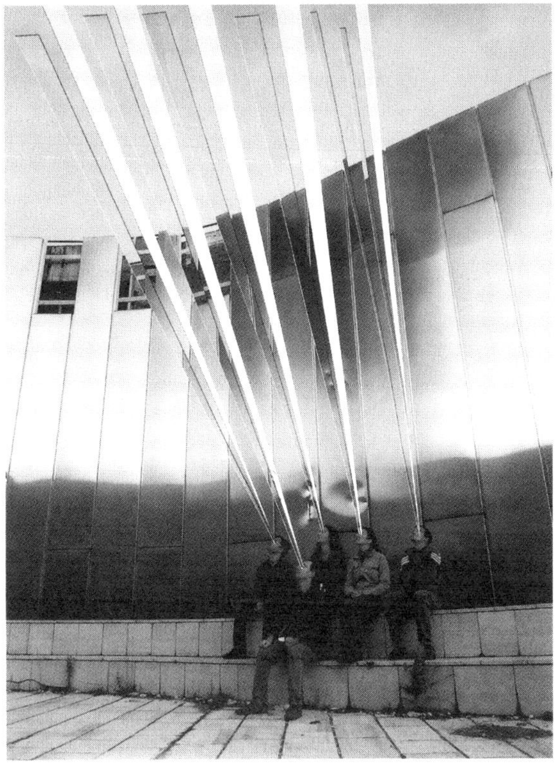

*Scene for New Heritage 3*, 2006, sketch for video set and collages

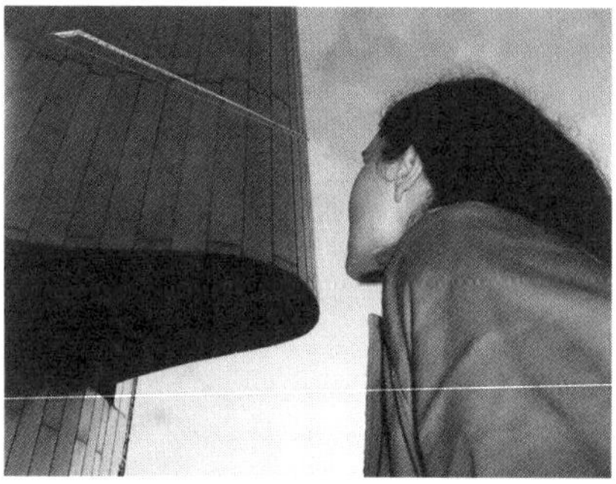

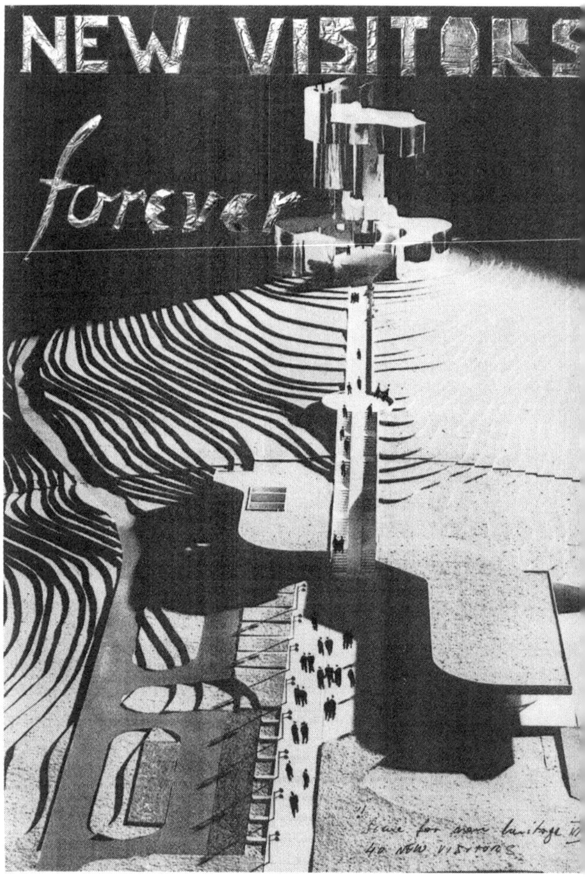
NEW VISITORS
forever
40 NEW VISITORS

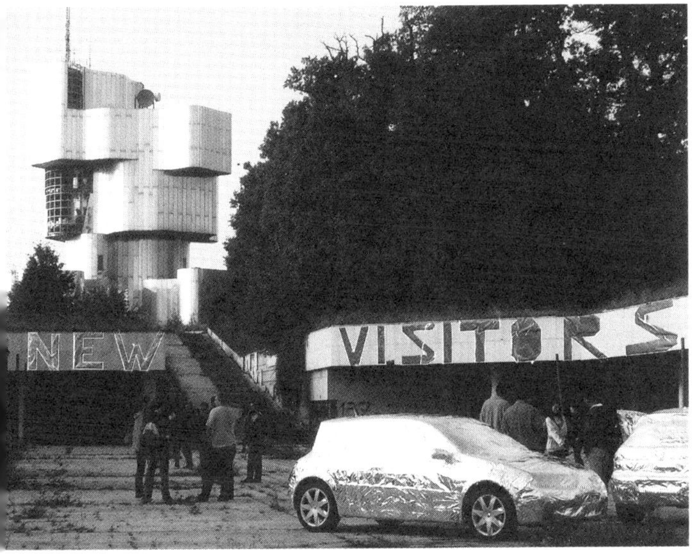


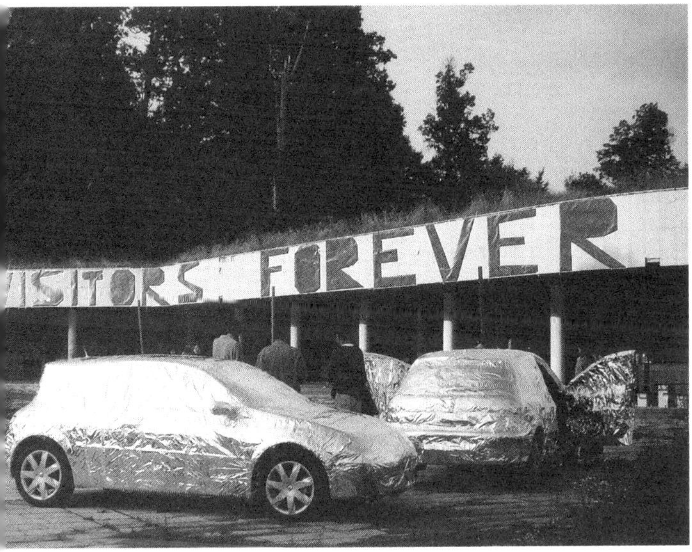




*Scene for New Heritage 3*, 2006, collages

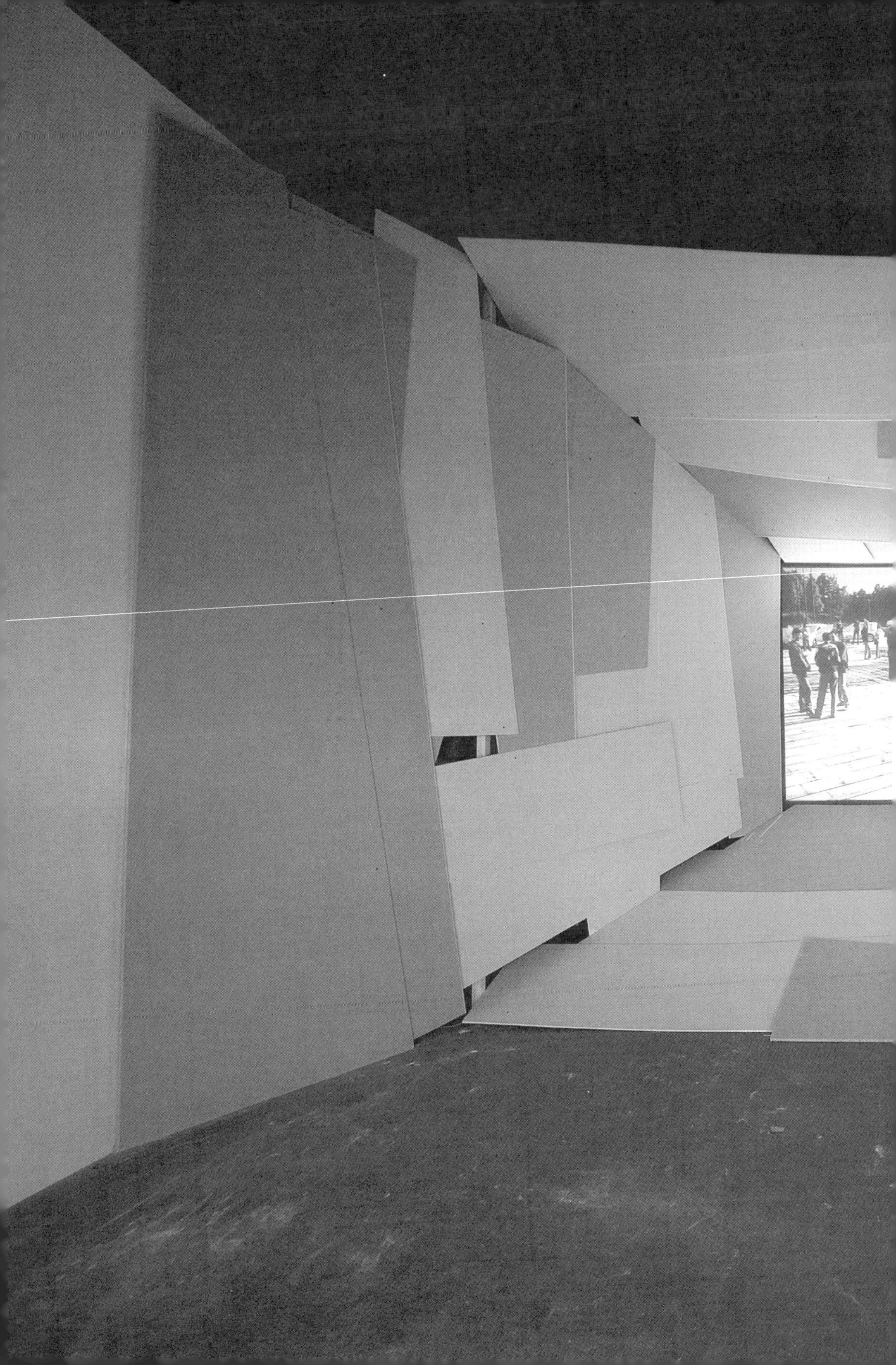

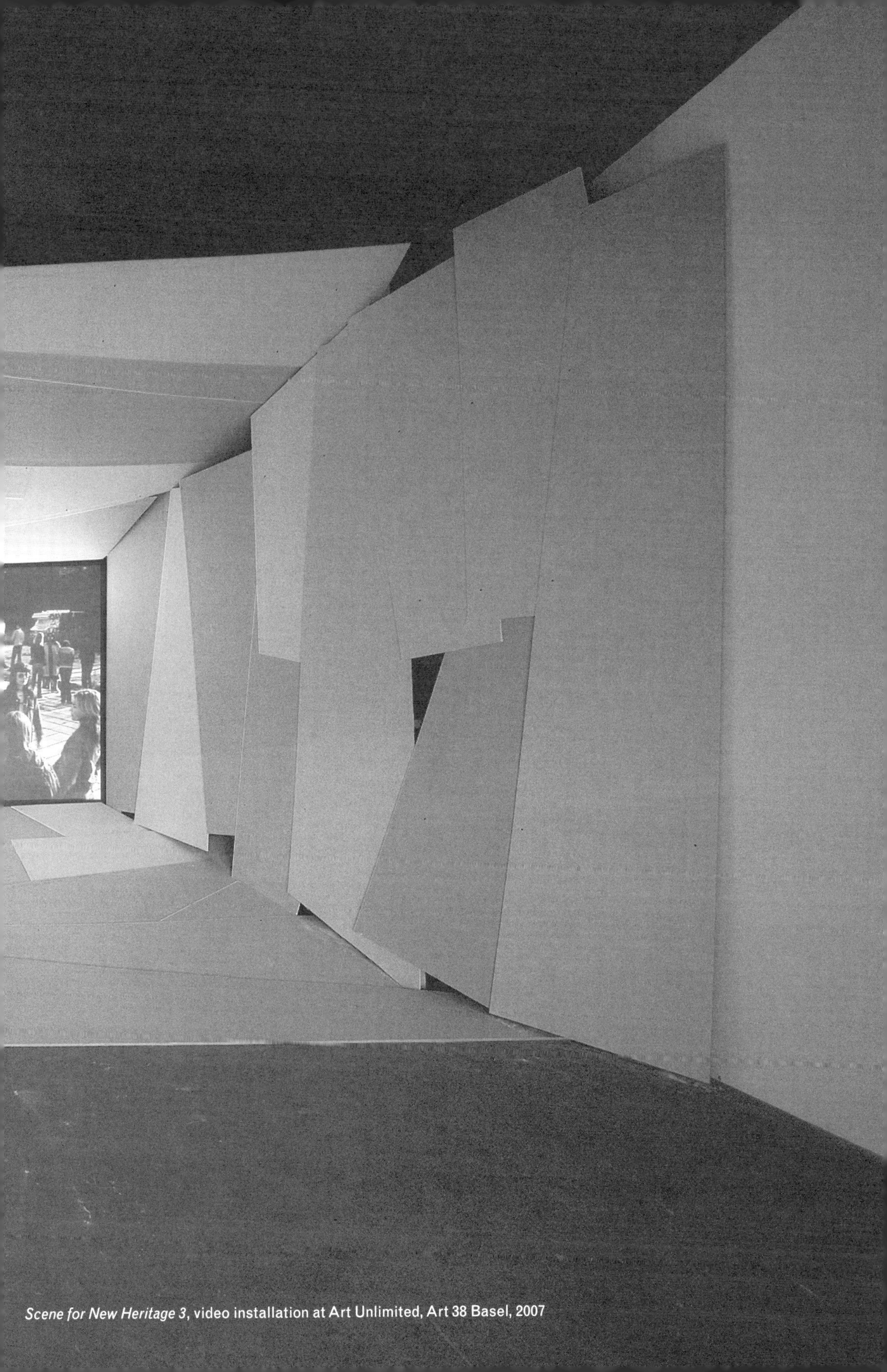

*Scene for New Heritage 3*, video installation at Art Unlimited, Art 38 Basel, 2007

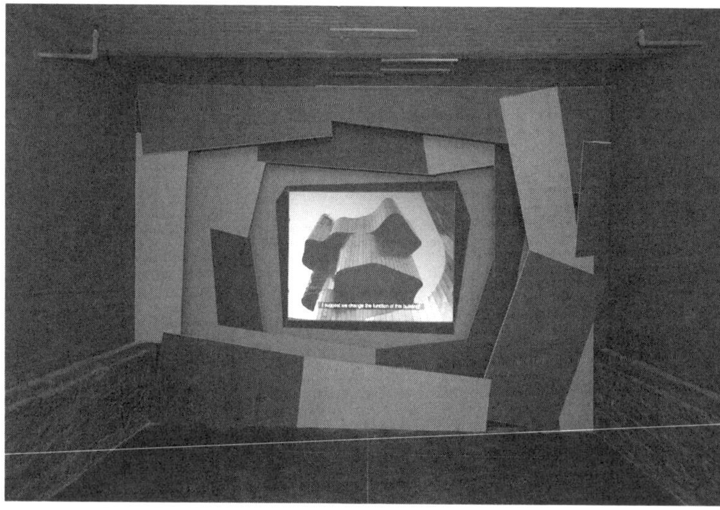

*Scene for New Heritage Trilogy*, video installation at P.S.1 Contemporary Art Center, New York, 2007

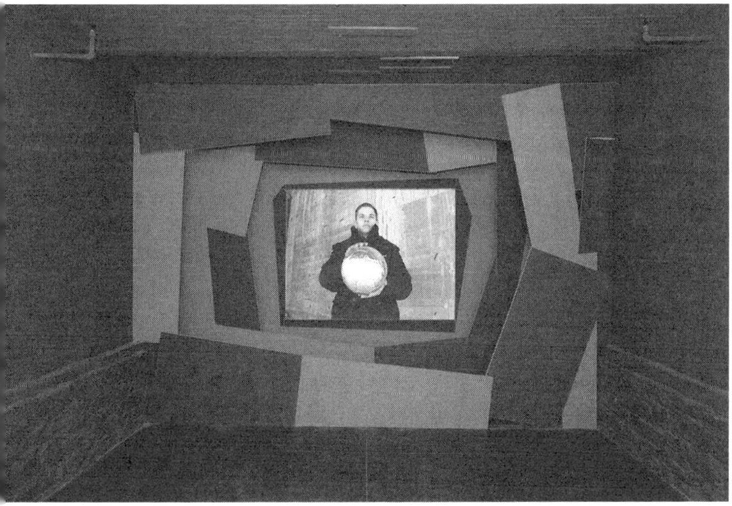

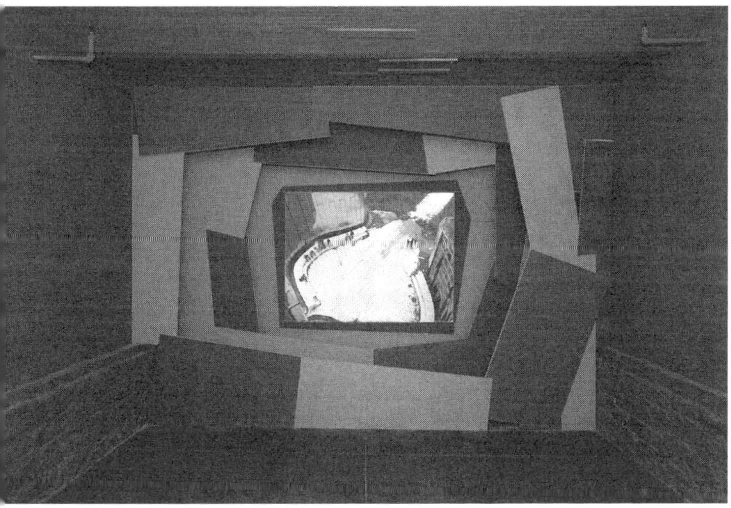

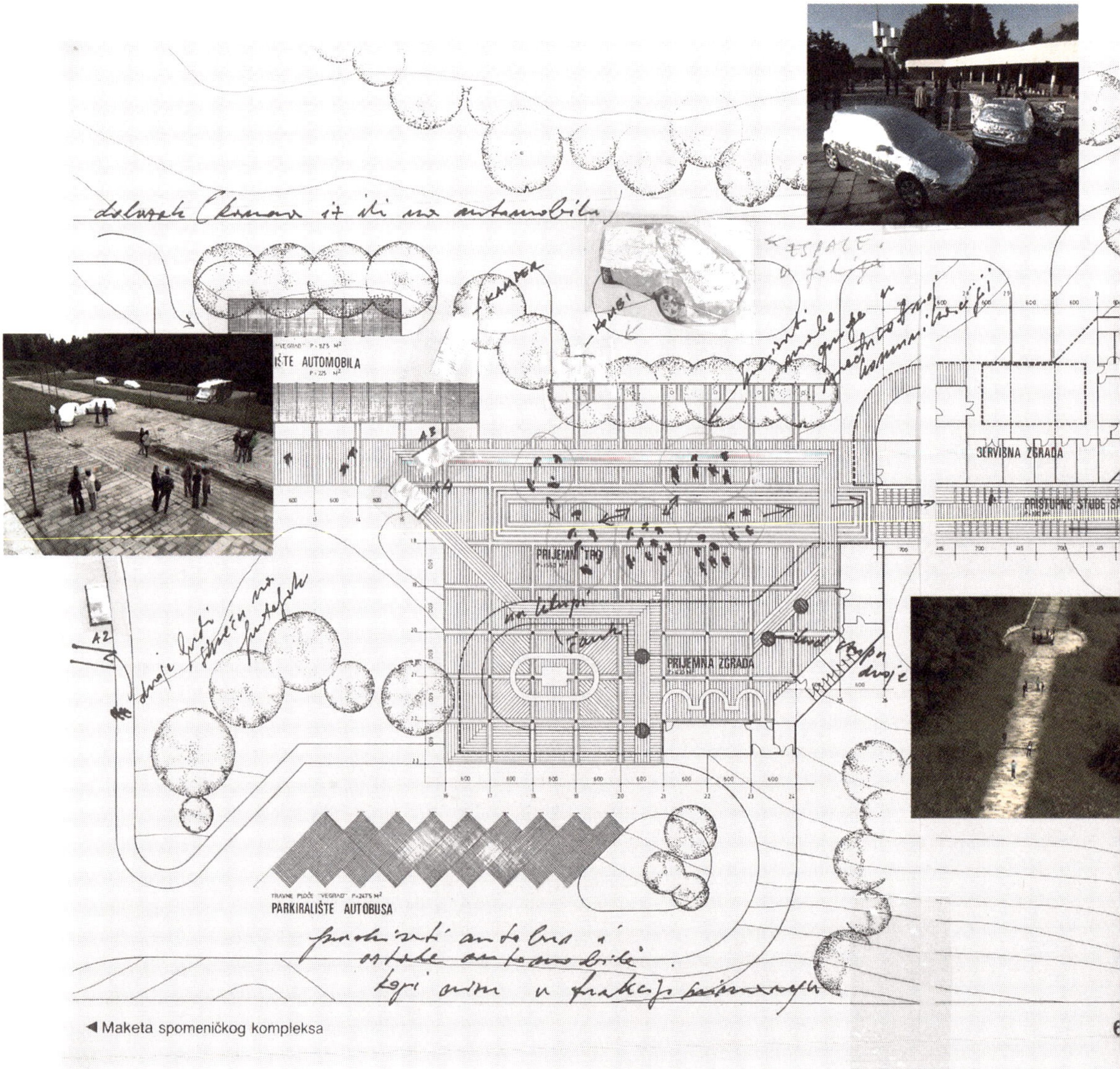


*Scene for New Heritage 3*, 2006, video stills and collage (preparation for video set)

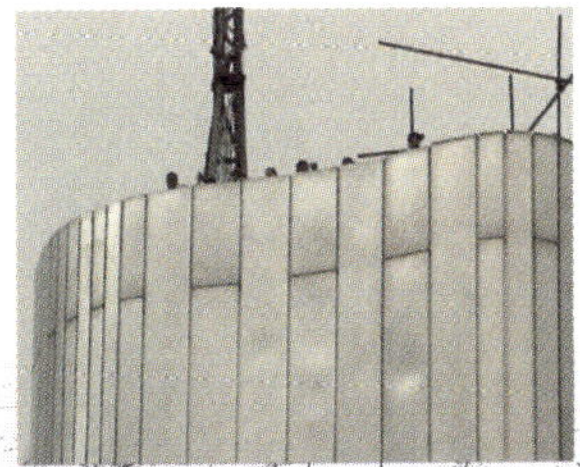

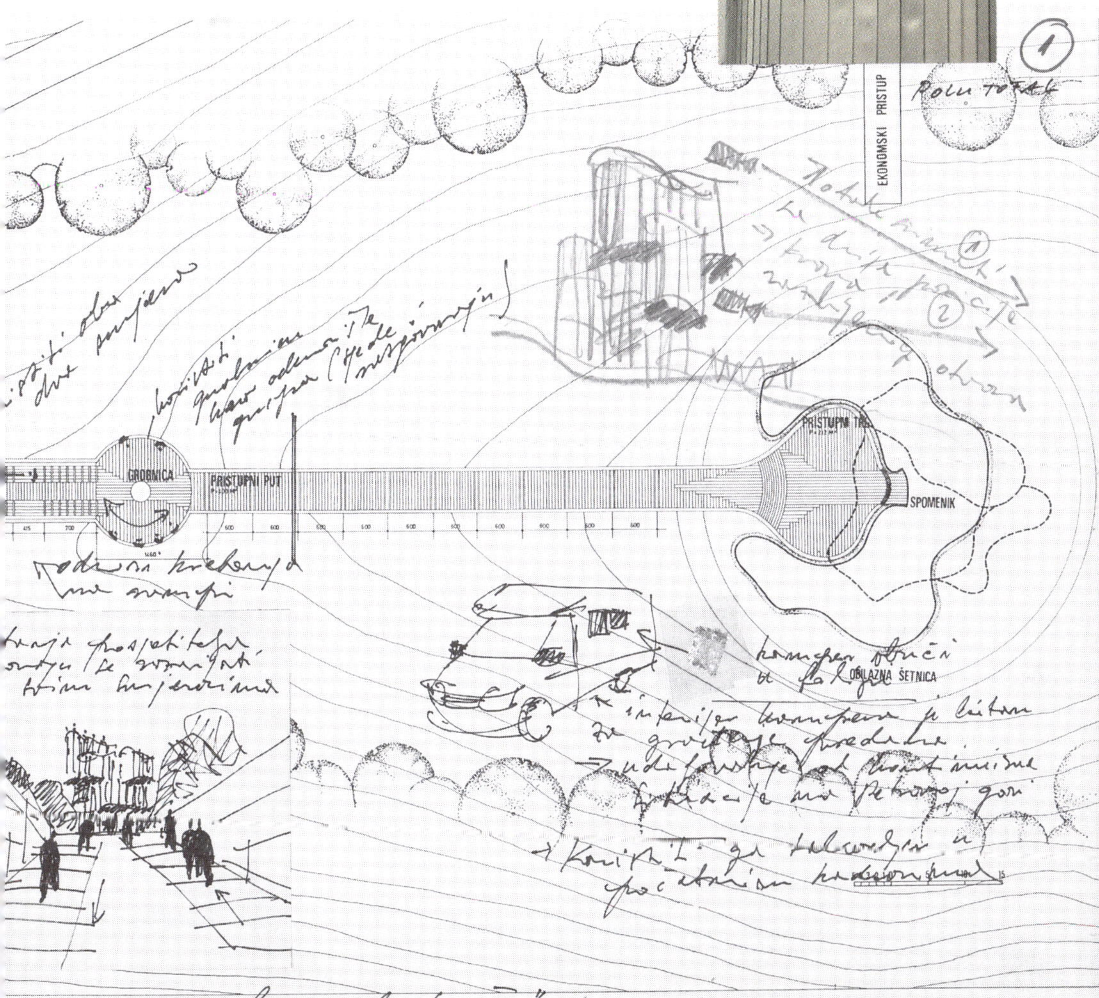


Situacija spomeničkog kompleksa

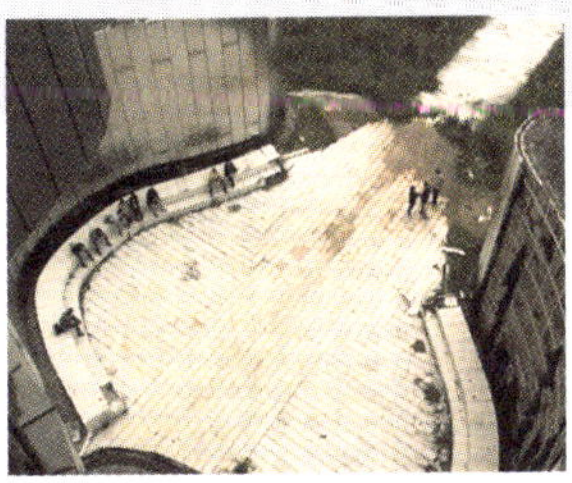

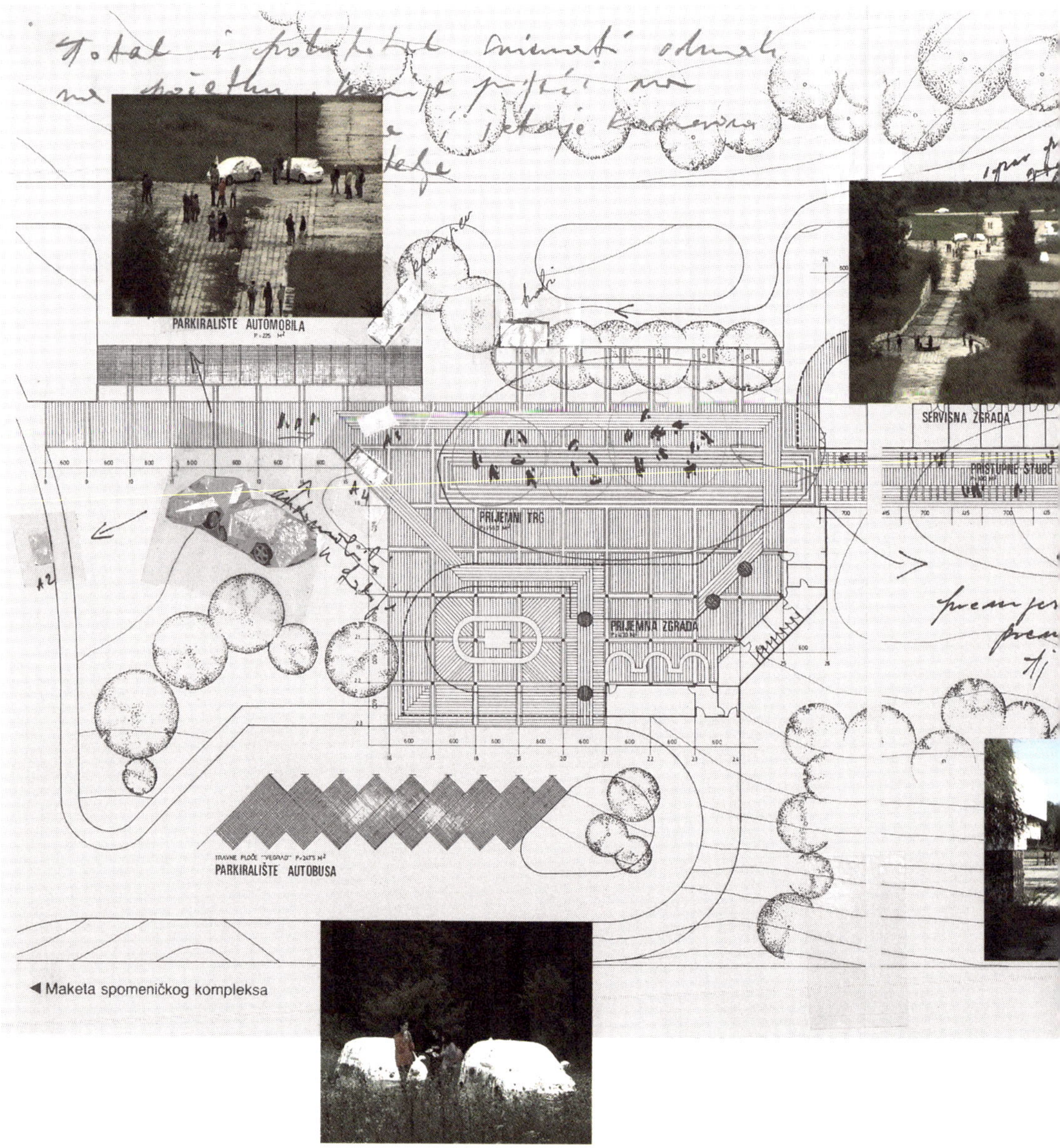


*Scene for New Heritage 3*, 2006, video stills and collage (preparation for video set)

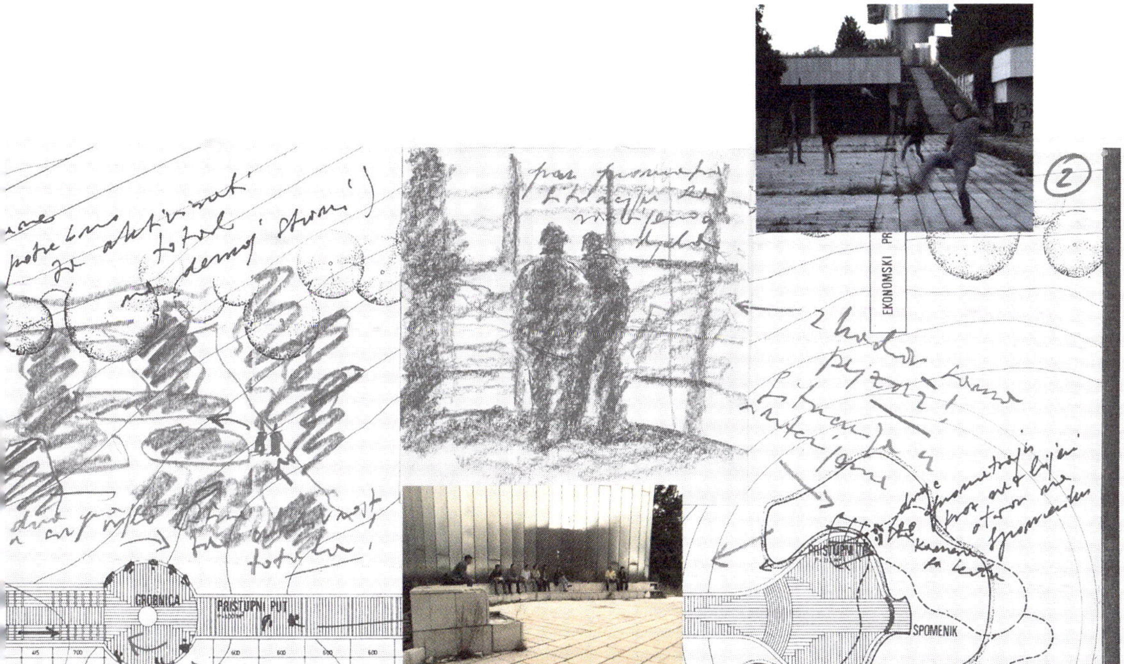
GROBNICA
PRISTUPNI PUT
SPOMENIK
OBILAZNA ŠETNICA
EKONOMSKI PR
"Scene for new heritage !!!"
Situacija spomeničkog kompleksa

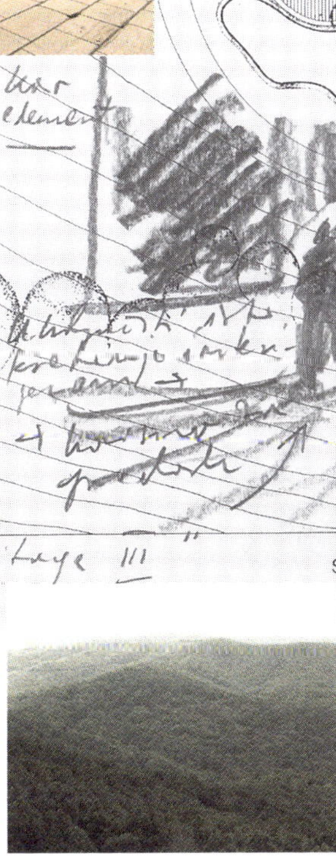

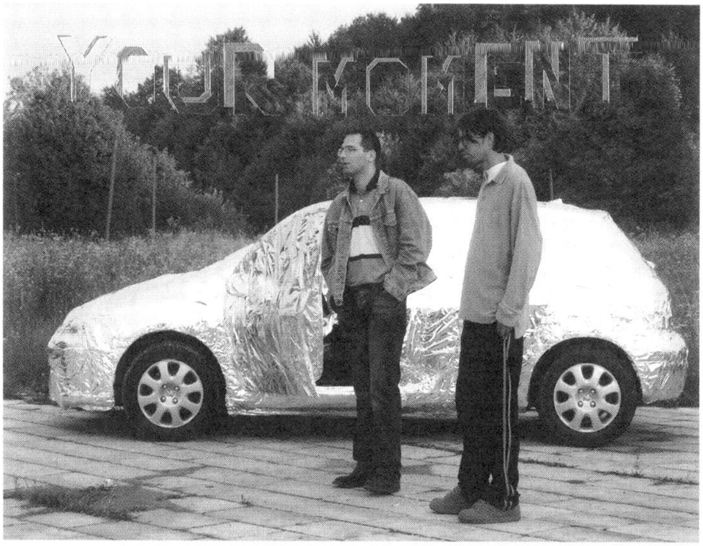
YOUR MOMENT

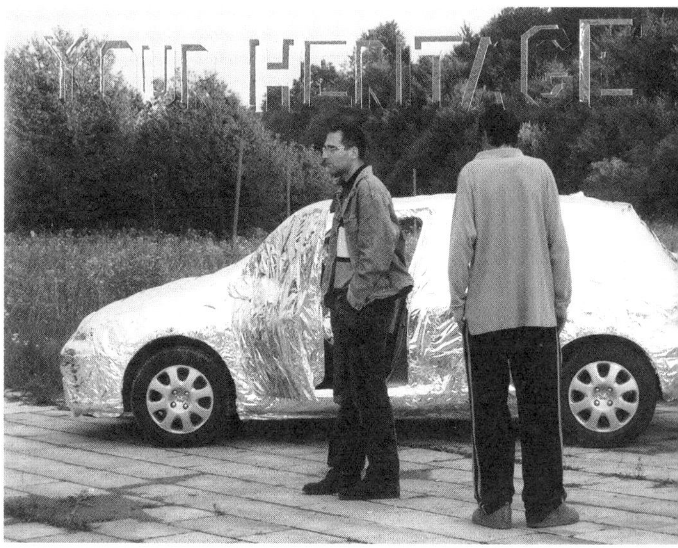
YOUR HERITAGE

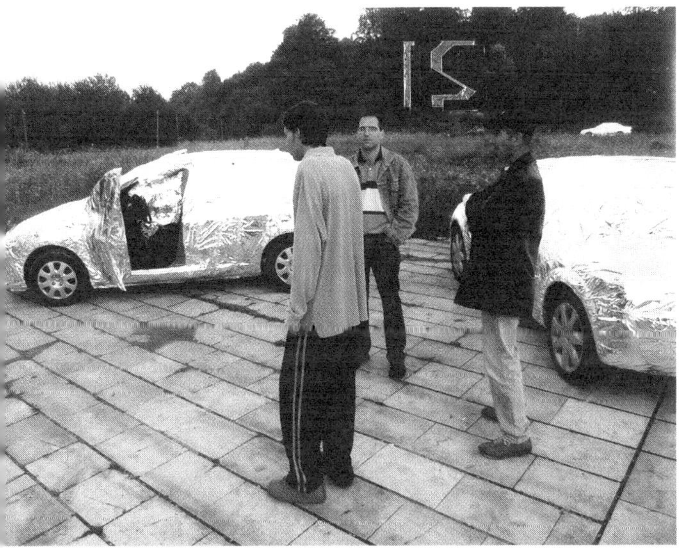

*Scene for New Heritage 3*, 2006, collages

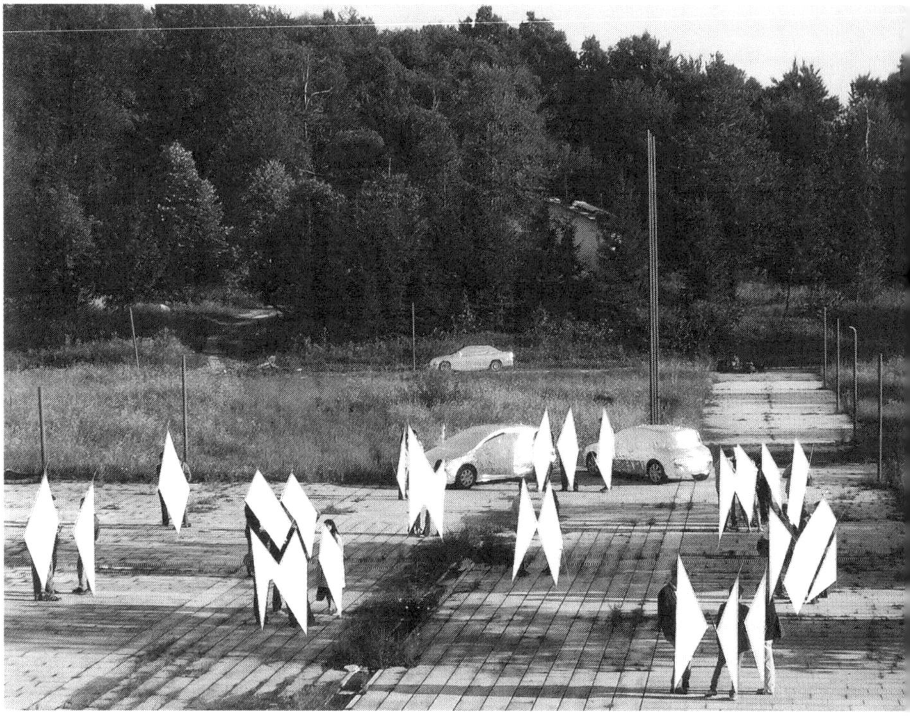

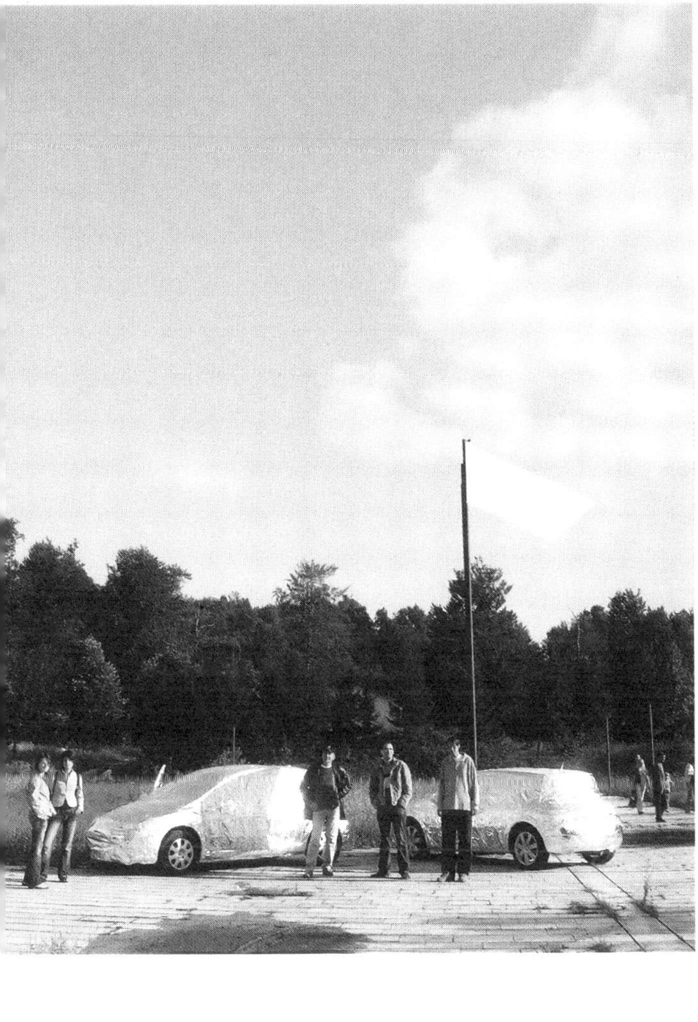



*Scene for New Heritage 3*, 2006, collages

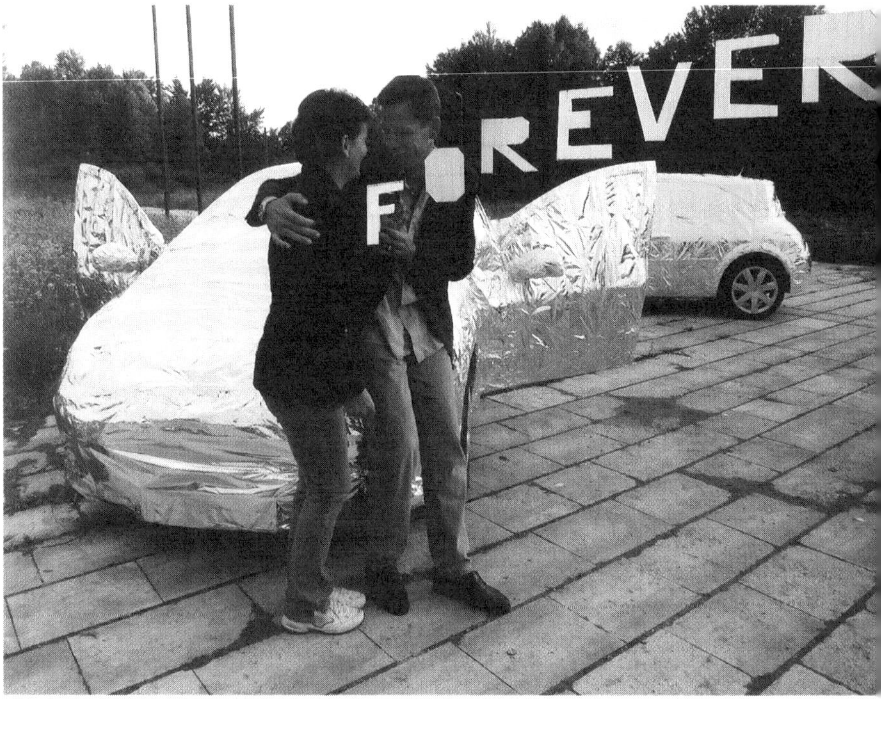
FOREVER

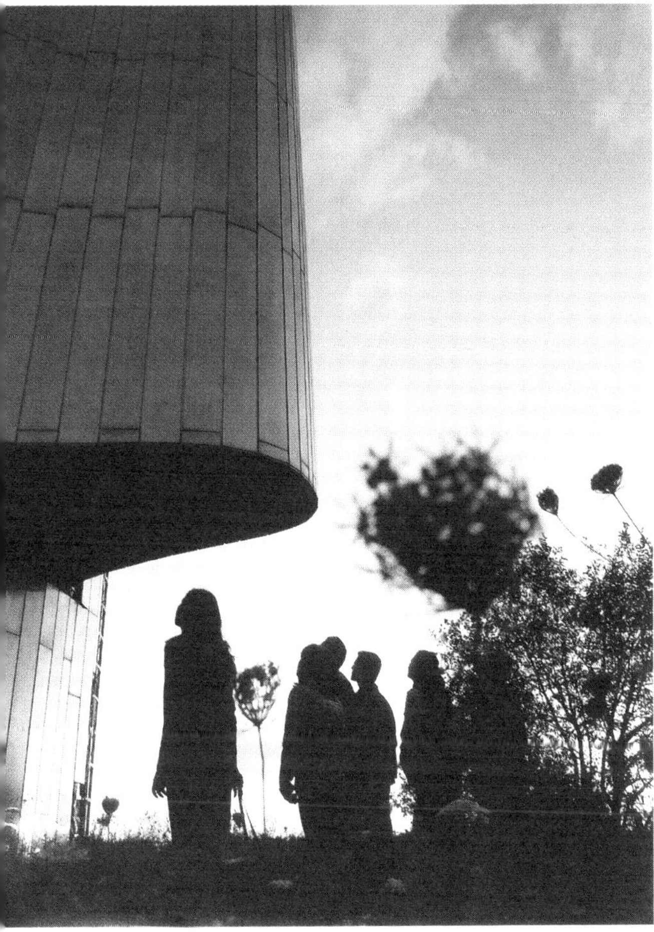



*Scene for New Heritage 3*, 2006, collage and photograph

# THE EMPTY SPACE OF THE FUTURE

## NATAŠA ILIĆ IN CONVERSATION WITH DAVID MALJKOVIĆ

Nataša Ilić

*I intended to start from the end, from our last conversation in which I had the impression that a chapter of your work had ended, a chapter that had begun, we could say, when you left for Amsterdam, to the Rijksakademie, and that a new story is about to begin. And you made a serious change when you stopped painting, went to the Rijks, retired for a while and stopped showing your work, and then started to produce new works, different from anything you had been doing before. Do you think this is a drastic change?*

David Maljković

I think I have always had some ruptures. We could call them linear oscillations, that was the title of my academy graduation thesis. I started in 1995 with some minimalist dislocations. The first work I did was to dislocate a whole classroom into a pedestrian passage. A while later I made a very minimal work in which I put police identification numbers into a gallery; this work was called *A Space Happened*.

Then I enrolled at the Zagreb Academy of Fine Arts, in the painting section. I happened to be in this medium and its questions and problematic began to preoccupy me. But I noticed that I was only considering the circumstances, what was going on around painting. When I first went to the Rijks, a crisis ensued. That was the first time I had had a more serious encounter with what we could call artistic ambition. We were raised in specific surroundings, educated to believe ambition was not such a good thing. At the Rijks I found that everybody was ambitious and I was astounded by this. I sensed competition for the first time.

*But isn't this normal for the competitive capitalistic market? Was this a relief for you, that you were allowed to be competitive?*

No, it wasn't any kind of relief. I needed some time to see what it was. It felt weird, everybody was doing something, and I wasn't doing anything, and I was supposed to, because I had been given an opportunity … This was a very serious crisis, I was wondering why I should do it anymore, I didn't see any reason for it, I couldn't sleep, my platform collapsed, everything I had been building up disappeared, or it didn't, but for me in that state it was as if it had really disappeared. Later, I saw what was good there and what was bad, but for a moment I had lost my base, I was completely naked. Simply put, I was stunned; I felt I was different, functioning differently … In Amsterdam I felt I couldn't exclude what I was and where I came from, I felt that I didn't have the same education, that I hadn't grown up in this system … And this was simply true, and my not getting on in this system was also true. During my second year, I loosened up and started to work on a series of experimental works that I later put in the artist book *Place With Limited Premeditation*. I called the book this because I had really begun to do something just to make something happen with me and my work.

*Then you stopped painting.*

I realized that a painting is, in principle, always a painting, no matter how much I surrounded it with something. There was the simple question: would I go directly into the painting, to the end? I was trying, I was constantly working on two paintings, but it just didn't move any further. This wasn't any kind of statement. Simply, the new content that started to integrate into my work did not communicate with painting. I went more and more into a fictitious form, and painting is an illusion by itself. These two contents – the space of painting and the fictitious content that I started to work on, they simply collided. I'm not saying that some other artist wouldn't have succeeded in reconciling this, but I was not able to do so. To enter a painting was as natural as stepping out of it.

*Do you now feel you are a video artist?*

I am often perceived as such, but I have never felt I was a video artist. This medium simply served me for projects I was working on; it gave me a way of expressing myself. When I started to work on *Scene for New Heritage*, I began it playfully, from my personal memory and intimate content. This is one of the first videos that I did and I allowed myself the luxury of this excursion, but when I found myself in these surroundings, I saw it wasn't going to be just an excursion. The second and third parts were made not because something more had to be said, and these works have no need to say something, but some relations and feelings prevailed, and I couldn't withdraw from them just like that. It was the same with the *These Days* video.

This experience brought me a kind of openness. People often wonder why I am still working on the same thing, and for such a long while; considering the rhythm of needs and happenings around us, artists often quickly change their works. But what these works brought me is that I am freer now, that I have articulated more precisely the relations toward myself and now I can – not any faster, but more easily – pin down the feeling I want to create in a relation.

*In what kind of relation?*

Towards a subject, problem or phenomenon.

*Or do you talk about a feeling you would like your work to incite?*

I include myself too; it is very important to me that everything works from the inside. A work can be more or less successful, but it is important to work all the time; it is important that you have an edge.

*In your last works,* Lost Memories from These Days *and* Scene for New Heritage 3 *you worked with numerous people. How did this affect the works?*

*Scene for New Heritage 3* was a drastic experience in this sense. I had some thirty sketches for a video, I was on site with the cameraman many times, I had prepared everything, but when these forty people came to the site, I completely froze. The first man I talked to told me that he had been fighting there in the '90s, and that nothing had changed there. I made the first shots with him, on top of the monument. I didn't use them later, they were cut out.

All the objects that I had in the form of models, sketches, preparations, all the plans I had, all that I thought I had under control, it vanished in a moment. I was really shocked by the reality. It was the first indication of how much I was immersed in my consciousness, in my fictitious world that collapsed when a number of real people came. The objects in my plan became subjects. The real people who came were defeating me all the time. I was fighting with all this and needed the whole day to get to the level where I wanted to be.

This was the first time that reality conquered fiction. The content that this space has, the relations it makes, the discontinuities and the impossibility of people to communicate with this place, all this was so intense that my intervention wasn't needed at all.

*How did you choose the actors?*

I did not choose them. When I needed forty extras for the Petrova Gora scene, I told the producer to bring me forty people. I like to find myself caught off-guard, although I have the need for control. I have long preparations, but I like to be caught off-guard when I shoot.

*Reality resisted your master plan. Was it because you imagine the future? Why do your works happen in the future, and on symbolically powerful dates? In your* Scene for New Heritage *the story takes place on 25 May 2045, in* Scene for New Heritage 2 *the date is 29 November 2063, and only in the third part the future is not determined.*

I had the need to express the content which this space has, and its relations and discontinuities, the impossibility of people to communicate with this space. But since the impossibility of communication with this place exists in the present, I thought one ought to position it in the future, because of other subjects, because of taking the burden off this whole complexity. In the third part I started to determine a year in the future, I thought of 2071, I had this year in my sketches, as a reference to the Croatian spring of 1971, the awakening, but it seemed too much for me and I gave it up. When I began to come to the location more often, I saw visitors there, very few of them though, but people came there, families with children, hikers … I had a subtitle for this work, *New Visitors – Visitors Forever*, but then I decided to give this up, as well as the year. This last part of the work I wanted to leave completely open, the plot may take place before or after. And I did not insist that the communication with the place must happen, I did not force this frustrated communication between the monument and the visitors. That is why I brought the hikers, the campers, people who stay there without asking what is this place and what to do there. I stopped developing the relation between the visitors and the location, and I let them develop their personal relation to the place, to be aware of it or not.

*The series of your videos and video installations* Scene for New Heritage *is formed around Bakić's monument at Petrova Gora. How did your interest for Bakić originate in the very first place?*

I had basic information on Bakić, but the first real interest started with reviving the memory of the location of the Petrova Gora Monument. This place was a part of the collective memory of my generation, and during the '80s it had been regularly visited by elementary school pupils, scouts and so on. But my cameraman, who was born in 1980, had never heard of the Petrova Gora monument. He was amazed when he saw it for the first time. I wanted to know what is happening with this memory and with the heritage which is not of interest anymore. At that time, in 2003, I lived between Amsterdam and Zagreb. I visited Petrova Gora once and saw that the location was completely neglected and out of use; its only function was to house a television transmitter. I interpreted this location as a place of fascinating absence, as a place that was completely absent. Then I started to work on the script for a video.

*Was Bakić important for you as an ultimate representative of universal modernism, in which he participated both with his works and with his career?*

Bakić is certainly one of our greatest sculptors, and Petrova Gora is one of our greatest modernist monuments. But for me, what was important was the personal memory which tied me to the location, and the historic part, and Bakić's place in it, all this just started to emerge. I was trying my best to use the empty space of the future. I wasn't concerned with history or politics, because these elements already exist in the monument itself and the Petrova Gora location, and I didn't feel the need to emphasize or manipulate them; they are simply there, strongly present by themselves. Petrova Gora during the '90s, the partisan hospital from the Second World War, King Peter … I was more interested in how to re-create all these elements on a new level than how to use their existing qualities and present them on the documentary level. I wasn't interested in the phenomenon of modernism in Yugoslavia and Croatia in a general sense; this isn't a relation that could motivate me personally, but creating new platforms for all this, that was a strong motivation for me. How to re-create this energy that already exists, how to give it a new colour. I conceived physical platforms in the collages.

*How are they formed?*

Very often as a preparation, but often they are a post-production. I have a long practice of two-dimensional works, and as I am not a trained video-artist, drawings and collages help me very much in using this medium.

*But you also exhibit them?*

Sometimes, if it makes any sense, if the space enables it. I don't want them to be didactic; I want them to open up other questions.

*The works at Petrova Gora deal with what Jelena Vesić calls production of the future. Do you see it like that?*

In the Petrova Gora works, the future is dodging the very subject, unburdening it of all historical and political connotations of Petrova Gora. This content cannot be annulled, it can't be avoided, but by going into the future it can be unloaded. I have not dealt with the future from the position of science fiction, but as a way to use an empty space.

*Some elements of low-tech aesthetics are present in a way, especially in* Scene for New Heritage.

Packing a car in silver foil is an expression of the need to intervene in the visitor/monument relation, to incite the third element, which is in a way a small incident within the picture, a suggestion whose need I had felt on a more intuitive level, so as not to create a 1:1 relation, to create a diversion by the third element.

*Still, it is about a journey into the future?*

Yes, it is a journey into the future; it questions the potential relation of visitors who will come in the future, but this relation is already present, the miscommunication and misunderstanding exist today. Relations between the visitors and the location, which were marginally present in the first two videos, cease to be important; I have ignored them. This is why the third part is the most diverse, the most open. The first two parts are more condensed.

*The image of travel is present in many works, from* Again for Tomorrow *to* These Days. *Why is this important to you?*

It is always about a mental journey, and it is always more about the impossibility of travelling, about immobility. The thing is being brought to the level of depression.

*Is the future a counterbalance to depression?*

I use the space of the future as an element of openness, a slight indication of potential optimism; what still does not exist gives a new sensibility, it makes all the facts that attacked us in those places softer. The future slowly grinds them down, as if the sharpness and the rough edges of the things were eroding.

If we are to elaborate the facts, we might say that these places do not exist anymore, that they exist only in a physical sense. If I had posited this as a fact, I would get a relation that would be, ultimately, defeating, I wouldn't feel any challenge to consider it; it would be a replica of reality, a space that doesn't have any relevance any more, a heritage that isn't relevant anymore. I tried to include a personal relation that is sometimes tangible, and sometimes very discreet. It is a kind of escape, a hole, a small crack through which it is possible to escape.

My relation towards the future is the constant imagining of what it could potentially be, examining these potentials and what could happen. And the element of dodging is constantly present. The time stamp is very symptomatic for my work.

*The text of the* These Days *video is almost a statement of the lost generation. An atmosphere of depression prevails; there are no elements of the future, but the statement that accompanies the video promises new beginnings.*

Texts from English tutorials served as preparation for a better tomorrow, with English as the language necessary for the preparations. This work elaborates a very banal situation, but it seems to me that an element of humour is essential, a mild irony around the whole situation. Such a view of a generation which sees itself in this is a potential for optimism. This is why I chose the location of the Italian pavilion at the Zagreb Fair, which was made during a period of post-war optimism.

*In* Lost Memories from These Days, *the feeling of tiredness is still dominant.*

I shot *Lost Memories from These Days* in the Italian pavilion at the Zagreb Fair again, but this time I intended to reconstruct a photograph I had found of an auto show from the '60s.

*With the hostesses?*

No, only the cars were there, but I went for the present story and I invited hostesses who work at auto shows, young women. The hostesses are a real element, they exist, this is how it is.

It was an intensive shooting. I was almost glued to the cameraman, behind him the whole time, I even guided him slowly, I held him, his whole body, and guided him. It was terribly hot and stifling, the pavilion had been closed for weeks and the air was stale. I thought, I would instruct the hostesses to act tired, to show the tiredness I wanted to give to the place, I wanted to make a reconstruction of tiredness, but because of the heat and the lack of air, tiredness, anxiety and nervousness started to emerge by themselves. This work gave me something which I could maybe do in some perspective, a lot of tactile levels and feelings which I hadn't known.

*Why is tiredness the leitmotif of the re-construction?*

I used a tired location. I intended to re-create an image from the '60s, that golden, successful period that is now simply gone. The feeling in the abandoned and empty pavilion is an expression of tiredness. I consider the tired place also to be an oasis, a place of potential pause, a place that has no ambition any longer; it has done its work. Although such places can have their trauma, their failure, they are nevertheless oases, places where one can take a break.

I have used tiredness in my earlier works, for instance, in the experimental work *Dead Race*. This work was never realized, it was presented only in the *Place With Limited Premeditation* book, and later at the Museum in Rijeka, as a model, as a hint. This work is not important in its physical sense, but in its mind-set. Tiredness is an element of pause, an element that contains failure, absence. It is a privilege to allow yourself to be tired; in this sense, tiredness is already a new beginning, a healthy element. Also in *Dead Race,* tiredness is an oasis in which you have the right to fail, you have a right to be tired, to say 'I don't know'... I used this later in my other works. Tiredness as an opportunity.

*You mentioned a tired gallery in your interview with Charles Esche in the book* Place With Limited Premeditation.

The idea of a tired gallery is to be given a space to do nothing, to be insecure, to say 'I can't', to have a crisis, to not know what you want, to not know where you are going. I've been thinking about a place that would make such states legitimate. This idea hasn't developed further; it exists only as a hint; it originated from the idea of a tired place, and Petrova Gora and Zagreb Fair are such places.

*In* These Days *and other works, cars have blocked wheels; in* Again for Tomorrow *a motorcycle is blocked by a construction.*

*Again for Tomorrow* is very important, but I do not see it as a work. It is a position from which I had started when I began with fiction and started to write a fictitious diary and texts, to complicate relations with the past and future ... Its structure hinted that it would become a model. In 2003 I made the *Again for Tomorrow* installation for the Open Studios at the Rijks, because I had to make something. There I began to work with immobility, with the impossibility of moving. *Again for Tomorrow* had its justification in a studio, in a private space. It was a hermetic, exploratory work; it didn't have any need to say something. When you invited me to the Cetinje Biennial, I decided to show it, and while it looked good visually, it had lost the energy it had in the studio. This experience taught me that the energy that existed in my studio is not necessary to be presented in a gallery. I wouldn't call it a mistake, rather a wrong assessment of feelings. The experience of Cetinje was important to me. I began to write fictitious diaries about locations where *Again for Tomorrow* went, and this work became an important position for what was happening later. This is why I later used it only in diary form, in the form of sketches, with a model that I prepared for the studio, with some diary texts and photographs, and it was much closer to the idea of a work.

*What is the role of the texts you write with the works?*

They are made during pre-production, or post-production; I then mix them, as a kind of summary. They are not made because I am an artist who writes; I do not really write. These texts are not a long diagnosis of what happened, of feelings that were dominant during the process of work, so as to make transparent a palette of invisible things that came up during the process. I need them to make visible what is not visible within the work or its presentation, and I think these things are important for a broader understanding of some kind.

*The constructions in which you put your videos create a 1:1 relation; they enable intimacy.*

In the videos, this element suggests a way of seeing, a suggestive positioning of a work. I do not want to justify these interventions, to say that they make sense because the content of a video corresponds with these installations. They originate on an intuitive, physical level, to find a place for a video within a space. A plaster board structure is not directly associated with a video.

*Why plasterboard?*

It appeared spontaneously when I worked in my studio on the *Again for Tomorrow* piece, and then it had its strongest justification. It is about the deconstruction of a wall, the feeling of frustration, the impossibility of moving. *Again for Tomorrow* is the matrix of all later works, and this structure has survived.

Generally, my decisions are tactile in their nature; they originate on an intuitive level; they have no justification, and I have no need to justify them. Something happens and later I can ascribe various meanings to it, but it is justified only by my feeling, even if it is a wrong one.

*Sound is very important in all your videos.*

Sound is something that intrigues me very much in my latest videos, especially in *Scene for New Heritage 3*. I am often intrigued when I am not an expert for something. I have no musical talent, but I am interested in music.

*Do you think that sound introduces a physical element?*

In *Scene for New Heritage 3* I used low frequencies and the first two minutes of the video can be heard only on the physical level. After these low frequencies there is a slow and gradual opening of the sound, and the third segment is electronic sound, that is, music. I have been deciding on whether to use music for a long time now; it is very risky and can be an unfortunate solution, but I was so afraid of it that in the end I had to do it. I was really losing control in this work, although I had set it out very precisely and thought it through. The work was defeating me, both in post-production and during the shooting; I was really fighting with it. A very difficult video, but it is important for me. And it is clear to me that someone could find it unacceptable as a work.

*Why?*

There are many illogical things; it doesn't flow easily, it isn't fluent. It is very disunified, and not only because I was disunified during the shooting. I needed this confusion in the whole situation, not only mine, but also the confusion of visitors regarding the locality. This bewilderment is present in the video. But it was made as if it didn't matter what anybody thinks.

*Why is Ganga music used in* Scene for New Heritage*? Ganga is an explicitly folk musical element with strong social connotations in Croatia today.*

It appeared out of a need for dialogue. I wanted to use an abstract dialogue and I didn't want to create an abstract language. I'm not a linguist and I wouldn't know where to start even if I tried. I didn't want any particular language that characters would speak. I didn't want them to comment on the monument in Croatian, I wanted to bring the language to a level of abstraction. The Ganga enabled me to use a totally primitive polyphonic form through which I created a dialogue. The Ganga has a long history. During the '70s it was used as a commentary on the political situation.

*What is the sound in* Lost Memories from These Days*?*

The first idea was to call it *Lost Projection*, but later I decided to use this title for a text or for something else. I put it on hold, but in forming the sound I took the original sound of the projector, subtracted it in the program, and it stayed as the basis and it seems like some kind of torture, some kind of frustrated sound, with a blocking action. The third level of the sound is its absence; some frames are totally without sound.

*How do you choose the titles for your works?*

I change them often. *Scene for New Heritage* is a title created before Petrova Gora, in a series of collages when I started to create lost landscapes, scenes that had passed and do not matter anymore, but I didn't complete it. When I started to do research on Petrova Gora, I found this title very suitable; the whole idea took hold and began to take shape. The *These Days* video was initially called *Waiting for Tomorrow*, but this was too explicit, and I later used it for a group of works.

*You work in classic exhibition spaces. Do you have the need to get out of the museum, the gallery?*

If I would get out, I would do it in a performative sense to construct a situation. In the book *Place With Limited Premeditation*, the performances that I did at the Rijks I called situations. I have never felt I was a performance artist. I have simply built situations in which I found myself. Building situational relations would be interesting to do in real-time, constructing situations that do not have to include me. This is something in which I see a potential space. But it is not defined; I am still not going in this direction.

*Can you imagine these situations as being architectural?*

I am not into architecture; it is secondary. I use architecture as a set for what I want. The location is architectural, but I have never dealt with architecture directly. My work communicates with architecture, but it does not deal with problems of architecture, its functions, etc. My contents just find themselves at architectural locations, but in any case, I'm interested in which way it is going to develop.

*It often seems that, in architecture, you are interested in its Utopian dimensions.*

Utopia is a part of art history, a signal, an element that we have in our subconsciousness. At one point, Utopia became a signal for me, when I needed it to solve some personal problems. I didn't include it, but it was summoned at one time.

*Do you have artistic role models?*

This is always changing. A book I read a lot in my youth was *The Great Experiment: Russian Art* by Camilla Gray. I wasn't doing any art then, I wasn't going to any art schools. The second thing that was important for me was a coincidence. In 1990, the new edition of *Start* magazine was published, a journal which, besides publishing serious articles on politics and culture, was the first in ex-Yugoslavia to publish naked beauties as its centrefold. I was 17 then, and I bought it to see what the new centrefold looked like. The paper became finer, the format smaller, but I was disappointed with the content, with its too glitzy photos; it was all too arty for me. There was also an interview with Vlado Kristl, entitled 'A Painter Must Always Be an Anarchist', and this really motivated me to become an artist. I have never become an anarchist, but his passion for art infected me. These were the first impulses, so to speak, external incentives which started the mechanisms that would have perhaps started by themselves, but they gave them some sense.

*Did you do any research on Kristl later on?*

I've been researching his work; it's not easy to obtain his films. It occurred to me that I should do a publication, but Kristl is a very sensitive subject; all of us owe him a lot. He was a dissident, he had to leave the country. Nobody has ever done any serious work on him.

*It is similar with Bakić.*

Bakić was neglected during the '90s, with the change of power, and Kristl was neglected in all the regimes.

*Did you feel an acute lack of information during the '90s?*

Yes, I wrote a paper about it, *The 90s without the 90s,* about the experiences that I and my generation had in Rijeka, about how the '90s for us were marked by a complete absence of any events. The Croatian scene had always been more or less well informed, but in the '90s this was suddenly interrupted and there was an absence of communication with the world of visual arts abroad. But, on the other hand, our own '90s began to happen. We were deprived of information, out of touch with world current events, and things began to happen from the inside. My generation started to refer to itself and to the world we were immersed in. The space determined us, we were oriented towards it. We didn't travel; there was no direct information.

Today the scene is different, as much as I am able to follow it. It seems to me that at the Academy there is the need for commercial success, but there are no institutions that could organize this in a sound way; there aren't any mechanisms and everything depends on chance. The Croatian scene is in a transitional phase.

*In what sense?*

Relations toward the West are still not developed in a healthy way; there is the constant fascination with everything that is 'abroad'. We need to smash the barrier between 'us' and 'them' and break this autism. The biggest problem we may encounter is to take the models from the West, because we must start from the situation we find ourselves in. We cannot exclude the place where we are. It seems to me that young artists are not aware of their heritage, and I think they are not interested in it. And the relation to the past must be constant; it doesn't have to be constantly present, but we must constantly be aware of it. This is also a problem of education and of how much the academy deals with these questions. While I was studying at the academy, the most important artists, and not only those connected with modernism, but also those connected with conceptual art, were completely invisible, they did not exist as a systematic part of the curriculum. Many students graduate at the academy without ever having heard of, for instance, Mangelos. And this is considered normal. The same thing holds for the avant-garde of the '20s and '30s, Klek, Micić ... and many others.

*Can you imagine yourself beginning to create works that do not deal with these locations and this milieu?*

I think that location is important for my work, but not necessarily. I think that the works we talked about made me free. It is difficult for me to define what I will do later on. There are some plans, but they do not necessarily matter. It would be insane to do something at home only because this is the most well-known ground. I am still very interested in this terrain; I didn't abandon it, but I think I have completed a large chapter.

# DER LEERE RAUM DER ZUKUNFT

## NATAŠA ILIĆ IM GESPRÄCH MIT DAVID MALJKOVIĆ

Nataša Ilić

*Ich möchte mit dem Ende unseres letzten Gesprächs beginnen, bei dem ich den Eindruck hatte, dass ein Kapitel deiner Arbeit zu Ende gegangen war, ein Kapitel, das, so könnte man sagen, begonnen hatte, als du nach Amsterdam an die Rijksakademie gegangen bist und eine neue Geschichte ihren Anfang nahm. Und du einen ernsthaften Wechsel in deiner Arbeit vollzogen hast, indem du aufhörtest zu malen, an die Rijksakademie gingst, dich für eine Weile zurückgezogen und nicht mehr ausgestellt hast, und dann anfingst, neue Arbeiten zu produzieren, die anders waren als alles, was du zuvor gemacht hattest. Hältst du das für einen drastischen Wandel?*

David Maljković

Ich denke, es gab bei mir immer irgendwelche Brüche. Man könnte sie als lineare Oszillationen bezeichnen, das war der Titel meiner Abschlussarbeit. Ich fing 1995 mit einigen minimalistischen Dislozierungen an. Die erste Arbeit, die ich gemacht habe, bestand darin, ein ganzes Klassenzimmer in eine Fußgängerpassage zu verwandeln. Eine Weile danach habe ich eine sehr minimale Arbeit gemacht, bei der ich Polizeikennziffern in eine Galerie versetzt habe; diese Arbeit trug den Titel *A Space Happened*.

Dann schrieb ich mich an der Kunstakademie in Zagreb ein, in der Malereiklasse. Ich fand mich in diesem Medium wieder, dessen Fragen und dessen Problematik mich zu beschäftigen begannen. Aber ich bemerkte, dass mich lediglich die Begleitumstände interessierten, das, was es mit der Malerei auf sich hatte.

Als ich zum ersten Mal an die Rijksakademie kam, folgte unmittelbar daraus eine Krise. Es war das erste Mal, dass ich eine ernsthaftere Begegnung mit dem hatte, was man künstlerische Ambition nennen könnte. Wir waren in einem speziellen Umfeld groß geworden, in dem Ehrgeiz nicht hoch im Kurs stand. An der Rijks stellte ich fest, dass jeder dort ehrgeizig war, und das erstaunte mich. Ich spürte zum ersten Mal Konkurrenz.

*Aber ist das nicht normal innerhalb des kapitalistischen Wettbewerbs? War es nicht eine Erleichterung für dich, dass du mit anderen konkurrieren durftest?*

Nein, es war überhaupt keine Erleichterung. Ich brauchte einige Zeit, um zu verstehen, was das war. Es war seltsam, jeder machte irgendetwas, und ich machte überhaupt nichts, aber es wurde erwartet, dass ich etwas machte, weil ich doch eine Chance dazu bekommen hatte ... Das war eine sehr ernste Krise, ich fragte mich, warum ich das Ganze überhaupt noch betreiben sollte, ich sah keine Veranlassung dazu, ich konnte nicht schlafen, meine Festplatte stürzte ab, alles woran ich gearbeitet hatte verschwand, oder auch nicht, aber für mich sah es in diesem Stadium so aus, als ob es wirklich verschwunden war. Später konnte ich unterscheiden, was daran gut, was schlecht war, aber für einen Augenblick hatte ich meine Grundlage verloren, ich war vollkommen nackt. Kurzum, ich war wie gelähmt; ich empfand mich als verschieden, als jemand, der anders tickt ... In Amsterdam spürte ich, dass ich nicht davon absehen konnte, was ich war und woher ich kam, ich spürte, dass ich nicht dieselbe Erziehung gehabt hatte, dass ich nicht in diesem System aufgewachsen war ... Und das war schlicht und einfach so und meine Unfähigkeit, in diesem System zurechtzukommen, war ebenfalls ganz real. Während meines zweiten Jahres wurde ich lockerer und begann an einer Reihe experimenteller Sachen zu arbeiten, die ich später in das Künstlerbuch *Place With Limited Premeditation* aufnahm. Ich nannte das Buch so, weil ich wirklich begonnen hatte, etwas zu machen, nur um etwas mit mir und meiner Arbeit geschehen zu lassen.

*Dann hast du aufgehört zu malen.*

Ich verstand, dass ein Gemälde grundsätzlich immer ein Gemälde ist, auch wenn ich es noch so sehr mit etwas anderem umgab. Es stellte sich die einfache Frage: Würde ich direkt in die Malerei hineingehen, bis zum Ende? Ich versuchte es, ich arbeitete ständig an zwei Gemälden, aber es ging einfach nicht weiter. Darin lag nicht irgendeine Art von Aussage. Es war einfach so, dass die neuen Inhalte, die in meine Arbeit einzufließen begannen, sich nicht mit der Malerei vertrugen. Ich fand mehr und mehr zu einer Form des Fiktiven, und Malerei ist eben selbst bereits illusionär. Diese beiden Dinge – der Raum der Malerei und der fiktive Gehalt, an dem ich zu arbeiten begonnen hatte – kollidierten einfach miteinander. Ich will damit nicht sagen, dass nicht ein anderer Künstler Erfolg darin hätte haben können, beides miteinander zu vereinbaren, aber ich war dazu nicht in der Lage. In ein Gemälde hineinzugehen war genauso natürlich, wie es wieder zu verlassen.

*Empfindest du dich inzwischen als Videokünstler?*

Ich werde häufig als solcher wahrgenommen, aber ich habe mich nie als Videokünstler gefühlt. Das Medium hat sich mir einfach für die Projekte, an denen ich arbeitete, angeboten; es eröffnete mir einen Weg mich selbst auszudrücken. Als ich an *Scene for New Heritage* zu arbeiten begann, war das spielerisch, ging von meiner persönlichen Erinnerung und intimen Gegenständen aus. Es ist eines der ersten Videos, die ich gemacht habe, und ich erlaubte mir selbst den Luxus dieser Abschweifung, aber als ich mich selbst in diesen Umgebungen wiederfand, merkte ich, dass es nicht bloß eine Abschweifung werden würde. Der zweite und dritte Teil entstanden nicht etwa, weil etwas über den ersten Teil hinaus gesagt werden musste, diese Arbeiten müssen nicht unbedingt etwas aussagen, sondern weil einige Bezüge und Gefühle, denen ich mich nicht ohne weiteres entziehen konnte, dazu Veranlassung gaben. Mit dem Video *These Days* war es genauso.

Diese Erfahrung brachte eine Art Offenheit mit sich. Die Leute wundern sich oft, warum ich noch immer an derselben Sache arbeite, und das seit so langer Zeit; in Anbetracht des schnellen Wechsels von Bedürfnissen und Geschehnissen um uns herum, verändern Künstler oftmals auch ihre Arbeit schnell. Mich selbst haben diese Arbeiten freier gemacht, durch sie habe ich die Bezüge zu mir selbst präziser artikuliert und jetzt kann ich – nicht etwa schneller, aber leichter – das Gefühl festmachen, das ich durch einen bestimmten Bezug erzeugen will.

*Was für einen Bezug?*

Zu einem Menschen, einem Problem oder Phänomen.

*Oder sprichst du von einem Gefühl, von dem du möchtest, dass es deine Arbeit hervorruft?*

Ich schließe mich selbst mit ein; es ist für mich sehr wichtig, dass alles aus dem Inneren heraus funktioniert. Eine Arbeit kann mehr oder weniger erfolgreich sein, aber es ist wichtig, die ganze Zeit über zu arbeiten; es ist wichtig, effektiv zu sein.

*In deinen jüngsten Arbeiten,* Lost Memories from These Days *und* Scene for New Heritage 3 *hast du mit zahlreichen Leuten zusammengearbeitet. Inwiefern hat das deine Arbeit beeinflusst?*

*Scene for New Heritage 3* war in dieser Hinsicht eine drastische Erfahrung. Ich hatte etwa dreißig Skizzen für ein Video, ich war mehrmals mit dem Kameramann vor Ort gewesen, ich hatte alles vorbereitet, aber als diese vierzig Leute an den Ort kamen, war ich vollkommen erstarrt. Der erste Mann, mit dem ich sprach, erzählte mir, dass er dort in den 1990ern gekämpft und dass sich nichts verändert hatte. Ich machte die ersten Aufnahmen mit ihm oben auf dem Denkmal. Ich habe sie später nicht benutzt, sie wurden herausgeschnitten.

Alle diese Objekte, die ich in Form von Modellen, Skizzen hatte, die Vorbereitungen, alle Pläne, die ich hatte – all das, von dem ich dachte, dass ich es unter Kontrolle hätte, verschwand im Handumdrehen. Ich war tatsächlich von der Wirklichkeit überwältigt. Das war das erste Anzeichen dafür, wie sehr ich in mein Bewusstsein, in meine erdachte Welt eingetaucht war, die zusammenbrach, als eine Anzahl wirklicher Menschen auftraten. Die Objekte aus meinem Plan wurden zu Subjekten. Die realen Menschen, die dort kamen, durchkreuzten ständig meine Pläne. Ich kämpfte mit alledem und brauchte den ganzen Tag, um das Level zu erreichen, das ich anstrebte.

Dies war das erste Mal, dass die Realität die Fiktion bezwang. Was es mit diesem Ort auf sich hat, was er für Bezüge stiftet, die Diskontinuitäten und die Unfähigkeit von Menschen, mit diesem Ort zu kommunizieren, all das war so intensiv, dass ich gar nicht eingreifen musste.

*Wie hast du die Darsteller ausgesucht?*

Ich habe sie nicht ausgesucht. Als ich vierzig Statisten für die Petrova Gora-Szene brauchte, sagte ich dem Produzenten, er solle mir vierzig Leute bringen. Ich lasse mich gerne von Dingen überraschen, obwohl ich zugleich das Bedürfnis nach Kontrolle habe. Ich bereite lange vor, aber auf dem Dreh mag ich es, wenn überraschende Dinge passieren.

*Die Realität widersetzte sich deinem Masterplan. Geschah das, weil du die Zukunft imaginierst? Warum spielen deine Arbeiten in der Zukunft und an symbolträchtigen Daten? In deiner* Scene for New Heritage *findet die Geschichte am 25. Mai 2045 statt, in* Scene for New Heritage 2 *ist das Datum der 29. November 2063, und lediglich im dritten Teil ist die Zukunft nicht determiniert.*

Ich hatte das Bedürfnis, den Anteil auszudrücken, den dieser Raum und den seine Bezüge und Diskontinuitäten haben, und die Unmöglichkeit von Menschen, mit diesem Raum zu kommunizieren. Aber insofern die Unmöglichkeit einer Kommunikation mit diesem Raum in der Gegenwart existiert, dachte ich, man sollte ihn, um anderer Menschen willen, und um die Last dieser ganzen Komplexität wegzunehmen, in die Zukunft versetzen. Im dritten Teil begann ich, ein Jahr in der Zukunft zu bestimmen, ich dachte an 2071. Ich hatte dieses Jahr in meinen Skizzen, als Referenz auf den Kroatischen Frühling von 1971, dieses Erwachen, aber es schien mir zuviel, und daher gab ich es auf. Als ich begann, öfter zu dem Ort zu kommen, sah ich dort Besucher, zwar sehr wenige, aber es kamen Leute dorthin, Familien mit Kindern, Wanderer ... Ich hatte einen Untertitel für diese Arbeit, *New Visitors – Visitors Forever*, aber dann entschied ich mich, ihn aufzugeben, ebenso wie das Jahr. Den letzten Teil der Arbeit wollte ich komplett offen lassen, der Plot kann also vorher oder nachher spielen. Und ich insistierte nicht darauf, dass eine Kommunikation mit dem Ort stattfinden musste, ich forcierte diese zunichte gemachte Kommunikation zwischen dem Denkmal und den Besuchern nicht. Deshalb bezog ich die Wanderer, die Camper, die Leute mit ein, die sich an diesem Ort aufhalten, ohne zu fragen, was es mit ihm auf sich hat oder was dort zu tun ist. Ich hörte auf, eine Beziehung zwischen den Besuchern und dem Ort herzustellen, ich ließ die Leute ihre eigene Beziehung zu dem Platz entwickeln, ob sie sich dessen nun bewusst waren oder nicht.

*Die Reihe deiner Videos und Videoinstallationen* Scene for New Heritage *entstand um Bakićs Denkmal in Petrova Gora herum. Was hat, ganz am Anfang, dein Interesse für Bakić begründet?*

Ich hatte Grundkenntnisse über Bakić, aber das eigentliche Interesse entwickelte sich, als man begann, das Gedächtnis am Ort des Petrova Gora-Denkmals wieder zu beleben. Dieser Platz war Teil des kollektiven Gedächtnisses meiner Generation; während der 1980er wurde er regelmäßig von Grundschülern, Pfadfindern usw. besucht. Aber mein Kameramann, der 1980 geboren ist, hat nie vom Petrova Gora-Denkmal gehört. Er war sehr erstaunt, als er es das erste Mal sah. Ich wollte wissen, was mit diesem kollektiven Gedächtnis geschieht und mit dem Erbe, das nicht mehr von Interesse ist. Zu jener Zeit, im Jahre 2003, lebte ich in Amsterdam und Zagreb. Ich besuchte Petrova Gora einmal und sah, dass der Ort vollkommen vernachlässigt und nicht mehr benutzt wurde; er diente nur noch dazu, einen Fernsehsendemast zu beherbergen.

Ich deutete diesen Ort als denjenigen einer faszinierenden Absenz, als einen Ort, der völlig abwesend ist. Dann begann ich an einem Drehbuch für ein Video zu arbeiten.

*War Bakić als genuiner Vertreter eines universellen Modernismus, an dem er sowohl mit seinen Arbeiten als auch mit seiner Laufbahn Anteil hatte, wichtig für dich?*

Bakić ist sicherlich einer unserer größten Bildhauer, und Petrova Gora ist eines unserer größten modernistischen Denkmäler. Aber für mich war die eigene Erinnerung wichtig, die mich mit dem Ort verband, und die historische Seite, und Bakićs Rolle in ihr, all das begann gerade erst wach zu werden. Ich setzte alles daran, den leeren Raum der Zukunft zu nutzen. Ich war nicht mit Geschichte oder Politik befasst, weil diese Elemente bereits im Denkmal selbst und am Ort Petrova Gora existieren und ich verspürte nicht das Bedürfnis, sie zu betonen oder zu manipulieren; sie sind einfach da, aus sich selbst heraus stark präsent. Petrova Gora während der 1990er, das Partisanen-Lazarett aus dem Zweiten Weltkrieg, König Peter … Ich war mehr daran interessiert, alle diese Elemente auf einer neuen Ebene wiederzuerschaffen, als daran, deren vorhandene Qualitäten zu benutzen und sie auf einer dokumentarischen Ebene zu präsentieren. Ich war nicht am Phänomen des Modernismus in Jugoslawien und Kroatien in einem allgemeinen Sinne interessiert; das ist kein Bezug, der mich persönlich motivieren könnte, sondern neue Plattformen für all dies zu schaffen, das war eine starke Motivation für mich. Ebenso die Frage, wie ich diese bereits existierende Energie wiedererschaffen, wie ich ihr eine neue Farbe geben könne. Mit den Collagen konzipierte ich physische Plattformen.

*Wie gestalten sich diese?*

Sehr oft als eine Vorbereitung, oft sind sie aber auch eine Nachbereitung. Ich produziere seit langem zweidimensionale Arbeiten, und da ich kein erfahrener Videokünstler bin, helfen mir Zeichnungen und Collagen sehr beim Gebrauch dieses Mediums.

*Aber du stellst diese auch aus?*

Manchmal – wenn es einen Sinn ergibt, wenn der Raum es erlaubt. Ich will nicht, dass sie didaktisch wirken; ich will, dass sie andere Fragen eröffnen.

*Die Arbeiten in Petrova Gora haben mit dem zu tun, was Jelena Vesić die Produktion der Zukunft nennt. Siehst du das auch so?*

In den Petrova Gora-Arbeiten überspielt die Zukunft das eigentliche Thema, entbindet es von allen historischen und politischen Konnotationen von Petrova Gora. Dieser Anteil kann zwar nicht annulliert, er kann nicht vermieden werden, aber indem man sich in die Zukunft begibt, kann er entladen werden. Dabei ist der Raum der Zukunft nicht als Science-Fiction zu verstehen, sondern vielmehr als ein Weg, einen leeren Raum zu nutzen.

*Speziell in* Scene for New Heritage *sind einige Elemente einer Low-Tech-Ästhetik präsent.*

Ein Auto in Silberfolie zu verpacken, zeigt, dass es nötig ist, in die Beziehung Besucher/Denkmal zu intervenieren, das dritte Element aufzustacheln, das gewissermaßen eine kleine Episode innerhalb des Bildes ist, eine Andeutung, deren Notwendigkeit ich auf einer eher intuitiven Ebene spürte, um so nicht etwa eine 1:1-Relation zu schaffen, sondern eine Ablenkung durch das dritte Element.

*Geht es dabei noch immer um eine Reise in die Zukunft?*

Ja, es ist eine Reise in die Zukunft. Sie befragt den potentiellen Bezug von Besuchern, die in der Zukunft kommen werden, aber dieser Bezug ist bereits gegenwärtig, die gestörte Kommunikation und das Missverstehen existieren heute. Die Bezüge zwischen den Besuchern und dem Ort, die am Rande in den ersten beiden Videos präsent waren, verlieren hierbei ihre Bedeutung; ich habe sie ignoriert. Deshalb ist der dritte Teil der vielfältigste, der offenste. Die ersten beiden Teile sind stärker komprimiert.

*Das Bild des Reisens ist in vielen deiner Arbeiten präsent, angefangen von* Again for Tomorrow *bis zu* These Days. *Warum ist es wichtig für dich?*

Es geht immer um eine geistige Reise, und es geht immer eher um die Unmöglichkeit des Reisens, um Unbeweglichkeit. Die Sache wird auf das Niveau einer Depression gebracht.

*Ist die Zukunft ein Gegengewicht zur Depression?*

Ich nutze den Raum der Zukunft als ein Element von Offenheit, einen verhaltenen Hinweis auf potentiellen Optimismus; was noch nicht existiert, gibt eine neue Sensibilität, es macht all die Fakten, die uns an solchen Orten betroffen haben, weicher. Die Zukunft schleift sie langsam ab, als ob die Schärfe und die rauen Kanten der Dinge erodieren.

Wenn wir die Fakten erläutern sollten, könnten wir sagen, dass diese Orte gar nicht mehr existieren, dass sie nur in einem physikalischen Sinne existieren. Wenn ich dies als ein Faktum setzen würde, würde ich einen Bezug bekommen, der schließlich abwehrend wäre, ich würde keinerlei Herausforderung wahrnehmen, darüber nachzudenken. Das Ganze wäre eine Replik der Realität, ein Raum, der keine Relevanz mehr hätte, ein Erbe, das nicht mehr relevant ist. Ich habe versucht, einen persönlichen Bezug einzubringen, der manchmal spürbar ist, und manchmal sehr diskret. Es ist eine Art Flucht, ein Loch, ein kleiner Spalt, durch den es möglich ist, zu entkommen.

Meine Beziehung zur Zukunft besteht in der konstanten Vorstellung dessen, was potentiell sein könnte, und darin, diese Potentiale zu erforschen, das, was passieren könnte. Das Prinzip der Ausflucht ist stets präsent. Die Prägung durch die Zeit ist sehr bezeichnend für meine Arbeit.

*Der Text des Videos* These Days *ist fast schon ein Statement der verlorenen Generation. Eine Atmosphäre der Depression herrscht darin vor; es gibt keine Zukunftselemente, aber das Statement, das mit dem Video einhergeht, verheißt einen Neuanfang.*

Die Texte aus englischen Tutorien dienten der Vorbereitung für ein besseres Morgen, und Englisch war als Sprache für die Vorbereitungen erforderlich. Diese Arbeit entwickelt eine sehr banale Situation ganz genau, aber ich habe eben den Eindruck, dass das Element des Humors wesentlich ist, die ganze Situation ist in eine milde Ironie gehüllt. Eine solche Sicht einer Generation, die sich selbst hierin wiederfindet, birgt ein Potential für Optimismus. Darum habe ich den Italienischen Pavillon auf der Zagreber Messe, der in einer optimistischen Nachkriegsphase entstand, als Ort gewählt.

*In* Lost Memories from These Days *herrscht dennoch ein Gefühl der Müdigkeit vor.*

Ich habe auch *Lost Memories from These Days* wieder im Italienischen Pavillon auf der Zagreber Messe gedreht, aber dieses Mal wollte ich ein Foto von einer Autovorführung aus den 1960ern rekonstruieren, das ich gefunden hatte.

*Mit den Hostessen?*

Nein, es waren nur die Autos darauf, aber es ging mir um die gegenwärtige Geschichte, so lud ich Hostessen ein, die bei Autovorführungen arbeiten, junge Frauen. Die Hostessen sind ein reales Element, sie existieren, das ist so.

Es war ein intensiver Dreh. Ich klebte förmlich an dem Kameramann, war die ganze Zeit hinter ihm, ich führte ihn sogar langsam, ich hielt ihn, seinen ganzen Körper, und führte ihn. Es war fürchterlich heiß und stickig, der Pavillon war über Wochen geschlossen gewesen und die Luft war abgestanden. Ursprünglich wollte ich die Hostessen anweisen, müde zu agieren, um die Müdigkeit wiederzugeben, die ich dem Ort verleihen wollte, ich wollte eine Rekonstruktion dieser Müdigkeit herstellen, aber angesichts der Hitze und des Mangels an frischer Luft, begannen Müdigkeit, Ängstlichkeit und Nervosität sich ganz von selbst einzustellen. Diese Arbeit vermittelte mir in mancher Hinsicht eine Idee davon, was ich machen konnte, eine Menge sensorischer Ebenen und Gefühle, die ich zuvor nicht gekannt hatte.

*Warum ist Müdigkeit das Leitmotiv der Rekonstruktion?*

Ich benutzte einen müden Ort. Ich wollte ein Bild aus den 1960ern wiedererschaffen, aus jener goldenen, erfolgreichen Periode, die mittlerweile einfach verschwunden ist. Das Gefühl in dem verlassenen und leeren Pavillon ist ein Ausdruck von Müdigkeit. Ich halte den müden Ort auch für eine Oase, den Raum einer potentiellen Pause, einen Raum, der nicht länger Ambitionen hat; er hat seine Arbeit getan. Obwohl solche Räume ihr Trauma haben können, ihr Scheitern, sind sie nichtsdestotrotz Oasen, Räume, in denen man innehalten kann.

Ich habe Müdigkeit auch in meinen früheren Arbeiten benutzt, beispielsweise in der experimentellen Arbeit *Dead Race*. Diese Arbeit wurde nie realisiert, sie wurde lediglich in dem Buch *Place With Limited Premeditation* präsentiert, und später im Museum in Rijeka als ein Modell, als eine Andeutung. Diese Arbeit ist nicht im physikalischen Sinne wichtig, sondern als geistiges Konzept. Müdigkeit ist ein Prinzip des Aufschubs, ein Element, das ein Scheitern enthält, Abwesenheit. Es ist ein Privileg, sich selbst zu erlauben, müde zu sein; in diesem Sinne ist Müdigkeit bereits ein neuer Anfang, ein gesundes Element. Auch in *Dead Race* ist Müdigkeit eine Oase, in der du das Recht hast, zu scheitern, du hast ein Recht, müde zu sein, zu sagen ›ich weiß nicht‹ … Ich habe das später auch in meinen anderen Arbeiten benutzt. Müdigkeit als Möglichkeit.

*In deinem Interview mit Charles Esche in dem Buch* Place With Limited Premeditation *hast du eine müde Galerie erwähnt.*

Die Idee hinter einer müden Galerie besteht darin, einen Ort zu bekommen, um nichts zu tun, unsicher zu sein, ›ich kann nicht‹ zu sagen, eine Krise zu haben, nicht zu wissen, was du willst, nicht zu wissen, wo du hingehst. Ich dachte an einen Ort, der solche Zustände legitimieren würde. Diese Idee hat sich nicht weiterentwickelt; sie existiert nur als Andeutung; sie entstand aus der Idee eines müden Ortes, und Petrova Gora und die Zagreber Messe sind solche Orte.

*In* These Days *und anderen Arbeiten haben Autos blockierte Reifen; in* Again for Tomorrow *ist ein Motorrad durch eine Konstruktion blockiert.*

*Again for Tomorrow* ist sehr wichtig, aber ich sehe dies nicht als eine Arbeit an. Es stellt einen Punkt dar, von dem ich ausging, als ich mit der literarischen Arbeit begann und anfing, ein fiktives Tagebuch zu schreiben und Texte, um die Bezüge zur Vergangenheit und zur Zukunft komplexer zu gestalten … Die Struktur legte nahe, dass daraus ein Modell werden würde. Im Jahre 2003 machte ich die Installation *Again for Tomorrow* im Rahmen der offenen Ateliers an der Rijksakademie, weil ich dafür etwas machen musste. Dabei begann ich mit Immobilität zu arbeiten, mit der Bewegungsunfähigkeit. *Again for Tomorrow* hatte seine Berechtigung in einem Atelier, in einem privaten Raum. Es war eine hermetische Forschungsarbeit; es gab dabei keine Notwendigkeit etwas auszusagen. Als du mich zur Cetinje Biennale eingeladen hattest, entschloss ich mich, die Arbeit zu zeigen, aber auch wenn sie optisch gut wirkte, hatte sie die Energie verloren, die sie im Atelier besaß. Diese Erfahrung lehrte mich, dass die Energie, die etwas in meinem Atelier hat, sich nicht notwendigerweise auch in einer Galerie zeigt. Ich würde es nicht als einen Fehler bezeichnen, eher als eine Fehleinschätzung von Gefühlen. Die Erfahrung von Cetinje war wichtig für mich. Ich begann, fiktive Tagebücher über die Orte zu schreiben, an denen *Again for Tomorrow* stattfand, und diese Arbeit wurde ein wichtiger Ausgangspunkt für das, was später passierte. Deshalb nutzte ich diese Arbeit später nur noch in Tagebuchform, in Form von Skizzen, in einem Modell, das ich für das Atelier anfertigte, in einigen Tagebuchtexten und Fotografien, und das kam der Idee der Arbeit viel näher.

*Welche Rolle haben die Texte, die du zu den Arbeiten schreibst?*

Sie entstehen während der Vorbereitung oder der Nachbereitung; dann vermische ich sie zu einer Art Zusammenfassung. Sie entstehen nicht, weil ich ein Künstler bin, der schreibt; ich schreibe nicht wirklich. Diese Texte stellen keine lange Analyse dessen dar, was passiert ist, der Gefühle, die während des Arbeitsprozesses vorherrschend waren, um etwa eine ganze Anzahl unsichtbarer Dinge, die währenddessen entstanden sind, sichtbar zu machen. Ich brauche sie, um sichtbar zu machen, was innerhalb der Arbeit oder in deren Präsentation nicht sichtbar ist, und wovon ich denke, das es für ein besseres Verständnis in irgendeiner Weise wichtig ist.

*Die Bauten, in denen deine Videos spielen, schaffen eine 1:1-Relation; sie ermöglichen Intimität.*

Diese Elemente in den Videos legen eine Sichtweise nahe, den suggestiven Ausgangspunkt einer Arbeit. Ich will diese Interventionen nicht rechtfertigen, nicht sagen, dass sie Sinn ergeben, etwa weil der Inhalt eines Videos mit diesen Installationen korrespondiert. Sie nehmen ihren Ausgang von einer intuitiven, körperlichen Ebene, in der räumlichen Suche nach einem Ort für ein Video. Eine Struktur aus Gipsplatten ist dabei nicht direkt einem Video zugeordnet.

*Warum Gipsplatten?*

Das kam spontan auf, als ich in meinem Atelier an *Again for Tomorrow* arbeitete, und bei diesem Werk hatte es seine stärkste Berechtigung. Es geht um die Dekonstruktion einer Wand, das Gefühl der Frustration, die Unmöglichkeit sich zu bewegen. *Again for Tomorrow* bildet die Matrix aller späteren Arbeiten, und diese Struktur hat sich erhalten.

Grundsätzlich sind meine Entscheidungen sensorischer Natur; sie nehmen ihren Ausgang von einer intuitiven Ebene; sie haben keine Rechtfertigung, und ich verspüre kein Bedürfnis, sie zu rechtfertigen. Etwas passiert, und später kann ich dem verschiedene Bedeutungen zuschreiben, aber alles ist nur durch mein Gefühl gerechtfertigt, sogar wenn dieses falsch ist.

*Der Soundtrack ist in allen deinen Videos sehr wichtig.*

Der Soundtrack ist etwas, das mich in meinen jüngsten Videos sehr beschäftigt, speziell in *Scene for New Heritage 3*. Ich bin oft neugierig, wenn ich mich mit etwas nicht so gut auskenne. Ich habe kein musikalisches Talent, aber ich interessiere mich für Musik.

*Glaubst du, dass der Soundtrack ein körperliches Element hineinbringt?*

In *Scene for New Heritage 3* habe ich niedrige Frequenzen benutzt; die ersten beiden Minuten des Videos können lediglich auf der rein physischen Ebene wahrgenommen werden. Nach diesen tiefen Frequenzen gibt es eine langsame, gradweise voranschreitende Öffnung der Musik, und das dritte Segment bildet elektronischer Sound, das heißt Musik. Ich habe jetzt lange Zeit vor der Entscheidung gestanden, ob ich Musik verwenden sollte; es ist sehr riskant und kann eine unbefriedigende Lösung sein, obwohl ich es sehr präzise geplant und durchdacht habe. Die Arbeit enttäuschte mich, sowohl in der Vorbereitung als auch während des Drehs; ich kämpfte wirklich damit. Es ist ein sehr schwieriges Video, aber wichtig für mich. Und es leuchtet mir ein, dass man es als Arbeit inakzeptabel finden kann.

*Warum?*

Es gibt viele unlogische Dinge darin; es fließt nicht einfach, ist nicht fließend. Es ist sehr uneinheitlich, und nicht nur, weil ich während des Drehs nicht im Einklang mit mir war. Ich brauchte diese Konfusion in der ganzen Situation, nicht nur meine, sondern auch die Konfusion der Besucher in Bezug auf die Lokalität. Diese Verwirrung ist im Video präsent. Aber gemacht wurde es so, als ob es egal wäre, was irgendjemand darüber denkt.

*Warum wird in der* Scene for New Heritage *Ganga-Musik benutzt? Ganga ist heutzutage in Kroatien ein ausgesprochen volkstümliches musikalisches Element mit starken sozialen Konnotationen.*

Das entstand aus dem Bedürfnis nach einem Dialog. Ich wollte einen abstrakten Dialog benutzen, und zugleich wollte ich keine abstrakte Sprache schaffen. Ich bin kein Sprachwissenschaftler und ich wüsste nicht, wie anzufangen, selbst wenn ich es versuchen würde. Ich wollte keine spezifische Sprache, die von Figuren gesprochen würde. Ich wollte nicht, dass diese das Denkmal in Kroatien kommentieren würde, ich wollte vielmehr die Sprache auf eine

Ebene der Abstraktion bringen. Ganga ermöglichte es mir, eine vollkommen einfache polyphone Form zu benutzen, mit der ich einen Dialog schuf. Ganga hat eine lange Geschichte. Während der 1970er wurde diese Musik als Kommentar zur politischen Situation benutzt.

*Woraus besteht der Soundtrack in* Lost Memories from These Days?

Zunächst hatte ich die Idee, das Video *Lost Projection* zu nennen, aber später entschloss ich mich, diesen Titel für einen Text oder für etwas anderes zu benutzen. Ich stellte ihn zurück, aber für die Gestaltung des Soundtracks nahm ich das Originalgeräusch des Projektors in das Programm auf, es blieb als Grundlage erhalten, es scheint wie eine Art Folter, eine Art von zunichte gemachtem, mittels einer Blockierung vereiteltem Sound. Die dritte Ebene des Soundtracks ist seine Abwesenheit; bei einigen Bildern gibt es gar keinen Soundtrack.

*Wie wählst du die Titel für deine Arbeit?*

Ich verändere sie oft. *Scence for New Heritage* ist ein Titel, den ich vor Petrova Gora fand, in einer Reihe von Collagen, als ich anfing, verlorene Landschaften zu erschaffen, Szenen, die zwar stattgefunden haben, aber nicht mehr interessieren; aber ich habe diese Sachen nicht fertig gemacht. Als ich anfing, Recherchen zu Petrova Gora zu machen, fand ich diesen Titel sehr passend; die ganze Idee bekam einen Halt und begann Form anzunehmen. Das Video *These Days* hieß ursprünglich *Waiting for Tomorrow*, aber dieser Titel war zu explizit, ich benutzte ihn später für eine Reihe anderer Arbeiten.

*Du arbeitest an klassischen Ausstellungsorten. Verspürst du nicht das Bedürfnis, aus dem Museum, aus der Galerie herauszukommen?*

Wenn ich dort herausgehen würde, würde ich es in einem performativen Sinne tun, um eine Situation zu schaffen. Im Buch *Place With Limited Premeditation* habe ich die Performances, die ich an der Rijksakademie gemacht habe, Situationen genannt. Ich habe mich nie als Performance-Künstler verstanden. Ich habe lediglich Situationen geschaffen, in denen ich mich selbst finden konnte. Es wäre interessant, situative Bezüge in Echtzeit aufzubauen, Situationen herzustellen, an denen ich selbst nicht notwendig beteiligt sein muss. Das ist etwas, worin ich einen potentiellen Raum sehe. Aber das ist nicht klar definiert; ich bewege mich noch immer nicht in diese Richtung.

*Kannst du dir diese Situationen als architektonische vorstellen?*

Ich beschäftige mich nicht mit Architektur; das ist zweitrangig. Ich benutze Architektur als Set für das, was ich will. Der Ort ist durch Architektur bestimmt, aber ich selbst habe mich nie direkt mit Architektur befasst. Meine Arbeit steht in Verbindung mit Architektur, aber sie beschäftigt sich nicht mit Problemen der Architektur, ihren Funktionen etc. Meine Inhalte finden sich lediglich an architektonisch bestimmten Orten wieder, aber ich bin in jedem Fall daran interessiert, in welche Richtung sich die Inhalte entwickeln werden.

*Man hat oft den Eindruck, dass dich die utopischen Dimensionen der Architektur interessieren.*

Utopie ist ein Teil der Kunstgeschichte, ein Zeichen, ein Bestandteil, den wir in unserem Unterbewusstsein haben. An einem bestimmten Punkt, als ich einige persönliche Probleme lösen musste, wurde Utopie für mich zu einem Signal. Ich habe sie nicht eingeschlossen, aber an einer bestimmten Stelle wurde sie ›aufgerufen‹.

*Hast du künstlerische Vorbilder?*

Das verändert sich immer wieder. Ein Buch, das ich in meiner Jugend oft gelesen habe, war *Das große Experiment: Russische Kunst* von Camilla Gray. Ich habe damals keine Kunst gemacht, und ich ging auch nicht auf irgendeine Kunstschule. Die zweite Sache, die wichtig für mich war, stellt sich als Zufall dar. Im Jahre 1990 wurde die neue Ausgabe des Magazins *Start* publiziert, eine Zeitschrift, die, neben ernsthaften Artikeln zu Politik und Kultur, als erste in Ex-Jugoslawien Centerfolds mit nackten Frauen veröffentlichte. Ich war damals 17 und ich kaufte die Zeitschrift, um zu sehen, wie das neue

Centerfold aussah. Das Papier wurde besser, das Format kleiner, aber ich war enttäuscht vom Inhalt mit seinen Hochglanzfotos; es war mir alles zu gewollt künstlerisch. Es gab dort auch ein Interview mit Vlado Kristl unter dem Titel *Ein Maler muss immer ein Anarchist sein*, und das motivierte mich wirklich, Künstler zu werden. Ich bin nie zu einem Anarchisten geworden, aber Kristls Leidenschaft für die Kunst steckte mich an. Das waren sozusagen die ersten Impulse, äußerliche Anregungen, welche die Mechanismen in Gang setzten, die vielleicht sonst auch von selbst losgegangen wären, aber diese Anregungen gaben ihnen einen Sinn.

*Hast du später noch zu Kristl recherchiert?*

Ich habe seine Arbeit studiert; es ist nicht einfach, seine Filme zu bekommen. Es kam mir der Gedanke, eine Publikation zu ihm zu machen. Kristl ist ein sensibles Thema, wir alle verdanken ihm eine Menge. Er war ein Dissident, er musste das Land verlassen. Niemand hat je irgendeine seriöse Arbeit über ihn gemacht.

*Das ist mit Bakić ähnlich.*

Bakić wurde während der 1990er, mit dem Machtwechsel, missachtet, Kristl wurde unter allen Regimen missachtet.

*Hast du während der 1990er einen akuten Mangel an Information verspürt?*

Ja, ich habe ein Papier dazu geschrieben, *Die 90er ohne die 90er*, über die Erfahrungen, die ich und meine Generation in Rijeka gemacht hatten, darüber, dass die 1990er für uns gekennzeichnet waren durch das komplette Fehlen irgendwelcher Ereignisse. Die kroatische Szene war immer mehr oder minder gut informiert, aber in den 1990ern wurde das plötzlich unterbrochen, und es gab keine Kommunikation mit der Kunstwelt außer Landes. Auf der anderen Seite begannen da allerdings unsere eigenen 1990er stattzufinden. Wir verfügten über keinerlei Informationen, waren nicht auf dem Laufenden über das aktuelle Weltgeschehen, die Dinge begannen, sich von innen heraus zu ereignen. Meine Generation begann, sich auf sich selbst zu beziehen und auf die Welt, in die wir verstrickt waren. Der Ort bestimmte uns, wir orientierten uns an ihm. Wir reisten nicht; es gab keine direkten Informationen.

Heute ist die Szene, soweit ich das verfolgen kann, anders. Es scheint mir, dass es an der Akademie das Bedürfnis nach kommerziellem Erfolg gibt, aber es gibt keine Institutionen, die diesen in einer soliden Form organisieren könnten; es gibt keine Mechanismen, alles hängt vom Zufall ab. Die kroatische Szene ist in einer Übergangsphase.

*In welchem Sinne?*

Die Beziehungen zum Westen sind noch immer nicht in einer zuträglichen Weise entwickelt; es gibt diese konstante Faszination für alles, was ›Ausland‹ ist. Wir müssen die Barriere zwischen ›uns‹ und ›denen‹ niederreißen und diesen Autismus durchbrechen. Das vielleicht größte Problem, mit dem wir konfrontiert sind, ist die Übernahme von Vorbildern aus dem Westen, denn wir müssen von der Situation ausgehen, in der wir uns selbst wiederfinden. Wir können den Ort, an dem wir uns aufhalten, nicht ausschließen. Es scheint mir, dass junge Künstler sich ihres Erbes nicht bewusst sind, ich denke, sie sind daran nicht interessiert. Die Beziehung zur Vergangenheit muss Kontinuität haben; sie muss nicht immer präsent sein, aber wir müssen uns dieser Beziehung immer bewusst sein. Das ist auch ein Problem der Ausbildung und ein Problem dessen, wie sehr sich die Akademie mit diesen Fragen befasst. Während ich an der Akademie studiert habe, waren die wichtigsten Künstler, und nicht nur diejenigen, die mit dem Modernismus verbunden waren, sondern auch diejenigen, die mit der konzeptuellen Kunst verbunden waren, völlig unsichtbar, sie existierten nicht als ein systematischer Teil des Curriculums. Viele Studenten schließen an der Akademie ab, ohne jemals beispielsweise von Mangelos gehört zu haben. Und das wird als normal angesehen. Dasselbe gilt für die Avantgarde der 1920er und 1930er, Klek, Micić ... und viele andere.

*Kannst du dir vorstellen, dass du anfängst, Arbeiten zu schaffen, die sich nicht mit diesen Orten und diesem Milieu befassen?*

Ich denke, dass Orte wichtig sind für meine Arbeit, aber nicht notwendigerweise. Ich denke, dass die Arbeiten, über die wir gesprochen haben, mich frei gemacht haben. Es ist schwierig für mich festzulegen, was ich später machen werde. Es gibt zwar einige Pläne, aber die werde ich nicht zwangsläufig in dic Tat umsetzen. Es wäre verrückt, etwas zu Hause zu machen, nur weil das vertrautes Gelände ist. Ich interessiere mich nach wie vor für dieses Gebiet; ich habe es nicht verlassen, aber ich denke, dass ich ein großes Kapitel beendet habe.

## David Maljković

Born/geboren in 1973, Rijeka, HR

### Education and residencies / Ausbildung und Atelierstipendien

2007 International Residence at Recollets, Paris FR
2007 Kunstzeitraum, artist residency, Munich DE
2006 – 07 KW Institute for Contemporary Art, studio program, Berlin DE
2003 – 04 Rijksakademie van beeldende kunsten, Amsterdam NL
2002 Cité Internationales des Arts, Paris FR
1998 – 99 Academy of Fine Arts, University of Zagreb HR, Multimedia Alternative
1996 – 2000 Academy of Fine Arts, University of Zagreb HR, Department of Painting
1993 – 96 Faculty of Philosophy, University of Rijeka HR, Art Department

### Solo exhibitions / Einzelausstellungen

2007 *These Days*, Present Future, Artissima 14, Torino IT
*Almost Here*, Kunstverein in Hamburg, DE
*Scene for New Heritage 3*, Art Unlimited, Art 38 Basel, CH
P.S.1 Contemporary Art Center, International and National Projects, New York US
*Scene for New Heritage Trilogy*, Whitechapel Art Gallery, London UK
*Days Below Memory*, CAPC, Musée d'art contemporain, Bordeaux FR
*Scene for New Heritage Trilogy*, The Physics Room, Christchurch NZ

2006 Salon of the Museum of Contemporary Art, Belgrade RS
Museum of Modern and Contemporary Art, Rijeka HR
*These Days* (with/mit Yael Bartana), Gallery Nova, Zagreb HR
*It's Gonna Happen* (with/mit Rosa Barba), Croy Nielsen, Berlin DE
*Scene for New Heritage 2*, Centre de Creation Contemporaine, Tours FR

2005 *Waiting Tomorrow*, Annet Gelink Gallery, Amsterdam NL
*The 90s Without the 90s*, MMC Palach, Rijeka HR
*Scene for New Heritage*, Van Abbemuseum, Eindhoven NL

2002 *Paintings for everyday use*, Miroslav Kraljević Gallery, Zagreb HR
*Your Moment Is Your Heritage*, Minimal, Ljubljana SI
*Space of Painting*, Moria, Stari Grad HR

2001 *Transplantation*, Kordić Gallery, Velika Gorica HR
*Three Paintings – Isn't a Trilogy*, Beck Gallery, Zagreb HR

2000 Juraj Klović Gallery (with/mit Tomislav Ćurković), Rijeka HR

1999 Otok Gallery, Dubrovnik HR
Gal Gallery, Rijeka HR

1998 *There Is Too Much of Me*, Lotrščak Tower, Zagreb HR
*The Dishes Are Thrown*, Palazzo Ploech, Rijeka HR

1997 *Jederman*, Caffe In, Rijeka HR

1996 Modern Gallery – Young Artists Club, Rijeka HR

### Group exhibitions / Gruppenausstellungen

2007 *Magellanic Cloud*, Centre Pompidou, curated by/kuratiert von Joanna Mytkowska, Paris FR
*Elephant Cemetery*, Artist Space, curated by/kuratiert von Christian Rattemeyer, New York US
*Der Prozess*, Prague Biennial 3, curated by/kuratiert von Marco Scotini, Prague CZ
*Ground Lost*, Forum Stadtpark, curated by/kuratiert von WHW, Graz AT
*Verbalno vokalno*, Galerija SC, curated by/kuratiert von Lala Raščić, Zagreb HR

*Inbetweeness*, Complesso di San Michele, curated by/kuratiert von Dobrila Denegri and/und Ludovico Pratesi, Rome IT
*Ground Lost*, Gallery Nova, curated by/kuratiert von WHW, Zagreb, HR
*On Lost Worlds*, CAPC Musée d'art contemporain, curated by/kuratiert von Charlotte Laubard, Bordeaux FR
*Artist in the wonderland*, curated by/kuratiert von Agata Rogos, Gdansk PL
42nd Zagreb Salon, Zagreb HR
*Made in*, Schloss Ringenberg, curated by/kuratiert von Marcus Lutkemeyer, Ringenberg DE
*The line of time and the plane of now*, Harris Lieberman, curated by/kuratiert von Ohad Meromi, New York US
*Kapitaler Glanz*, Kunstverein für die Rheinlande und Westfalen, Düsseldorf, curated by/kuratiert von Vanessa Joan Müller, DE
*Stalking With Stories*, apexart, curated by/kuratiert von Antonia Majaca and/und Ivana Bago, New York US
*Nature & Society: Parallel Lines*, Gliptoteque of the Academy of Sciences and Arts, Zagreb HR
*Nature & Society: Parallel Lines*, Muzej Rupe, Dubrovnik HR
*Art Protects*, Yvon Lambert, Paris FR

2006 *Contemporary Surrealists*, Mali salon, curated by/kuratiert von Branko Franceschi, Rijeka HR
*New Ghost Entertainment – Entitled*, Kunsthaus Dresden, curated by/kuratiert von Katrin Pesch, Dresden DE
*Art is always somewhere else*, 2nd Biennial of Young Artists, Bukarest RO
47th October Art Salon, curated by/kuratiert von René Block, Belgrade RS
*Everywhere*, Busan Biennale 06, curated by/kuratiert von Manu Park KR
*Ideal City – Invisible Cities*, curated by/kuratiert von Sabrina van der Ley and/und Markus Richter, Potsdam DE
*Downloads from Future*, Kunsthalle Winterthur, curated by/kuratiert von Oliver Kielmayer, Winterthur CH
*Ideal City-Invisible Cities*, curated by/kuratiert von Sabrina van der Ley and/und Markus Richter, Zamoch PL
*Monument to Nikola Tesla*, Gallery Nova, curated by/kuratiert von WHW, Zagreb HR
*Phantom*, Charlottenborg, curated by/kuratiert von Soren Andresen and/und Jasper Rasmussen, Copenhagen DK
*Modern Lovers*, Three Colts Gallery, curated by/kuratiert von Pil and/und Galia Kollectiv, London UK
*Downloads from Future*, Townhouse Gallery, curated by/kuratiert von Oliver Kielmayer, Cairo EG
*Mercury in Retrograde*, De Appel, Amsterdam NL
*Again for Tomorrow*, Royal College of Art, London UK
*Interrupted Histories*, Gallery of Modern Art, curated by/kuratiert von Zdenka Badovinec, Ljubljana SI
*A picture of War is not War*, Wilkinson Gallery, London UK
*Wild Man in the Looking Glass*, Art 2102, Los Angeles, US
*Synergy*, 40th Zagreb Salon, Zagreb HR

2005 *Mixed Pickles*, K3 Project Space, Zürich CH
*Go Inside*, Tirana Biennale 3, curated by/kuratiert von Hou Hanru, Tirana AL
*Insert*, Retrospective of Croatian Video Art, Museum of Contemporary Art, Zagreb HR
*Snapshot*, Museum of Modern Art, Dubrovnik HR
Istanbul Biennial 9, curated by/kuratiert von Charles Esche and/und Vasif Kortun, Istanbul TR
*Present Perfect*, T293, Napoli IT
Artists Books, Art 36 Basel, curated by/kuratiert von Lionel Bovier, Basel CH
International Biennial of Contemporary Art, National Gallery, Prague CZ
La Plateau (with/mit Joan Jonas), curated by/kuratiert von Caroline Bourgeois, Paris FR
*The Imaginary Number*, KW Institute for Contemporary Art, curated by/kuratiert von Anselm Franke, Berlin DE
*Telegram*, Rosa Barba Studio, Amsterdam NL
*Linear Structures*, Riga Gallery, Riga LV
Annet Gelink Gallery, Amsterdam NL
*Fin de siecle, end of painting?*, The Croatian Fine Arts Centre, curated by/kuratiert von Zdenko Rus, Zagreb HR

2004 *Love it or Leave it*, Cetinje Biennial 5, curated by/kuratiert von René Block and/und Nataša Ilić, Cetinje ME
*Exhibition of Nature and Society*, Exit Gallery, curated by/kuratiert von WHW, Peja, Kosovo
*Normalisation*, Gallery Nova, Zagreb HR
*Painting and Object*, Museum of Modern Art, Dubrovnik HR
*Open Studios*, Rijksakademie van beeldende kunsten, Amsterdam NL

2003 *Emerging Artists*, Museum of Modern and Contemporary Art, curated by/kuratiert von Nataša Ivančević, Rijeka HR
*Dislocation*, Town Museum of Zagreb HR
*Open Studios*, Rijksakademie van beeldende kunsten, Amsterdam NL

2002 36th Zagreb Salon, curated by/kuratiert von Andrej Medved, Zagreb HR
*Slow Watching*, Casal Balaguer, Palma de Mallorca ES
*Start*, Mestna Gallery, curated by/kuratiert von WHW, Ljubljana SI
*Filip Trade Collection of Contemporary Croatian Art*, Manes Gallery, curated by/kuratiert von Zvonko Maković, Prague CZ
*Here Tomorrow*, Museum of Contemporary Art, curated by/kuratiert von Roxana Marcoci, Zagreb HR
*Space and Walls*, Mali Salon, curated by/kuratiert von Branko Franceschi, Rijeka HR
16th Blue Salon, Zadar HR

2001 26th Salon of Young Artists, curated by/kuratiert von Jurij Krpan, Michal Kolocek and/und Slaven Tolj, Zagreb HR
2nd Salon of Young Artists, Sisak HR

2000 4th International Student Biennial, Skopje MK
SC Gallery, curated by/kuratiert von David Maljković, Zagreb HR
*New Beginning*, SC Club, curated by/kuratiert von Marijan Crtalić, Zagreb HR
*Filodrammatica*, curated by/kuratiert von David Maljković, Rijeka HR
*Millenium*, Gelo Gallery, curated by/kuratiert von Željko Jerman, Split HR
*Vice-chancel prize*, Vladimir Nazor Gallery, Zagreb HR

1999 2nd Croatian Triennial of Drawings, Zagreb HR

1998 *Ars Futura*, Matrix Croatica, Trieste IT
*Exhibition of Young Artists*, Kortil Gallery, Rijeka HR
Otok Gallery, curated by/kuratiert von Žarko Violić, Dubrovnik HR

1995 *The Day of Planet Earth*, Pedestrian Underpass, Rijeka HR

**Screenings / Projektionen**

2007 Fiac Cinema, Palais de Tokyo, Paris FR
*Back to the Future*, Borderline Festival of Movig Images, curated by/kuratiert von Jelena Vesić, Beijing CN

*Coffe Break*, Sibiu Urban Ambient project, Sibiu RO
*Just Around the Block*, curated by/kuratiert von Magdalena Ziolowska, Bijlmer NL
*Normalization*, LACE, curated by/kuratiert von WHW, Los Angeles US
*Normalization*, 16 Beaver, curated by/kuratiert von WHW, New York US
*Strange Weather*, NBK, selection by/Auswahl von Michelle Cotton, Berlin DE
*Normalization*, Platform Garnati Contemporary Art Centre, selection by/Auswahl von Minna Henrikson, Istanbul TR
*Challenging the East-West Art Map*, U-Turn, selection by/Auswahl von Angelika Richter, Copenhagen DK

2006 *Glocal Realities as Periferal In-Betweeness*, Tranzit, selection by/Auswahl von Antonia Majaca, Prague CZ
*Stories from Neigbourhood*, De Balie, selection by/Auswahl von Jelena Vesić, Amsterdam NL
*Rituals*, The Artists Cinema, Frieze Art Fair, curated by/kuratiert von Cristina Ricuperto, London UK
*Zagreb Calling*, Maison populaire, selection by/Auswahl von Ivana Mestrov, Montreuil FR
*Visura aperta*, Momiano HR

2005 *Imaginary is Potential*, MUU, selection by/Auswahl von Henrikke Nielsen, Helsinki FI
*Imaginary is Potential*, Nikolaj centre of contemporary art, Copenhagen DK
*Imaginary is Potential*, W139, Amsterdam NL

*Imaginary is Potential*, Halle für Kunst, Lüneburg DE
*Stories from Neighbourhood*, Kunsthalle Tallinn, selection by/Auswahl von Jelena Vesić, Tallinn EE
*Serial Cases*, selection by/Auswahl von Antonia Majaca, Usti nad Labem, Istanbul, Iasi, Graz, Sofia, Holon, Novi Sad, Zagreb
*Normalisation and Its Discontents*, selection by/Auswahl von Nataša Ilić, Askalalwan, Beirut RL

**Bibliography/Bibliografie**


2007 Luca Cerizza, 'David Maljković: CAPC Musée d'art contemporain, Bordeaux', *Frieze*, no./Nr. 110.
Artist Project, *Bidoun*, no./Nr. 11.
Jantine Kremer, 'De grenzeloosheid van het bouwen', *Kunstbeeld*, no./Nr. 5.
Teresa Gleadowe, 'David Maljković: Whitechapel Art Gallery, London', *Art Monthly*, no./Nr. 306.
Joanna Mytowska, *Magellanic Cloud*, cat./Kat., Centre Pompidou, Paris.
Charles Esche, 'Looking Back: Emerging Artists', *Frieze*, no./Nr. 104.
Ami Barak, 'The Displaced Issue', *Parabol*, no./Nr. 2.
Christian Rattemeyer, *Elephant Cemetery*, cat./Kat., Artists Space, New York.
What, How and for Whom, *Ground Lost*, cat./Kat., Forum Stadtpark, Graz.

2006 Goska Charylo, 'Ideal City: Various Venues, Zamosc, Poland', *Frieze*, no./Nr. 102.
Ivet Curlin, 'A Dead End Is a Good Start', *Oris*, no./Nr. 41.
Jelena Vesić, *Nothing Is More Remote than Yesterday Nothing Is Closer than Tomorrow*, cat./Kat., Museum of Contemporary Art, Belgrade.
Branko Franceschi, *Tired Places*, cat./Kat., Museum of Modern and Contemporary Art, Rijeka, 2006.
Douglas Heingartner, 'Mercury in Retrograde: De Appel, Amsterdam', *Frieze*, no./Nr. 100.
Max Andrews, 'A Picture of War Is not War: Wilkinson Gallery, London', *Frieze*, no./Nr. 99.
Jasna Jakšić, *Feral Tribune*, no./Nr. 1072.
Jonathan Carrol, *Again for Tomorrow*, cat./Kat. Royal College of Art, London.

2005 Eleanor Heartney, 'Artist in the City: Engagement With the Urban Environment and the Local Public Was the Theme of This Year's Istanbul Biennial', *Art in America*, December.
Cay Sophie Rabinovich, 'Address – Unknown', *Texte zur Kunst*, no./Nr. 61.
Charles Esche, *Istanbul Biennial 9*, cat./Kat.
Charles Esche, *Place With Limited Premeditation*, Artimo, Amsterdam.
Anselm Franke, *The Imaginary Number*, cat./Kat., KW Institute for Contemporary Art, Berlin.
Branko Franceschi, *Again for Tomorrow*, cat./Kat., International Biennial of Contemporary Art, Prague.
Branko Franceschi, *Linear Structures*, cat./Kat., Riga Gallery, Riga.
Zdenko Rus, *Fin de siecle, end of painting?*, cat./Kat., HDLU, Zagreb.

2004 What, How and for Whom, *Normalisation*, cat./Kat., Nova Gallery, Zagreb.
Antun Maračić, *Painting and Object*, cat./Kat., Museum of Modern Art, Dubrovnik.
Sabina Salamon, 'Emerging Artists', *Kontura*, no./Nr. 80.
Zlatko Wurzberg, 'Emerging Artists', *Nedjeljni Vjesnik*, 11 January.

2003 Natasa Ivančević, *Emerging Artists*, cat./Kat., Museum of Modern and Contemporary Art, Rijeka.
Maja and/und Reuben Fowkes, 'Here Tomorrow, Museum of Contemporary Art, Zagreb', *Frieze*, no./Nr. 72.

2002 Roxana Marcoci, *Here Tomorrow*, cat./Kat., Museum of Contemporary Art, Zagreb.
Andrej Medved, *What Is There Left of Croatian Painting*, cat./Kat., 36th Zagreb Salon, Zagreb.
What, How and for Whom, 'Aperto Zagreb', *Flash Art*, vol. 34.
Rebecca Heald, 'Tale of 12 Cities: Zagreb', *Art Review*, vol. 53.
Branko Franceschi, *Paintings for Everyday Use*, cat./Kat., Miroslav Kraljević Gallery, Zagreb.
Branko Franceschi, *Space and Walls*, cat./Kat., Mali Salon, Rijeka.
Marina Baričević, 'Ni jedno vrijeme ne moze najaviti smrt slikarstva', *Novi List*, no./Nr. 17493.

Mladen Lucić, *Slow Watching*, cat./Kat., Casal Balaguer, Palma de Mallorca.
Leila Topić, *Kontura*, no./Nr. 71.
Iva Boras, 'Trenutak upisan čavlima', *Zarez*, no./Nr. 83.

2001 Leila Topić, 'Transplantacija umjetničkih djela', *Zarez*, no./Nr. 52.
Zlatko Keser, *David Maljković*, cat./Kat., Beck Gallery, Zagreb.

2000 Zlatko Wurzberg, 'Virtualni i aktualni prostor', *Vjesnik*, 28 April.
Natasa Ivančević, *David Maljković*, cat./Kat. Juraj Klović Gallery, Rijeka.
Zlatko Keser, *Vice-Chancel Prize*, cat./Kat., Vladimir Nazor Gallery, Zagreb.
Nataša Šegota, 'Nova Apstrakcija', *Novi List*, 14 April.

1999 Damir Stojnić, *David Maljković*, cat./Kat., Otok Gallery, Dubrovnik.

1998 Branko Cerovac, *Made in Ri: Nova likovna situacija*, cat./Kat., Rijeka.
Ana Dević, *There Is Too Much of Me*, cat./Kat., Lotrščak Tower, Zagreb.

1997 Branko Cerovac, *Jedermann*, cat./Kat., Caffe In, Rijeka.

**Works in public collections/**
**Werke in öffentlichen Sammlungen**

Centre Pompidou, Paris
Fonds municipal d'art contemporain, Ville de Paris
Museum of Modern Art, New York
Museum of Modern and Contemporary Art, Rijeka
Stedelijk Museum, Amsterdam
Van Abbemuseum, Eindhoven

# Credits/Nachweise

### Video credits/Videonachweis

*Scene for New Heritage*
2004, DVD, colour/Farbe, sound/Ton, 4'33"
Produktion/Production: Rijksakademie van beeldende kunsten, Amsterdam
Camera/Kamera: Hrvoje Franjić
Editing/Bearbeitung: Sanjin Stanić

*Scene for New Heritage 2*
2006, DVD, colour/Farbe, sound/Ton, 6'06"
Production/Produktion: Centre de Creation Contemporaine, Tours
Camera/Kamera: Hrvoje Franjić
Editing/Bearbeitung: Sanjin Stanić
Sound/Ton: Igor Fabris

*Scene for New Heritage 3*
2006, DVD, colour/Farbe, sound/Ton, 11'29"
Production/Produktion: Centre Pompidou, Paris and/und Annet Gelink Gallery, Amsterdam
Camera/Kamera: Hrvoje Franjić
Editing/Bearbeitung: Sanjin Stanić
Sound/Ton: Boris Wagner
Sound extract/Tonausschnitt: Jan St. Werner

*These Days*
2005, DVD, colour/Farbe, sound/Ton, 5'31"
Production/Produktion: What, How and for Whom, Zagreb
Camera/Kamera: Hrvoje Franjić
Editing/Bearbeitung: Sanjin Stanić

*Lost Memories from These Days*
2006, DVD, colour/Farbe, sound/Ton, 6'45"
Production/Produktion: Museum of Modern and Contemporary Art, Rijeka
Camera/Kamera: Hrvoje Franjić
Editing/Bearbeitung: Sanjin Stanić

### Photo credits/Fotonachweis

Marko Ercegović, B. Fontanel, Peter Hauck, Renaat Jansen, David Maljković, Geer Oskam, Ilya Rabinovich, Matthew Septimus, Willem Vermaase, Branko Vilus.

# Sources/Quellen


Vojin Bakić, *Monument Petrova Gora: Architectonic Project 1:200*, from the Bakić family archive/aus dem Archiv der Familie Bakić.

Vojin Bakić, *Projekt spomenika na Petrovoj gori*, from the Bakić family archive/aus dem Archiv der Familie Bakić, 1981.

*Devětsil*, exhibition catalogue/Ausstellungskatalog, Zagreb: Gallery of Contemporary Art, 1989.

Living Language, *Easy English*, New York: Living Language.

Tonko Maroević, *Vojin Bakić* , Zagreb: Nakladni zavod Globus, SKD Prosvjeta, 1998.

Memorijalni park Petrova gora, *Petrova gora: Historijske fotografije*, 2nd edn./Zweite Auflage, Beograd: Niška turistička štampa, 1982.

Stefan Schulze, *Peugeot 4002* <http://www.fast-zination.de/articles/ ssc_special/ 4002/4002_11_1600.html>, 2002.

*Slobodni Zagreb*, Zagreb: Stvarnost, 1965.

# Colophon/Impressum


This catalogue is published on the occasion of the exhibition/Dieser Katalog erscheint anlässlich der Ausstellung

*David Maljković: Almost Here*
15 September – 18 November 2007
Kunstverein in Hamburg

Kunstverein in Hamburg
Klosterwall 23, D-20095 Hamburg
Tel. +49 (0)40 338 344, Fax +49 (0)40 322 159
hamburg@kunstverein.de
www.kunstverein.de

*Director/Direktor*
Dr. Yilmaz Dziewior

*Board members/Vorstand*
Stephen Craig, Dr. Harald Falckenberg, Anna Gudjonsdottir, Prof. Dr. Susanna Hegewisch-Becker, Dr. Ernst-Josef Pauw, Markus Peichl, Claudia Reiche, Jürgen Vorrath, Dr. Hans-Jochen Waitz

The exhibition and catalogue of David Maljković have been sponsored by the Alfried Krupp von Bohlen und Halbach-Stiftung / Die Ausstellung und der Katalog von David Maljković wurden von der Alfried Krupp von Bohlen und Halbach-Stiftung gefördert.

**Exhibition/Ausstellung**

*Curator/Kurator*
Yilmaz Dziewior

*Exhibition coordination/Ausstellungskoordination*
Corinna Koch

*Press and public office/*
*Presse- und Öffentlichkeitsarbeit*
Meike Behm

*Curatorial assistance/Wissenschaftliche Assistenz*
Eva Birkenstock

*Internship/Praktikum*
Lisa Thieme

*Bookkeeping/Buchhaltung*
Gesche Früchtenicht

*Exhibition technology/Ausstellungstechnik*
Robert Görß

*Cashier/Kasse*
Yilmaz Balkan, Kay Ruchholtz

*Cleaning/Reinigung*
Maike Nuppnau

Courtesy of all works Annet Gelink Gallery, Amsterdam and the artist/Courtesy für alle Arbeiten Annet Gelink Gallery, Amsterdam und der Künstler.

**Catalogue/Katalog**

*Editor/Herausgeber*
Yilmaz Dziewior

*Editing/Redaktion*
Meike Behm

*Lectorship/Lektorat*
Meike Behm, Eva Birkenstock

*Bio- and bibliography/Bio- und Bibliografie*
Meike Behm

*Texts/Texte*
Yilmaz Dziewior, Anselm Franke, Nataša Ilić, David Maljković

*Translations/Übersetzungen*
G–E/D–E: Kirsten Scheffler, Nikolaus G. Schneider
E–G/E–D: Michael Eldred, Daria Torre
C–E/K–E: Magdalena Skoblar, Nataša Ilić

*Graphic design/Grafische Gestaltung*
Toni Uroda with/mit David Maljković

*Typesetting/Satz*
Toni Uroda

*Typefaces/Schriften*
Bureau Grotesque, Monotype Grotesque, Times Ten

*Paper/Papier*
Munken Lynx, Manteca

*Printing/Gesamtherstellung*
Die Keure, Brugge/Brügge

*Binding/Buchbinderei*
Binderij Hexspoor, Boxtel

*With special thanks to/Mit besonderem Dank an*
Ana Martina Bakić & Bakić family, Christiane Berndes, Collection De Bruin-Heijn, Charles Esche, Anselm Franke, Annet Gelink, Nataša Ilić, Višnja Šporer Maljković, Magdalena Skoblar, Gijs van Tuyl, WHW – What How and for Whom, Zagreb, Floor Wullems

Cover illustration/Umschlagabbildung:
*Scene for New Heritage*, 2004, collage (detail/Detail)

© 2007 David Maljković, Kunstverein in Hamburg,
authors/Autoren & DuMont Buchverlag, Köln

© 2007 for the reproduced works of/für die
abgebildeten Werke von David Maljković:
the artist/der Künstler

Die Deutsche Bibliothek – CIP – Einheitsaufnahme.
Ein Titelsatz für diese Publikation ist bei Der
Deutschen Bibliothek erhältlich.

ISBN: 978-3-8321-9055-2

Published by/Erschienen im DuMont Buchverlag
www.dumont-buchverlag.de